The
Complete
Roadside
Guide to Nebraska

The
Complete
Roadside
Guide to Nebraska

and comprehensive description of items of interest to one and
all travelers of the state, whether native or transplant, senden-
tary or transient,

including:

a mile by mile tour of all major roads and side roads, lanes, avenues, highways
and interstates, distinguishing for the traveler all sights both ordinary and unusual,

profusely illustrated by James Exten

and compiled and written for the edification and
pleasure of the reading public by

Alan Boye

59-155

"They camped one night on the banks of the Platte
Where Ike found a place that was muddy, but flat
When Ike in his robes, 'neath the snow did lie
Said Betsy, 'Dear Ike we'll move on by and by.' "

SALTILLO PRESS

Printing history:
First edition, 1989

SALTILLO Press
57 Lafayette
St. Johnsbury, VT
05819

ISBN 0-913473-10-3

For my brothers

Acknowledgements

The sheer volume of information in this book owes its existence to a large number of kind people who, over the last 4 years, have helped in a thousand different ways. Without their efforts and selflessness, this book would simply not have been possible.

In the initial research of this book hundreds of people across the state of Nebraska set aside extra time and effort in order to provide me with information, books, maps, letters, telephone conversations and encouragement.

I would first like to thank those members of county historical societies and local museums, far too numerous to mention in this short space, who made such a sacrifice to answer my countless letters and queries. From your generousity and hard work, with your books of local history and photographs, and to your hand written letters of correction and praise, you were the audience for whom the book was written. Without you and your support, this project would have remained incomplete.

The research staff at the Nebraska State Historical Society helped in a similar fashion with their tireless patience and diligent work. Information and assitence was never lacking from any of the members of the variety of Chambers of Commerce across the state who provided invaluable information.

Lyndon State College and the University of Texas at El Paso were kind and generous in their support as well.

Thanks are graciously extended to staffs at the Oregon State Library, the Lincoln and Omaha City Libraries, the Nebraska State Library and the University of Texas Library system, and to Jim Exten and Thomas Whitby.

A special thanks to the Lincoln City Library Nebraska Heritage Room staff for their support of me and my writing over the past decade.

To Wright Morris for his kindness and generosity.

And the greatest thanks is extended to my family:

For my research assistant David Boye for his tireless and uncomplaining footwork.

For my mother who first taught me about the hidden places where love of the land might bloom.

For my wife and companion Linda Wacholder's unbending love and support.

And for the gentleman out around Harrisburg in Banner County, who offered me a place to stay at his ranch, just so I could see how beautiful the sunset looked from his backporch, keep the door open, I'm coming.

Preface

In a note to me, Alan Boye described his *Complete Roadside Guide to Nebraska*, as one the traveler might carrry in the glove compartment of a car. Would that it had once been in *my* glove compartment in those days, in the 1940s, when it would have been a welcome companion. Nebraska was hardly a tourist mecca at that time, nor is it now, but today even native sons and daughters take the time to look freshly about them. Since *my* time, for example, there has been a bit of history and visible change. More than change, there is now new interest in what was once taken for granted.

The town of Schuyler, for example, once

known to me as the location (if I could find it) of the empty piano box where I—for most of one long 4th of July morning—concealed myself while I smoked *punk* in neatly rolled sheets of toilet paper. This may well still be frowned on. I was not in the condition the rest of the day to speak publicly about my experience. Places of concealment have always been special to me, and in these Nebraska is still not lacking where there are front porches with a fence of cross slats at the bottom. The culverts that once ornamented street crossings might well now be gone, signifying progress. Mr. Boye's comment, in his guide, sites Schuyler as having once been a rip-snorting cowboy town. That would have been of keen interest to me, in 1917, but it comes a little late for me to act on it.

A fine example of touring literature at its best will be found on page 247, where he sites Duncan as a small village between here and there. How beat that? Precisely what a good guide should do, if given the chance.

April, 1989
Wright Morris

Contents

Roads Heading **East and West** That Are:
South of the Platte

North of the Platte

How To Use This Book

This book is designed so that a person may start using it from any point on nearly any highway in all of the state's 93 counties.

To locate a particular highway:
Look for the name of the higway listed in the contents.

To use the Guide as you travel:
The chapters always read from east to west, or from south to north. If you are traveling in either of these directions, simply read **down** the page.

If you are traveling south, or east, read from entry to entry going **up** the page.

Distances given are between entries. If you are reading **up** the page, follow the distiacnes in the **parentheses**. The distance between entireis are in **bold**.

Sites which are off the main road or highway a fair distance are given in *italics*. The distances to these sites are in ***bold***.

Please see below for a sample page description.

While a great many of these sites have been visited by the author in order to test the distances, the wise traveler will not explore without a map of the state close at hand, or travel too far afield without stopping to ask for directions locally.

Because of the variety in maps and automobile audometers there may be slight differences from the distances indicated in the book, so always hunt around a bit if a site is not immediately visible.

Because the landscape is a changing and living being, time, progress, erosion and the elements may make some of the sites in the book less than immediately discernable. Get out of the car and look around. Use your imagination. Get down on your hands and knees and search among the prairie grasses. If you still can't find the site get up and brush the dust off your knees and take a deep breath of the clear Nebraska air, as it does its part at replenishing the earth.

Boldface ——————— *West of Tyron 22 miles* on State Highway 92 to turn off to the
indicates   south for Diamond Bar Lake vicintiy. Good fishing and hunting. Inquire
distance   locally. Ten miles southeast of here, accessible on backroads only,
                                was the small town of Forks, located at the forks of the East and West
Italics ——————— Birdwood Creeks. It had a post office until the early 1920s.
indicate
sites off the   *West of Tryon 28 miles* to Flats, another near ghost town.
main road.   Because of an early pioneer named Lombard the area was called
                                Lombard Flats. The US Post Office, in its infinite wisdom cut off the
                                Lombard part because it was too long and simply left Flats.

Distance from – Twenty nine miles (5 miles.)
previous entry,   Take the narrow paved road leading off to the west. **Down**
while traveling **this road 15 miles** to the banks of the North Fork of the Dismal River,
north cross the river and continue another **eight miles** to the banks of the
                                South Fork and the site of the North and Cody Ranch.
(distance from   This grassy expanse of hills was once the range of thousands
previous entry of buffalo, antelope and deer. In 1877 William F. Cody, who would
traveling south 126
in parentheses.)

later become world renowned as Buffalo Bill, along with Major Frank North, purchased a herd of cattle at Ogallala and spent a good part of their summer driving them to this range land. Here the men started a ranch that would become known as the North and Cody Ranch. Not much is known about the success of this ranch, or Buffalo Bill's part in it, but for years the ranch was made welcome to any traveler who happened this way. In later years many dignitaries were entertained here. Today the quiet and peaceful river flows through beautiful country of grasslands and thickets along the banks.

Five miles (0 miles.)

Mullen.

Junction with State Highway 2 and the end of State Highway 97.

For information about Mullen, see entry for State Highway 2.

*North of Mullen the road continues as county roads into the vast Cherry County. Under most weather conditions the road is passable, although it might be a bit washboardy in spots. In **forty miles** is the Samuel McKelvie National Forest, the hideout spots for the state's most famous outlaw, Doc Middleton, and other interesting sites.*

For a full discussion of the area North of Mullen see the entry for Valentine and US Highway 20.

Distance from previous entry, while traveling north (distance from previous entry traveling south in parentheses.)

Italics indicate sites off main roads.

Reference to intersecting roads. See index or contents for those chapters.

Chapter Heading for US Highways

Chapter Heading for State Highways

Zero miles (5 miles.)

Kansas Border. For five miles Route 73 is joined by US Highway 159. For information about the strange and interesting southeast tip of Nebraska, please see the entry for US Highway 159.

Five Miles (9 miles.)

Falls City.

If you are the type of person who wants to know exactly where the falls is when a town has a name like Falls City, it is nearby on the Nemaha. Prichard Museum is open midafternoons weekdays, and by appointment.

The special collections at the Falls City Library include art collections by artists John Falter, Alice Cleaver and others. Included in the collection is the *Saturday Evening Post* cover collection.

The True Value Hardware store in downtown Falls City is located in the Gehling Opera House, built in 1892. The capacity was 700 to 800 and as was the case with most local opera houses, the upstairs was used for productions and stage shows, and the downstairs for restaurants and saloons. A grand spiral staircase once went from the center of the main floor to the second floor. Some of the frescoes can still be seen on the second floor walls, and some of the old time equipment used to run shows is still in storage. William Jennings Bryan spoke here, and many vaudville shows stopped at this grand hall in Falls City.

The city became the county seat after a battle with Salem, in 1860.

Nine miles (2 miles.)

The intersection of 73 and state 67.

*North on State 67, **six miles, then east five miles** to Barada. On the way you will pass old red brick church at about **2 miles.***

Barada was named for Antonine Barada and his story is one of the most interesting and strange tales of the state's history. Barada's father was a French nobleman, well trained in the arts and culture, and destined for a high rank in the finest circles of French society.

During the reign of Louis XVI Barada was strolling about Paris one day when a rose fell at his feet. He picked it up, looked about, and determined that the rose had been flung there by the most beautiful woman he had ever seen. She stood above the street in a window and smiled down at him. She had the blackest hair he had ever seen, and a dark, brown skin the color of wild and free nature itself.

He went about his business and returned to the same place the next day. The window was boarded up. He inquired at the house and learned that the woman who he had seen was gone, and he would never see her again. "Why not?" he demanded.

The man in the house laughed. "That woman was called Taeglena. She was an Indian from Louisianna, in America. She has left to return to her buffalo and campfires."

Barada sold what possessions he could, gathered his money, and within days was on a boat for America. He knew nothing about the woman, except for her name, and that she lived somewhere in the vast expanse of French territory in the New World.

Eventually Barada worked himself into the far north Canadian woods, working as a trapper and hunter, and traveling among the Sioux. He became rather well known as a good shot, and as the strange Frenchman who searched relentlessly for an Indian woman.

Barada roamed the vast territory of Louisianna for ten years, learning a bit of the language of the Sioux and about the wild country,

2

so different from his long-lost, distant France.

He searched every village of Indians. Once, in an Omaha village in Iowa, he passed by a teepee. An old woman sat in front of it, working on some hides and talking. "Taeglena," she said just as he passed. "What was that?" He glared at the woman.

The doorway of the teepee flipped back and there, after ten years of searching stood the woman who had thrown him the rose. They were married, and lived in various locations along the Nebraska side of the Missouri River.

One of their sons was Antoine. At age seven he was kidnapped by the Sioux and held ransom for six months until his father paid two ponies for his return.

At nine Antoine worked with a fur trading company and made excursions up the Missouri River.

Antoine was renowned for his extraordinary strength. Legends abound to this day about his powers. He was known to be able to snap a canoe paddle in his hands. Even his toes were so strong that he once pinched a man with them until the man pleaded for mercy.

Some say they saw him pick up a derrick that was being used to drive piles into the Missouri. In St. Louis there remains today a stone doorsill which he lifted from the ground. On the side of the stone is carved the words: Antoine Barada lifted this stone, 1,700 pounds, 1832."

Antoine worked for a while in California, trying, along with thousands of others, to strike it rich in the gold fields. Shortly after that he settled here, in the small town that still bears his name, on his parents' land. He and his French wife lived here until his death in 1887. He is buried next to his wife in the Barada cemetery, but his legend lives on and on in the tales and folklore of the people for miles around.

Northeast from Barada, **three miles:** southern edge of Indian Caves State Park. See entry for US 136 for information about this wonderful state park.

Two miles (7 miles.)

Verdon. Just west of here is Verdon State Recreation Area. A small, natural lake which makes a nice get-away.

Seven miles (1 mile.)

Intersection with US 75.

For a continuation of sites to the north, please see the entry for US Highway 75.

US Highway 75

Zero miles (4 miles.)
> Kansas border.

Four miles (5 miles.)
> Junction with State Highway 8.
> *East on State Highway 8 **seven miles** to Salem. From the Bible, meaning "peaceful." The name was given to suggest to the local Indians what the pioneers hoped they might be.*
> *West on State Highway 8 **seven miles, then three miles south** on State 105. A large Boy Scouts of America Reservation. These 370 acres are temporary home to those who promise to obey, cherish, etc.*
> *West on State Highway 8 **nine miles,** two miles west of the Boy Scout Reservation to Kinters Ford State Wildlife Management Area. Just four miles southwest of here, at DuBois in Pawnee County is the Iron Horse Trail Wildlife Area.*

Five miles (1 mile.)
> Junction with US Highway 73.
> These two highways are joined together from here to the northern edge of Omaha. This is a busy road, but with plenty to see along its path. For information about sites along US Highway 73, south, please see the entry for US Highway 73.

One mile (4 miles.)
> Just west of here is an ancient stone house, believed to be one of the oldest in the area. Ask locally for directions.
> *West on county road **seven miles** to Kirkman's Cove Recreation Area.*

Four miles (11 miles.)
> Junction with State Highway 62. East to Indian Caves State Park and Barada, named for one of the most interesting characters in American history. Please see entry for US Highway 73 for further information.

Eleven miles (5 miles.)

Auburn.

There is something wonderful about coming into this town from the north along US 73/75, passing the city park and slowing down for the center business district. Something about the place that reminds one of a day from youth, long ago when the future was endless and unimportant, and the present was a five dollar bill in your pocket and the chance to meet up with a new friend, a chance to find that someone of your dreams.

It may be that kind of reckless and priceless freedom of being able to stick out your thumb on that highway and catch a ride for just about any place you wanted to go, or it may be the way the sun gleams off the store fronts and the courthouse, but Auburn still glistens with a bit of that sense, that exhilarating feeling of being young.

Auburn is the county seat of Nemaha County and its original limestone courthouse still serves as the center of county politics. Auburn was originally two towns, Sheridan and Calvert. Sheridan was the older of the two, founded in 1868, and Calvert was settled sometime later. A lumber company was formed in 1881 and is still in existence as the oldest business in Auburn. In 1882 the two towns agreed to merge into a single entity. The courthouse was built on the land equal distant between the two town centers. The current court-house, built in 1900, is at that same location. Auburn's city center is a bustling area yet and has the charm of a bygone era.

The Nemaha Valley Museum, south of the county court-house, features two three-story buildings and a number of outstanding displays. It is open most Sundays, or by appointment.

Junction with US 136, please see that entry for information about sites along this route.

Five miles (1 mile.)

Junction with State Highway 67 east. East here to the most beautiful town in the state, Peru. Please see the entry for US Highway 136 for information about this area.

One mile (14 miles.)

Junction with State Highway 67 west.

Six miles west on 67 to Brock.

Brock is located in a belt of timber and the timber originally attracted the town's founders to the area. The name of the town has changed seven times since it was formed in 1855. At one time Brock was called Podunk. Podunk, Nebraska.

Three miles south *of Brock on county roads is privately owned but free Coryell Park. Coryell Park supporters claim that for the first-time visitor the Park is nothing short of amazing. The park is an unusual one as it was formed when the original homesteaders, the Richard Coryell family, decided to donate their land as a park for all the people.*

The old homestead house was reproduced out of lumber which grew on the land, and the house in which several of the children were born, was moved to the site. They added picnic grounds, swings as well as a tower, a reproduction of a prairie schooner, and a chapel. The chapel was built so that it would last for ages. The front wall of the stone building is 28 inches thick, the side walls, two feet. The inner walls are made of the same limestone as the state capitol building. The foundation is six feet deep and the walls are reinforced with steel and concrete. The floor is seven inches thick and the pews made from oak.

It was the intent of the builders that the chapel be made free and for the sacred nondenominational worship of God. It is available for weddings and special events. The park boasts an auditorium, a museum and a bell purchased in the memory of one of the Coryell children.

Four miles (10 miles.)

Take the county road to the ***east*** *from this intersection and soon it will swing north close to the river. It is a breathtaking and beautiful drive. There are camping areas along these roads. Inquire locally. The route is a pleasant way to get to the lovely town of Peru (see entry for US Highway 136) or you may continue* ***north, 12 miles*** *to Nebraska City.*

Ten miles (1 mile.)

Nebraska City.

No tour of the state of Nebraska can be complete without a stop and a look at Nebraska City, one of the oldest and most important cities in the state. Nebraska City was founded by William Nuckolls in the early 1850s as a trading post and river boat stop. Soon the town began to grow. Its convenient docks and natural land access to the Platte, Nemaha and other ways west, made it quickly bloom into a full-fledged, snorting, cursing river town. The trails which led west out of Nebraska City made it the jumping off place for trail drivers, bush-wackers, mule skinners, pioneers, gold rushers, and an entire host of con men.

In 1860 a Nebraska City gentleman tried to combine two important current items: the covered wagon and the steam engine. He was a few decades too early, and made several mistakes in design, so his steam-powered wagon was a dismal failure. The machine had four engines, front wheels six feet in diameter, rear wheels 12 feet in diameter, and was supposed to run for eight hours on a cord of wood. It was designed to run between Nebraska City and Denver, and made its maiden voyage on July 22, 1862. Ten miles west of here a drive shaft broke and since New York was the closest place to replace the shaft, and since the inventor soon learned his wife and family had been captured during a raid by Indians, the project was put on hold. By the time he was able to resume his steam wagon, the railroad had started up in earnest and the project was abandoned.

But transportation is what made Nebraska City. Two important trails led out of Nebraska City. The Nebraska City Cut-off of the Oregon Trail started in Nebraska City and zig-zagged in a more or less straight line due west until it joined the more frequently traveled branch of the Trail near present-day Kearney.

The Oxbow Trail, which connected Nebraska City with the Oregon Trail, but swung north toward Columbus, also started here.

The site of the old Fort Kearney Blockhouse is marked on the corner of Central Avenue and 5th Street. The original Ft. Kearney was built in 1847 at this site but abandoned in 1848 when the government decided that a better location for the fort would be some 200 miles west. The government then abandoned this fort and moved everyone west, a mere year after building and stocking this place. Nice to know that some things, like competency of governments, don't change.

Nebraska City was the location of the first high school in the state, and possibly the first one west of the Missouri. It was built in 1864.

North of the cemetery on South 19th Street is the site of John Brown's Cave which is where Brown hid runaway slaves from Kansas and Missouri for the Underground Railroad. The "cave" was essentially a small cellar under a house which until the 1930s had no windows or doors to the outside. A 30 foot tunnel went from there to Table Creek. If there was danger, someone on the floor above would tap out a prearranged signal on the floor and the slaves would escape down the tunnel to the creek and eventually to the river. From here the slaves were taken into Iowa where they were given the final preparations for flight into Canada. It is good to remember that there were those who sought to help the mistreated in our nation, but it is also good to remember that only a few decades ago there was a kind of life

7

that made it necessary for men and women to stay hidden and in fear of their lives just in order to gain their freedom in Canada.

The Wildwood Center on Steinhardt Park Road, open daily from spring until autumn, features a ten room historic brick house and a barn in which the exhibits are changed to present a varied display for the return visitors.

Nebraska City is the center for Nebraska's finest apple growing area. Without mentioning specific names, the country roads in Otoe County are filled with fruit and juice stands and it is an unfortunate traveler who zips past these roadside meccas without stopping for a taste of utter ambrosia.

Nebraska City is the county seat of Otoe County, which almost seems secondary to the distinct historic river town feel of the place. There are many fine smaller restaurants here, as well as many fine parks. Do not leave Nebraska City without going down to the river and sitting for a spell to watch the water flow.

Just north of the city is one of Nebraska's shrines: Arbor Lodge.

The Lodge was the home of one of the state's wealthiest and 'best known early-day citizens, J. Sterling Morton. Morton moved to the area in 1855 and became a squatter on this strip of land near the young Nebraska City. After a bit he built a three room house with a view of the river, and the Iowa hills. He added an unusual feature for that time and place: a shingled roof. The land he claimed did not have the rich timber that the river bottom land, just a few miles distant had, so Morton began to transplant a few trees. Soon he brought more trees, then more, then more. He added an orchard. Shade trees. Vines, shrubs, flowers, evergreens and hedges.

In 1874 Morton had become quite the well-rounded citizen. So much so that he was appointed President of the State Board of Agriculture. While in that position he persuaded Governor Furnas to proclaim a day of tree-planting. It became a regular feature of the state and in 1885 the state legislature declared it a state holiday and moved the date to April 22, Morton's birthday. Morton later became the Secretary of Agriculture during the second term of Grover Cleveland.

It may be difficult for us to understand just how big a celebration Arbor Day was at the turn of the century, but across the country, and especially in the west, the holiday caught on like wildfire. In San Francisco, for example, such notables as author Jack London and naturalist John Muir encouraged the city to declare the day a holiday of great importance.

Across the bay in Oakland a poet little known today, but of international celebrity status back then, Joaquin Miller organized his own celebration of the day by getting the city's school children to have a day away from classes and out in the parks, streets and yards planting trees. Oakland owes most of its greenery to Arbor Day.

For years in Lincoln and other communities fifth graders were given free trees to plant at home, and although the prohibitive costs of such a program have eliminated it from schools, Lincolnites can direct you to pine trees, beautiful blooming red buds, crab apples and cherry trees in yards all across the city that date from the program.

The mansion is open to the public and tours are given often. It is quite a house, with hand-hewed timbers, a beautiful staircase or two and semicircular porches. It took Morton and his heirs 50 years to bring the original three room house (which is still a part of the structure) to the 52 room monster that was donated to the state in 1923.

Morton's son Joy was the founder of Morton Salt, and became something quite less than poverty-stricken himself.

The land around the house is either nicely manicured, or left to retain a native and wild atmosphere. There are over 200 varieties of trees on the grounds, as well as an equal number of shrubs and, at last count, a million or two flowers. Other gardens, buildings and monuments are scattered about the park which is run by the State.

One mile (10 miles.)

One half mile north of Arbor Lodge is the site where the Table Creek Treaty with the Pawnee was signed in 1857. This treaty, which was signed by Hawk Chief, Grey Eagle and others, ceded all Pawnee claims to land except for a small parcel along the Loup River. In essence this meant the three or four chiefs were giving up about a third of the state for an area a little larger than Otoe County. In exchange the government gave the Pawnee $40,000 a year for five years. What happened to the money is not clear, but the land became the State of Nebraska.

Ten miles (2 miles.)

Cass County line.

The earliest documented exploration of Nebraska mentions a location in Cass County. Pierre and Paul Mallet reached the mouth of the Platte on June 2, 1739. They went up the river for 70 miles.

Later Long's expedition reported that Nebraska was "uninhabitable for people depending on agriculture for subsistence," a line similar in style to Custer's "what Indians?"

US Highways 73 & 75

In 1854 the Government made a treaty with the Omaha and Otoe Indians in which the Indians gave up the lands bordering the Missouri River. "They received as an equivalent a stated amount of provisions and other necessities." This consisted of pork and sugar.

Cass County's Indian history not only includes the Omaha and Otoe, but the Winnebago, recent arrivals to the state, often walked here from their reservation in the northern part of the state to visit relatives and friends. The sight of these travelers stayed in the memories of many a Cass County resident for a long while.

But before these tribes ancient Indian peoples lived here thousands of years ago. Their flint arrow heads and tools can still be found scattered over newly plowed spring fields. They are now known as the Nebraska Culture. The first north/south auto highway, the "King of Trails" from Omaha to Kansas City passed through the county. It was built in 1911.

Two miles (7 miles.)

Junction with US Highway 34. To the west Highway 34 travels the length of the state. It joins highways 73 and 75 here until Plattsmouth, where it swings into Iowa.

For information about sites along this route, please see the entry for US Highway 34.

This junction is at the town of Union. For information about Union, please also see entry for US Highway 34.

Seven miles (1 mile.)

Murray, the site of the first county school, 1856.

One mile (7 miles.)

*East on this county road **one mile** to Rock Bluff.*

This is a ghost town, or better yet, a ghost field, now, since all but the school house and a few scattered sites remain of this once prosperous river boat town. The existence of a thriving grain elevator cause some to hope that the site may once again produce a town.

The school is listed on the National Register of Historic Places. It was built in 1870; and was once a two story building. A tornado took away the top floor in 1872. Further twister damage was done in 1896 and 1913. The outside of the building is a kind of historic landmark. Please do not add your name to the walls. Let us leave our legacy in the fact that we were the ones who cared about not defacing such monuments.

Seven miles (3 miles.)

Plattsmouth.

Home of the Cass County Museum, 646 Main Street. An excellent museum in a historically rich county. The Museum is open every day except Wednesday.

The Museum is also the location for the start of a short walking tour of the town. At the SW corner of 6th and Main is the Old Bank Building built around 1885. As you walk down Main Street toward 5th Street, you will pass buildings on either side of street which date from the 1880s and 90s. This one block stretch has so many of them, that one can easily get the impression that the year is 1910.

The building at 525 Main was once Pepperberg Cigar factory. Continue down Main to 4th and take a left. At the SW corner of 4th and Main is the old Waterman Opera House built in 1882, and home for the best entertainment ever seen in Plattsmouth. It housed 1,500 people and had one of the largest stages of any hall in the state. The Cass County Courthouse is catty-corner from the Opera House and was built in 1892. It is probably the best example of Romanesque architecture in the state.

The city library, at Ave. A and 4th, is a Carnegie library and was built in 1922. On the SE corner of Ave. C and 4th is the Walhaus House built in 1886. One block further on 4th brings you to the Heights, 1887, and across 4th street, "The Surveyor General's House."

Turn left on Ave D and walk two blocks to 6th Street. Turn left. The houses along the next two blocks date from 1885-1900. Turn left on Ave. B. On the right is Church of the Holy Spirit Rectory, formerly St. John's Convent, built in 1889.

Turn right on 5th. The church at the corner of 5th and Ave. A was built in 1897, and across the street the interesting Anderson house, 1867.

Turn right on Ave. A. Walk to 7th, turn left on 7th. You will pass several older homes and businesses, and the First Methodist Church at the corner of 7th and Main which was built in 1903.

Turn left on Main and return to your car. See? No reason to lock your doors in this fine community!

Plattsmouth history goes back a long ways. This juncture of the Platte and the Missouri must have been a significant spot for perhaps thousands of years before the arrival of the whites. The Pawnee and the Otoes who dwelled here when the first white men pushed their boats up the river knew the area well. A Mormon, Libias Coon, ferried other Saints across the river near here in the late 1840s.

In 1853 a log trading post was established here which grew

so that it soon served not only the Indians, but the new white settlers as well. The trading post was located on Indian land, and with its establishment came the first step of the Indian's eventual subjugation.

Plattsmouth was a popular river crossing spot and so the town grew around the industry of outfitting pioneers headed west on what was known as the South Platte Trail, or Oxbow Trail, which eventually connected with the Oregon Trail just west of Hastings. The town was well established by the late 1850s and a bustling metropolis of 474 by 1860.

Try to imagine a warm day in May, 1865. On that day 125 covered wagons crossed the Missouri. The banks on both sides of the river were lined with wagons and mules and oxen and families. During that single month, a total of 2,360 wagons crossed the Missouri at Plattsmouth.

Steamboats headed up river for the Yellowstone, the Black Hills and other frontier locations, filled the Missouri, using cord wood to stoke their fires. On any given day the docks along Plattsmouth were filled with stern wheelers and side wheelers getting up a head of steam, filling the air with noise and black smoke. At that time the river was just east of where the Burlington railroad tracks run. The river is now east of town.

In the old days a series of streams ran alongside of the boardwalks on the main streets of town. They merged and flowed into the river. Now those streams have been confined underground. The streams did serve to run several grist mills which opened here in the heyday of pioneer migration west. The first Democratic Territorial Convention was held here in 1858. One of the first automobiles in the state, (back then called a "gig") scared the horses here in 1901. It was still around in order to cross over the first wooden auto bridge across the Missouri, built in 1911. The first railroad bridge was built in 1880, it was replaced in 1903.

Plattsmouth also had an ironworks foundry and much of the fancy ironwork that still exists in this part of the state came from there. It was in existence in the late 1800s. Another major industry here was cigars. Several factories, including the once famous "Acorn" brand, were located here.

The big annual event in these parts is the Kass Kounty King Korn Karnival, which has been held almost every year in September since 1932. One of the early Plattsmouth businesses, a clothing store, kept a tree with several monkeys in it in the store window. It was quite an attraction for miles around.

Feel a little shakey? Well, this is the location of a Nebraska earthquake. The quake started in the early morning in the spring of 1877. It was sufficient enough to cause some cracking on the southeast corner of the brick school house, which was later rebult.

Many of the town's several churches date to the late 1800s.

Three miles (5 miles.)

The Platte River. Just east of here the Platte enters the Missouri. This is a wonderfully wild bit of land surrounded by settlement. The closest one can get to the junction without getting wet, or riding a canoe, is onboard Amtrack. The train crosses the Platte near the mouth.

Five miles (1 mile.)

Offutt Air Force Base and the headquarters for the Strategic Air Command. For those of you who would want to be first hit in a nuclear war, this is the place to stand.

The Presidential plane, Air Force One is sometimes kept here. There are actually more than one One. Look closely and you will see planes with large radar discs sitting on top. A museum is on the grounds which features "some of the fastest missiles and largest bombers ever flown." It is located at 2510 Clay St.

It was just after 6:30 in the evening on September 8th, 1958 when Major Paul Duich sat down with his dinner at Offutt Air Force Base at SAC Headquarters.

He sat with a couple of buddies. They were talking about baseball scores. Major Duich then got up to go outside to get a newspaper from a vending machine in order to find out the latest scores. He left his plate of food on the table and went outside.

As he came back from the lobby of Officer's Quarters he glanced up into the clear sky and saw what at first he thought was a vapor trail. "I have seen thousands of vapor trails, but somehow this one was peculiar. I did a double take, for suddenly it occurred to me that this short "vapor trail" was actually a brilliant source of light. I stopped dead in my tracks and watched."

Instead of dissipating like a vapor trail would, the light grew in intensity and was motionless.

The Major called to other officers passing by. Soon there was a small crowd gathered gazing at the phenomenon in the sky.

He hurried back into the lobby and quickly called the Offutt tower. He described the object to the operator, and soon the members of the tower had it sighted too.

13

The color was changing to a yellow-orange and the fuzzy outline was growing into a solid, cigar-shape. One end was blunt and the other was not. The Major hurried back outside. By now nearly 20 men were gathered, looking at the object. As they all watched a swarm of black specks appeared at the lower end of the object. They looked like gnats, and after a minute or so they disappeared.

Then the object, which had been motionless, began to move. It had been in a vertical position and now swung to an angle to the side. It moved westerly, and slightly to the south.

It remained in the sky for about another 5 minutes. As it approached the horizon it continued to swing around so that it was nearly parallel with the distant corn fields. It faded from view as it moved farther and farther to the west.

The object had been in the sky for nearly 10 minutes. Toward the end a colonel had taken photographs which were never seen by any witnesses. However a full 25 people, including officers and civilians saw the events of that September evening.

One mile (3 miles.)

Bellevue.

An early Spanish explorer, Manuel Lisa, who came this way trapping, claimed the area near the confluence of the Platte and Missouri rivers was a pretty view, or Belle View, hence the name of this community.

The first governor of the territory of Nebraska, Francis Burt, was sworn in here on October 7, 1854. He died two days later.

The new governor liked Omaha as a territorial capitol and moved the legislature there. The folks in Bellevue were mad enough that they insisted they be separated from Omaha by a county line, and although the two towns were once in a single county, a new county, Sarpy, was formed and Bellevue became its first seat.

True to form, a rivalry soon developed over which town should have the courthouse. As was almost always the case, tempers rose and words and fists flew. The folks over at Papillion thought they were better suited for a county seat.

According to a newspaper account of the day Bellevue and Papillion "measured their tongues against each other, and vituperations flew thick and fast. The air was about as sulphurous as adjectives and epithets not to be found in the grammars of the day were thrown back and forth."

Modern Bellevue offers plenty of opportunities to explore its historic past. Tours of the city start at the Sarpy County Museum at

2402 Clay.

Fontennelle Forest, northeast of town offers 17 miles of hiking trails, including a Braille Trail.

Three miles (11 miles.)

Omaha.

At Omaha are the junctions of US Highways 75, 73, with US Highways 6, 275, and Interstate 80. Please see those entries for information about sites along those routes.

Omaha is Nebraska's largest city, at an estimated population of about 350,000. That makes Douglas County the most populated county in the state, and hence the number one in the first digit of local license plates. There is a lot to see in Omaha and the city has had quite an interesting past. Below are just a few of the notable things about the city. Ask downtown for a map of the city to help you find your way around town.

Lewis and Clark reported seeing a hill with 200 Indian houses on it and some believe these were the bluffs of present-day Omaha. It was here that Lewis wrote in his journal: "The musquitors so thick & troublesom that it was disagreeable and painful to Continue a moment still." That is hardly even true anymore.

The Omaha Indians once roamed this area in the time before the white man's arrival. The last remaining Omaha Indians who originally lived here were moved to their reservation in 1854.

Omaha was founded to serve as a town on the west side of the Missouri from the town of Council Bluffs. No one thought the new town would grow, but it did quite well for itself.

In 1825 a trading post was built between 9th and 10th on Dodge and Capitol.

The earliest large group of settlers in the area were the Mormons who had decided to go west until they found a place to live unmolested. Most of them started their journey west in caravans of hand-pulled carts from the Mississippi River. The Missouri served as a good spot to regroup and rest before the next long haul.

Their first settlement in this area was a spot just south of Ak Sar Ben, then they moved to west of present Forest Lawn Cemetery, and finally to Winter Quarters, in the northeast corner of the present city. At Winter Quarters they set up a permanent settlement to serve as a resting place for their fellow pioneers moving west toward Salt Lake City. The town was later renamed Florence and is now incorporated as a part of greater Omaha.

An excellent book on Winter Quarters, and the struggle of the early settlers is Conrey Bryson's *Winter Quarters.*

The Florence Museum was built as a bank in 1856 and is the oldest bank building in the state. The Mormon Pioneer Cemetery holds countless graves from the Mormon settlement days. The Florence Mills, built in 1846 by the Mormons, still stand.

In 1854 Omaha was selected as the location for the meeting of the Territorial Legislature. Thus began the long battle over just where the capitol city should be. The "South Platters" eventually won and Lincoln became the site, but not before the "North Platters" held a number of sessions.

Perhaps it is best understood why the capitol was moved to Lincoln when one realizes that among other activities the Omaha legislature succeeded in eliminating the entire criminal code, and on several occasions the sessions had to be stopped because of fist fights. In 1867 the capitol was moved to Lincoln. The state seal had to be taken by force. The North Platters/South Platters dispute was quite a thing back then and nearly led to Nebraska's own private civil war.

At 9th and Douglas was the site of a two story Territorial Statehouse, and at 22nd and Dodge, the first Territorial Capital.

On December 2, 1863 the Union Pacific started its move west toward building the first transcontinental railroad from Omaha. Later the courts decided the railroad had to start at Council Bluffs. As a result the Union Pacific had to build a bridge across the River.

The Union Pacific headquarters are in Omaha. They operate a wonderful train museum at 1416 Dodge Street. It is free and open seven days a week.

Railroad supporters were quite vocal in the early days, but none so vocal as a man with the unlikely name of George Francis Train. Train lived in Omaha for a time. He was quite a flamboyant character and taken to spontaneous actions. Once, when he had a dispute with an Omaha hotel owner he vowed to have a new hotel built right across the street in three months. His 120 room hotel opened in 90 days.

The Union Pacific Station at 801 S. 10th now serves as the Omaha History Museum. The building is one of the few Art Deco style buildings in the midwest. The museum houses the Byron Reed coin collection, a fine photographic exhibit and two major exhibits on Omaha's history. It is open the entire year.

Not only did the town serve as a trailhead and the start of many railroad journeys, but by 1870 Omaha was a very busy steamboat town with trips up river to the wilds of America leaving constantly, and trips down river to civilization equally as frequent.

In addition to a helper, the River often times can turn into an enemy. In April of 1881 a dam of ice in South Dakota, which had held the Missouri River behind it, broke, sending a cascade of water downstream. It flooded the town. The Missouri at Omaha was 5 miles wide and was 24 feet above low water.

That record was broken in 1952 when it reached 30 and a half feet, but by then the town had learned to take more precautions against high water. A flood in 1877 formed Carter Lake to the northeast. It took the Supreme Court to decide that since the land east of the lake was a part of Iowa before the flood, it should remain so. Consequently there is a little bit of Iowa surrounded by Omaha even today.

Omaha was always considered being on the edge of the vast American wilderness, and its history reflects that location:

—For years the Omaha Public Library displayed the scalp of a man who had survived a scalping by the Indians near Lexington. Today the beautiful main library is one of the showpieces of the modern downtown, despite the fact the scalp no longer resides there.

—The Nebraska Humane Society for the Prevention of Cruelty to Children and Animals was founded in Omaha in the 1870s. The "Children" part wasn't dropped until 1957.

—In 1890 the 16 year old son of the meat packing millionaire Edward Cudahy was kidnapped and held for $25,000 ransom in gold. The money was paid and the boy was returned.

Soon a former Cudahy employee, Pat Crowe was captured. He was not tried until 1905 and by that time he had become a legend as a working man's Robin Hood. When he was acquitted the courtroom burst into thunderous applause.

—One of the last lynchings in the country took place in Omaha in 1891. A crowd of 10,000 took a black man from jail and hung him from a street post.

Omaha's location on the edge of the wilderness made it the logical location for a base of operations for the Army. The General Crook House Museum at 30th and Fort Streets was built in 1878 to serve as a residence for the Commander of the Department of the Platte and is named after the first occupant. The museum is operated by the Douglas County Historical Society and charges a small fee.

The first performance of Buffalo Bill's Wild West Show where admission was charged was at the race track which eventually became the Ak Sar Ben track. Ak Sar Ben was formed in 1895 as a charitable organization designed to promote the best of Nebraska and its people. Each year the members crown a king and queen in a ceremony worthy of London.

Ak Sar Ben is Neb Ras Ka spelled backwards. The Ak Sar Ben track and facilities are at 63rd and Center. The Ak Sar Ben Aquarium is south of Omaha at Exit 432 on Interstate 80.

In 1898 the Trans-Mississippi and International Exhibition was held here. It was one of those grand World's Fairs where numbers of buildings were built to celebrate the American West. Included was a gigantic teeter-totter which held 200 people.

There have been many famous Omahans, but in 1911 when she died, Anna Wilson had a heart of gold and knew many of Omaha's leading male citizens in ways not even their wives knew...if you get the meaning here.

To give you an idea just how many men knew her so well, Wilson's estate was worth $1 million, which she left to local charities. Wilson is buried in Omaha's Prospect Hill Cemetery next to her lover Don Allen, a gambler. For years after her death each Memorial Day people would decorate her grave. That tradition faded out until the late 1970s when a group of people, led by members of the Prospect Hill Brass Band, decided to renew the tradition. Since then every Memorial Day 100 people or so gather at the Madam's gravesite to clap hands and sing along while the brass band plays old favorites.

Omaha has been the setting for a wide variety of unexplained phenomenon. At 4:30 a.m. on August 25, 1877 a "balloon shape" came up the Missouri and knocked over a bridge without doing damage to anything else in the area. One eye witness said "it disappeared as quickly as it had come." Some say it was a tornado, others claim it was a UFO.

In 1897 a group of people, including members of Ak Sar Ben, reported seeing a large flying craft in the skies above Omaha. It was 90 feet long, eliptical in shape, with four wings, two on each side. It shone with a bright light. This vehicle was also sighted through out Nebraska and in Kansas City and Denver at around the same time.

The night after the Omaha sighting a farmer in Kansas and his two sons reported witnessing a spacecraft descend from the sky and capture a cow. They watched a clear, cigar shaped vessel containing six creatures, hover over the cow and then capture it with a cable before the craft rose straight up and disappeared.

For other reports of UFO sightings at this same time see entry for US Highway 136 at Inavale and US Highway 281 at Hastings.

On May 28, 1966 at four in the morning two Douglas Co.

sheriff patrolmen saw a bright blue object, which had a long orange tail, move across the sky in the western part of the county. At that same moment an employee of Western Electric saw a blue-green object in the sky. It had a long reddish tail.

One noon-day in August of 1952 a crew of workmen working on a county bridge saw a round puff of smoke streak across the sky. It moved very quickly.

Some of Omaha's other phenomena have been explained. In 1913 a gigantic tornado touched down at Ralston and cut a 7 mile path of destruction, 1,000 feet wide from 55th and Center to Iowa. Over 2,000 homes were destroyed and 185 people were killed.

That storm stood as the worse until 1975 when a twister touched down and demolished 2,459 buildings. Thanks to early warning systems, only three died in the later storm.

The tornado of 1975 came only a month after one of the worst snowstorms ever to hit the city. There were 11 inches of snow driven by 50-60 mph winds. The strong winds lasted for hours. The drifts from this storm were over 20 feet high.

One of the world's most famous charitable organizations is in Omaha. A Catholic priest by the name of Father Flanagan started a home for boys on the western edge of the city in 1917. The home, soon known as Boys Town, was helped by a 1938 movie and expanded to its present size. It is at 132nd and Dodge. There are many other Omaha sites to see.

The beautiful Joslyn Art Museum at 22nd and Dodge was built in 1930 and houses a vast collection of art including an extensive Western Art collection. It was named after a city founder. His home, called the Joslyn Castle, is at the site of the Omaha Board of Education Offices, 3902 Davenport.

Among many other notable citizens Gerald Ford, the only man who held the office of President of the United States without having to undergo the electoral process for the office, was born in Omaha. His birthplace, at 32nd and Woolworth, is now a mini-park.

Memorial Park at 63rd and Dodge streets was the site of a 1971 demonstration to legalize the use of drugs on public property. Strange times, those early 70s.

In 1966 a white Omaha policeman shot and killed a 14 year old black girl which helped to touch off the city's worst riots. Since then the wounds of the city have healed, although there is much room for improving the way all races treat one another.

The unique and fine Great Plains Black Museum opened in 1976 as the largest Black American cultural institution west of the Mississippi. In addition to the museum, it offers facilities for community meetings and exhibitions. It is open to the public on weekdays. It is located at 2213 Lake Street.

The Omaha Children's Museum is at 551 South 18th Street. It provides a hands-on experience for youngsters of all ages. It is opened year around except Mondays.

At 1600 Abbott Drive in Freedom Park is the World War II minesweeper the *USS Hazard*. This is the largest ship to ever make it this far inland, and serves as a monument to veterans who have fought to keep America free.

At 33rd and Dodge is the Mutual of Omaha Dome which houses artifacts from the television show "Wild Kingdom." It is covered by the largest glass dome of its kind.

The Henry Doorly Zoo is the largest zoo in the state and is one of the nation's finest zoos. It is a natural environment zoo, which means that the animals are allowed to walk around in open spaces, and are not held in small cages. It has the largest enclosed aviary in North America and many other interesting sites. It is located at Deer Park Boulevard and 10th streets. It is open seven days a week.

If the River made Omaha, then livestock made it big and kept it going. You can visit the stockyards at 29th and N streets. Although the Market is much smaller than in its heyday, it still features the 11 story Exchange Building and many fine steak restaurants.

One of the most unique shopping areas anywhere can be found in the Old Market area centered on Howard Street from 10th to 13th in Downtown Omaha. Great bookstores, cafes, galleries and other shops are included in an antique area still used for various sewing and other factories.

Omaha is the site for the College World Series which is held in late spring at Rosenblatt Stadium, 13th and Bert Murphey Drive.

The stadium is also the home of the Omaha triple A baseball team, the Royals.

Famous people seem to come from Omaha in droves. Famous people born in Omaha include Gerald Ford, Marlon Brando, Fred Astaire, Nick Nolte, Inga Swenson, Melvin Laird, Julie Wilson, Paul Williams, Roger Williams, and Buddy Miles.

The University of Nebraska at Omaha includes the Medical Center. The main campus is at 60th and Dodge and the Medical Center at 42 and Emile. Creighton University was founded in 1878 and is located at 24th and Cass. Among many fine programs they are also noted for their basketball teams.

Eleven (3 miles.)

Junction with Interstate 680.

Three miles (6 miles.)

*East on this road **two miles, then north for four miles.***

On top of this hill is believed to be the site of the Ft. Lisa trading post established by Manuel Lisa. Lisa went up the Missouri to the Yellowstone and established a trading post near the Big Horn in 1807.

In 1812 he established this trading post to service the Indians in the area, and became the representative of the U.S. government to the Indians.

Lisa was very important to the Indians and earliest whites over the entire midwest. His wife lived at this spot for a number of years, and died here in 1819. She was quite possibly the first non-Indian woman to ever see this area.

Somewhere near here was also the trading post of the American Fur Company, established in 1825.

This place was visited by Prince Maximilian of Germany in 1833. He wrote: "We saw a crowd of Otoe and Omaha Indians. A small brook with steep banks flows down to the river from a pleasant little wide valley in which are the corn plantations."

***A few miles north of** here was the campsite of S.H. Long who was commissioned by the government to explore the Platte River and the mountains beyond. The name of Long's Peak in Colorado bears the imprint of this expedition.*

Long brought along biologists, painters and geologists on his expedition. To reach this point the troup traveled in a steamboat up the Missouri. This first steamboat to reach Nebraska had its bow carved into the likeness of a dragon, and a short smokestack was placed in its mouth. As the steamboat moved up the river the dragon breathed

21

fire and smoke. One can imagine the effect such a sight might have had on the local native population. One recorded reaction to Long's boat from an Omaha Indian was: "The White man is a bad man, he keeps the spirit of fire chained and forces the spirit to paddle his boats."

Long camped here during the winter of 1819-1820.

Six miles (3 miles.)

Fort Calhoun.

This high and dry town used to be located on the banks of the Missouri when it was incorporated in 1858. The town has long had an importance as a trade center for local farmers, and remains unique and independent, despite its proximity to Omaha.

The Washington County Historical Museum is located in the old Ft. Calhoun State Bank. The displays include a gallery containing relics and artifacts dating from 22,000 years B.C. The museum has a fine collection of Indian work, artifacts from nearby Ft. Atkinson (see below) as well as many items from the county's pioneer period. One of the best collections of barbed wire in the state is also on display. The museum is open from April to December Sundays, Wednesdays, Fridays and Saturdays.

One -half mile east of Ft. Calhoun: Fort Atkinson.

Legend has it that the Fort was built on the location of Lewis and Clark's famous "council" with the Indians at Council Bluffs. Truth of the matter is that no one knows for sure, or knew for sure even when this fort was built, where that meeting took place. Ask any historian and you will be bound to get a heated discussion as to the precise location of Council Bluffs.

Ft. Atkinson was established in 1819 as a result of some pretty tricky international arms deals. The Hudson's Bay Company gave guns to thousands of Indians in the territory surrounding this area. They hoped to have a good chance at controlling the Northwest fur trade.

The United States passed a law which said it was illegal for any non- U.S. citizen to travel in the wilderness without a passport. To enforce this law, and to keep the Canadians, French, and Spanish out of the territory, a series of forts were established. The first of these was Ft. Atkinson, built near the site of Council Bluffs on the Missouri River.

The Fort had a brickyard, a kiln, a sawmill, a gristmill rock quarries, a school and a library of over 500 books. In a sense the 1,000 soldiers, Indians, trappers, hangers-on and traders who lived here composed Nebraska's first town.

The fort lasted from 1820 until 1827 when the entire number of troops were moved to better serve the pioneers who already were starting to move west. The troops were stationed at Leavenworth, in Kansas Territory.

Soon after the soldiers left, the Indians burned the fort to the ground. Later, in 1855, the first settlers of Ft. Calhoun used what remained for building materials for their new town. Time and the elements slowly converted the last remnants of the Fort to dust. It remained nothing but a field until the 1960s when local citizens worked together to have the site saved. The Game and Parks Commission agreed to pay for half of the land.

Things really picked up during the 1970s when a series of archeological excavations began to determine the outline of the fort, and to learn more about the people who occupied it.

Under the able direction of the Nebraska Historical Society field crews searched in the dust and dirt under the hot Nebraska sun for some trace of the earlier occupation. Through their diligent work, and the work of others, much of the life of the fort has been reconstructed.

With considerable expense and volunteer work, the Game and Parks Commission has started on a massive project to reconstruct the fort. What you will see will be their efforts at rebuilding the fort exactly as it once looked, in precisely the same spot.

One of the newest and most interesting state parks run by the Game and Parks Commission, Ft. Atkinson is a "must see" of the area.

Five miles west of Ft. Calhoun: Allen Cemetery. In this cemetery the ruts of the old Ft. Atkinson Trail which led to the Platte River trails to the west are visible..

Three miles (6 miles.)

The former town of DeSoto, once the county seat of Washington County and now nothing more than a memory. This town once had two newspapers, a hat factory and a sizable population.

Near here the Mormon encampment at Winter Quarters (later Florence, near Omaha, see above) raised corn in order to survive the Nebraska winters before moving on to Salt Lake City.

Six miles (6 miles.)

Blair.

Blair is the home of Dana College, northwest of downtown.

US Highways 73 & 75

The college began in 1884 as a seminary for the Danish Evangelical Lutheran Church. The Danish flavor of Dana and Blair is from the largely Danish pioneers who settled here in the 1870s.

Blair is also the location of the Tower of the Four Winds. This commemorative venture is located in Black Elk-Neihardt Park near the college campus. The tower is 45 feet tall, and was constructed to promote world peace, brotherhood (and we assume sisterhood) and understanding. The tower is made from native rock. A mosaic on the east face, constructed of nearly 50,000 pieces, is based on a figure from the Oglala Sioux holy man Black Elk's vision as recorded by John Neihardt (see entry for US Highway 77 for more on these gentlemen). In a vision Black Elk once saw a person standing in front of the tree of life with hands outstretched: the spirit of the universe, the holy one. This tower represents that vision.

An interesting side trip can be had by following State Highway 91 west from Blair:

*West of Blair on State Highway 91, **four miles.** Orum.*
The site of the only crossroads store still operating in the county. A one-room school is preserved here as a museum.

*West of Blair **15 miles** on State Highway 91 are the remains of the small village of Fontanelle. This is the site of Nebraska's first college and was originally called Nebraska University. (They did not have a football team, however.) The college was later moved to Crete and became known as Doane College.*

The Fontanelle Orchard is one of the oldest continuously operated apple orchards in the midwest. The apple juice and other fruit delights available here all year around are something like finding a bit of Nirvana in Nebraska.

Fontanelle was a misspelling of Logan Fonenelle, who was the inerpreter for the Winnebago in the 1850s.

Fontanelle made an attempt to become the territorial capital. They lost.

The Fontanelle Store was built of concrete blocks in 1906 to replace an earlier structure which had burned to the ground. The main floor was the store, and the second floor was used as a meeting hall and theater.

The Fontanelle Cemetery, south of town, has graves from the 1850s.

***Four miles west** of Fontanelle is US Highway 77. Please see* *that entry for further information for sites in this area.*

Six miles (4 miles.)

Take the county road to the west to Neils Miller Cabin-Museum. This log structure, the oldest in the county, was built in 1857.

Four miles (7 miles.)

Herman.

Named for a conductor on the Omaha and Northwestern Railroad, Herman is a German and Danish settlement. On June 13, 1899 Herman was struck by a tornado which demolished every single building in town except for the school and the church which were at opposite ends of the town.

Seven miles (11 miles.)

Tekamah.

The poetic name probably comes from an Indian word meaning cottonwood, or large cottonwood.

Tekamah is the county seat of Burt County. The Burt County Museum is located in a 14 room mansion, and contains many fine exhibits. It is free and open several days a week.

*East of Tekamah, **two miles.** This is the site of an Omaha Indian Village. This village near the river was attacked by hostile Yankton and Santee on December 12, 1846. The village suffered many casualties since many of the men were on a buffalo hunt. Eighty or more of the villagers were killed. The burial ground for these Indians is just west of Tekamah.*

North of here, three miles to Arizona, Nebraska. Retirement center of Burt County.

West of Tekamah on State Highway 32:
Please see entry for US Highway 77.

Eleven miles (5 miles.)

Golden Springs.

This historic springs is on the face of a sandstone bluff on the west side of the road. Traces of the old stagecoach trail can still be found nearby as this was a popular stopping place for early-day travelers. Names were carved in the rock here, and Indians claimed that some of the faintest scratchings are those of the French and the Spanish who came 150 years before the American pioneers.

Five miles (8 miles.)

Decatur.

This is the second oldest town in the state. Decatur was founded in 1855 and was an important and strategic point on the Missouri River. In 1927 a bridge was to be built across the Missouri at Decatur. As these things go, the 20 years which ensued before it was built wasn't that long. However, shortly thereafter the river changed its course leaving the bridge a dry-land bridge. Ten years after that, in 1955, the U.S. Corps of Engineers changed the course of the river, diverting it back into its old channel and Decatur's bridge finally became a bridge across the Missouri.

Just north of Decatur is the southern boundary for the Omaha Indian Reservation.

One Omaha Indian in the late 1960s created quite a stir in Lincoln when he carefully plotted out a series of five foot archeological squares over several graves in the city's Wyuka cemetery. He was ready with note pad, trowel and shovel when the police took him in for questioning. His point was a good one: "If you can dig up the bones of my grandfathers, there should be no reason I can not do the same to yours."

Eight miles (2 miles.)

*Turn off to the **east** for Blackbird Hill State Park, **three miles.***

The story is that this area was the burial of a famous, but disliked, Omaha chief, Blackbird. When he died he was tied onto his favorite horse. The horse was led to this bluff, and then killed. The people then piled rocks and stones and dirt around the bodies until a large hill was formed. On top of the mound they placed all of the scalps Blackbird had traken, and then buried them. This was in 1800.

When Lewis and Clark came up the Missouri in 1804, they mentioned this hill. In 1832 the painter George Catlin climbed up here from the river and found a human skull, believed to be that of Blackbird. The skull was given to the Smithsonian.

*Near here to the **west** are petroglyphs on the sandstone hills including signs of the Thunderbird and Elk Hunter.*

Blackbird Hill is the site of one of Nebraksa's most famous, and perhaps oldest, ghost story.

In the earliest days of this territory, two men loved the same woman. The men were best friends. When the best man, the one that the woman truely loved, was away hunting, some disaster happened. Members of his party came back and said that he had been killed, he had drowned in the river. After a while the girl married the other man.

Some years later the best man returned, having survived the drowning, and having wandered for months. The other man, the one married now to the girl, was insane with jealousy, and fearing that his wife might return to his friend's arms, he cut her throat, and jumped from the top of Blackbird Hill with her in his arms. His bloodcurdling scream could be heard for miles. Her blood spilled on the grass as they crashed down the hillside.

For years afterwards, some say to this day, no grass would grow where her blood stained the earth.

For the past 200 years there have been reports from visitors to this area who hear the faint, yet distinct scream of a man whose voice seems to carry off and over the edge of this hill.

North of here (ask directions from a park ranger) is Indian Cave, or Robbers' Cave. Today it is nothing more than an over used indentation in the side of the sandstone cliff, but for years it served as a hide out for river highjackers who waited for boats coming up and down river. They would attack the boats, and steal furs or supplies.

There is good evidence that Jesse and Frank James hid out in this cave after their ill-fated and bloody attempt to hold up the bank at Northfield Minnesota.

This area is also the southern border of the once proposed Lewis and Clark National Park. (see description in the entry for US Highway 77 for details.)

Two miles (10 miles.)
Macy.

Macy is the main center for the Omaha Indian reservation, adjoining the Winnebagos.

Long before Columbus, the Omaha lived along the banks of the Ohio River. They migrated to the Mississippi, into Minnesota, the Black Hills, and finally, into the northeast corner of Nebraska, where they had been for at least 200 years before Lewis and Clark made contact with them in 1804.

The Omaha Indians have a custom similar to what Indians in the Pacific Northwest call the Potlatch. During the annual pow wow the Omaha may give away most, and sometimes all, of his prized possession. This is an indication of spiritual wealth and strength.

The story is told of an Omaha man, Amos Two Trees, who was married to a beautiful woman, Morning Star.

Once, while Amos Two Trees was away on a hunt, a white trapper took Morning Star away. For a long while Morning Star lived

27

with the trapper, although Amos Two Tree's heart was broken. Then, after a long while, Morning Star, torn with grief for her actions, drowned herself in the Missouri River near here.

Amos Two Trees, so distraught that his wife had killed herself, forced the trapper into the river where he too drowned. For the next 75 years, they say, there was no peace between the Omaha and the whites.

One of the Omaha's great leaders lived east of here on the banks of the river. Son of an Omaha leader, Big Elk, a man by the name of Iron Eyes had his home on the sandstone cliffs above the river. He eventually became the leader of the Omahas and during his term he instituted an Indian police force to serve the tribe, rather than use the BIA agents.

In addition he wrote a monumental history of the Omaha tribe and did studies on their language, customs and rituals. His sons and daughters became some of Nebraska's leading doctors and lawyers.

Ten miles (0 miles.)

Junction of US Highways 73 and 77.

You have entered the Winnebago Indian Reservation. The Winnebagos, transplanted here from their ancestral home in Wisconsin, are good friends with their neighbors the Omahas.

One half mile south of the junction of US 73 and 77, *turn east* on county road and travel *3 miles* to a large depression, lined with trees and bushes.

This is Big Bear Hollow, named after Nebraska's version of Bigfoot, Sasquash, or the Abominable Snowman. According to legend, a large creature, half man and half bear once lived near here. This depression, five miles in diameter, was his home. It is said that he would come into nearby villages and take off children and young girls. One time he took a young girl. The girl's boyfriend trained two bears to scour Big Bear Hollow. The Big Bear/Man ran out of a covering of brambles and the Indian killed him. Who knows, perhaps that story represents the only known killing of a Bigfoot...

The annual Winnebago Pow wow is held near the inteersection of 77 and 73.

This is from the 1928 book *Winnebago Tales:*

Almost every Indian family lived in a lodge of the old-time oval shape made with a framework of slender poles stuck in the ground in a circle, their tops bent over the center and bound together with strong strings or cords made from the fibers of the basswood bark. This frame was strengthened by other poles placed around the sides horizontally, in as many rows as the builders saw fit to use. These poles were then covered with elm bark or mattings made of rushes which overlapped until the lodge roof was rain-proof. At the top a place about two feet square was always left open for the smoke hole. Some of the lodges were made in oblong shape with two or more fireplaces within, and even now the Indians speak of old-time lodges with as many as ten fireplaces, for Indian families were large in those days.

For a continuation of sites to the north, please see the entry for US Highway 77.

Zero miles (13 miles.)
    Kansas border.

Thirteen miles (3 miles.)
    Pawnee City.
    Home of the Pawnee County Historical Society museum which includes 15 buildings. The home of Nebraska's first governor is one of the buildings. Who was he? Answer at the end of the paragraph! Other buildings include Pawnee County's first school building. A barbed wire collection of considerable fame resides in the museum's collection, as do displays on early farm equipment and turn-of-the-century store goods.
    Give up? Nebraska's first governor was David Butler.

Three miles (15 miles.)
    Junction with State Highway 65.
    East three miles *to Table Rock and the Table Rock Museum. Seven buildings make up this museum including the 1893 Opera House which is filled to the gills with antiques and items from yesteryear.*

Fifteen miles (1 mile)
    Cross the Nemaha River which joins the Missouri near the extreme southeastern corner of the state.

One mile (20 miles)
    Junction with US Highway 136. Please see the entry for this highway for information about sites along its route.
Twenty miles (7 miles.)
    Syracuse. For more information about sites in this area, please see the entry for State Highway 2.

The Nebraska City Cutoff of the Oregon Trail crosses State Highway 50 at the southern edge of Syracuse.

Seven miles (3 miles.)

State Highway 50 crosses the Oxbow Trail which connected the Missouri River at Nebraska City with the Oregon Trail, through the area near Columbus, Nebraska.

Three miles (4 miles.)

Junction with US Highway 34. For information about the sites in this area, please see the entry for US Highway 34.

Four miles (8 miles.)

Junction with S-13K. Two miles east: Weeping Water.

Somehow this quiet town with the poetic name could typify all that is beautiful and quaint about the eastern half of the state. It is located on the creek the French called L'Eau qui Pleure—The Water That Weeps—which is a translation of the Otoe name for the creek Ni-gahoe, or water that runs over a small falls. This name was confused by the French for another Otoe word which meant water that weeps.

The ground under your feet in Weeping Water, as well as a great part of the surrounding area, holds the purist limestone in the state. As early as the 1880s this stone was quarried for construction, as a feed lot supplement and for its use in paints. All around the city remnants of past quarries, and the wounds of current ones can be found.

Weeping Water is proud of its native daughters and sons. Among those from here are such folks as Ian Campbell, a reverend whose life has taken him to Turkey and India, and who was known for his love of coins. He was, and yes, there was such a position, the Curator of Coins at the Nebraska State Museum in Lincoln.

Marvin Kivett, a native of Weeping Water, is one of the best anthropologists and archeologists there have been. Kivett, who for years served as the Director of the Nebraska Historical Society, could walk over a field which had been searched by archeologists for a month, sniff the air, glance at the earth and point. "Dig here," he would say, and although others mumbled under their breath, shovels would fly. In a moment an entire earth lodge from a thousand years ago would slowly be

31

exposed.

However, there is perhaps no other Weeping Waterite like Dr. Lloyd Kunkel. Earthy, gnarled, profane, and profound, this gentleman's career included everything from being shot in the head by a bullet fired by Pancho Villa, to surviving a flu epidemic onboard a slow freighter carrying troops to fight in the First World War; from playing in silent moviehouse bands, to making some of the finest violins and cellos in the nation; from discovering and unearthing many of the pre-Columbian Indian dwellings of eastern Nebraska, to practicing medicine for 50 years.

The Weeping Water Historical Complex would not be what it is today without the support and the contributions of Doc Kunkel.

Eight miles (1 mile.)
Louisville.

The case gained national attention and became a rallying point for fundamentalist religious zealots.

One miles (5 miles.)
The Platte River. The river here is sluggish and wide as it approaches its confluence with the Missouri, 15 miles east of here, after its 700 mile journey from the peaks of the Rocky Mountains.

There is growing evidence that this area was visited by Francisco Coronado in 1541. Certainly it was traversed by French fur trappers as early as 1700, far earlier than any easterner (or south-westerner, for that matter) would want to believe possible of the great American desert.

Five miles (5 miles.)
Turn-off for Springfield and Richland.

One mile west of Richfield is the location of the once thriving town of Sarpy Center, one time contender for the county seat, and thought to be the best rival to topple Bellevue as the jewel of the state.

Five miles (1 mile.)
Junction with State Road 370, east to Papillion. Please see entry for Interstate 80 for information about this area.

One mile (0 miles.)
Junction with Interstate 80.

Zero miles (3 miles.)
    Kansas border.

Three miles (6 miles.)
    Junction with State Highway 8.

    East *on Highway 8* ***three miles,*** ***then one mile north*** *to Big Indian Recreation Area. The facility has boating, fishing, and picnicing.*
    East *on Highway 8* ***less than one mile*** *past recreation site turn off:*
    Barneston. This town is at the location of one of the largest Otoe villages. The village stood here in the 1800s. There was once an agency here, as well as a trading post. Later this was the center of the Otoe Reservation. The reservation existed from 1854 until the end of the century when it became apparent to most of the white leaders that

the Otoes would be much happier in Oklahoma.

The town was founded by a fur trader who was married to an Otoe woman.

Five miles east *of Barneston on Highway 8,* ***then north, 3 miles*** *on county road to Liberty. On Cub Creek: site of early trading post around 1855. Most of the early town founders were sympathizers with the Confederacy during and after the Civil War. There is some evidence that the Jessie and Frank James gang spent time here among friends.*

The original post office was one half mile west of the present town site. The mail ran two times a week. Liberty was quite a boom town, as it was located on one of Burlington Northern's main Chicago/Denver routes. Today it is hard to imagine that this sleepy burg was once one of the largest and busiest towns in southeast Nebraska.

Along the route of the Burlington tracks near Liberty the work crews unearthed the skeleton of a mastodon. It was 18 feet in length and over ten feet tall.

To the west on Highway 8 is Route 112 and Odell. For information about these sites, please see below.

Six miles (1 mile.)

Wymore.

Wymore started out because a man named Wymore offered part of his farm to the railroad to use as a connecting site between two railroads. The town once had a street car line, two railroad stations and one of the largest hotels in the area. Near the firehouse is a small stone building which was once the beer cooler for the old hotel. On May 26, 1900 a total of 63 trains stopped in Wymore.

Wymore is the home of Nebraska's only gold rush. A man, drilling for water south of town in 1907, brought up some gravel from the shaft and there, sparkling amid the black sand, was the yellow glimmer of gold. Soon, glory-dreams of nuggets the size of a man's fist danced about a lot of heads. For the next 20 years men tried to dig deep into the earth, and several mines were started, but with no results. Finally the last of the dreamers loaded up their shovels and pickaxes and drifted off into the distance, headed for another dream-stake.

Arbor State Park near Wymore is a fine place to play baseball.

West *of Highway 77, at Wymore* ***two miles, and then 1 1/2 mile south,*** *is the Lester Shalla rock house, one of the oldest structures, if not the oldest structure in the state. It was built in 1829.*

It has been used as a home, a church and a school.

Along highway 77 is pleasant McCandless Park, your last chance to stop and rest in beautiful Nebraska if you are speeding back toward Kansas.

One mile (4 miles.)

Blue Springs. The town is located on the original trail from Marysville Kansas through Otoe Country to Beatrice. The Otoes once had a village at this site.

One mile west of Blue Springs is a log cabin which is over 100 years old. It is now located in the city park where it had been moved from its original location just north of here.

Four miles (4 miles.)

Highway 77 turns sharply from the east to the north here, but those who know, go south on State Highway 112 if they are going any place west of Kansas City, for here is one of the most widely used shortcuts in the state. Several miles can be saved by knowing just how to get from here to the Kansas border. It has happened that people get lost going this way, but people around here are friendly and are used to being asked how to get to Kansas.

Six miles south on Highway 112 is Kriter Hill, one of the tallest spots for miles. This is a spot known for as long as there have been human beings in this area for the beauty of the view. During the 1930s the WPA straightened the road to the top and moved Indian Creek further to the west to prevent flooding. The construction project was carried out with horse-drawn wagons.

One mile east of the hill, in a pasture along the creek the bank is still dug out where the area's best known brick kiln once stood. The "Kriter Kiln" bricks can still be found in many of the older brick buildings in the county.

After seven miles south along State Highway 112, the road makes a junction with State Highway 8.

Turn west on Highway 8. Three miles to Odell. Another town created by the railroad. There is a nice and quiet city park here, a good place to stretch the legs and listen to the landscape of Nebraska.

The Old Odell Bank, built in 1885, is a fine example of a common early Nebraska building trait: using local limestone for local

*building projects. This limestone came from a quarry a few mile.
outside of Odell. The bank is two blocks north of the railroad tracks or
the west side of the street.*

*Across the street from the Old Odell Bank is the Apres Bag
Factory. They make canvas bags here. Although the main factory i.
in Kearney, this place produces 250 different designs of bags in si.
different colors. It employes 30 people.*

*The short cut into Kansas goes south out of Odell on a paved
but bumpy road. On this route is the village of Lanham which started
as a trade center for area farmers. Lanham is half in Nebraska and ha.
in Kansas. Main Street is the state line.*

Three and a half miles to the west *of Odell, on Highway 8
on the south side of the dam on the State Game Preserve, is the place
where, with a bit of walking and some luck, you can still find some o.
the strange and famous "Odell Diamonds", a pink or clear stone
usually with four flat sides. Unfortunately, the best site for these stone.
was covered with water when the dam was built, but many can still be
found.*

*For a continuation of this route, and of sites nearby including
sections of the still-visible Oregon Trail, please see the entry for State
Highway 15.*

Four miles (2 miles.)

Turn off for Homesville on Homesville Road.

Take this road for **two miles, then turn north** *on the gravel
road and follow the road to Iron Mountain. Keep in mind that some
pioneers hadn't seen the Rockies yet and called a number of items
"mountains." Still, this mountain makes an invigorating hike and the
view, especially at dawn, is well worth it.*

***Return to Homesville Road and continue East for five
miles****: Homesville, on Cedar Creek and the Blue River. This was an
alternative route for the Oregon Trail. The area was settled by several
families from England.*

*The limestone quarries these families started became well
known during the years when so many buildings were being con
structed of the rocks of the earth. The first state capitol building in
Lincoln was made of the rocks from here, as were hundreds of other
buildings all over the nation.*

*During the Great Depression the WPA employed hundreds of
workers here to lift out the rock. The town grew to become one of the
largest towns in the area. But the demand for the fine stone gave way
to steel and concrete and plastic, and the importance of the railroad*

faded, so that now a glance at this once thriving town would convince you it couldn't have happened here.

Two miles (8 miles.)
Beatrice. Junction with US Highway 136. Please see entry for US Highway 136 for information about Beatrice.

Eight miles (7 miles.)
Pickrell. When the Zion Lutheran Church was built in 1917 it was said to be the largest church in open country west of the Mississippi. That's pretty easy to believe since the bell towers can be seen for quite a distance. Some classic church art is represented at the church, including a large oil canvas "Christ Knocking at the Door," and fine stained-glass windows.

Try to get a hold of a copy of the interesting and entertaining book which tells the church's history. The book is for sale at the church for $2.00. Pickrell was the site of an early lumber mill, and its existence is what attracted the people to start the town.

Seven miles (3 miles.)
Eleven miles east *of here on State Highway 41 is the town of Adams. Near here was the first land cultivated by the whites in the area. Do you even have to ask? What else? Corn.*

West *on State Highway 41 is Wilber, home of the Czech festival, and DeWitt, home of the Vice Grip. For information about each of these locations, please see entry for State Highway 15.*

Three miles (2 miles.)
Cortland.

This town dates from 1884, and was first a railroad stopping place and location of a general store which attracted much local business. The creek to the west of here, Soak Creek, was given its name when a pioneer fell off his wagon and into the water. His friends named the creek, since what the pioneer called it was not really an appropriate name for anything.

Two miles (3 miles.)
Turn off to the west for Hallam.

A Lincoln businessman, Herbert Gold tried to have Hallam become the site of the first nuclear power plant in the country. In a close vote by the Atomic Energy Commission ,a site in Pennsylvania was selected to be first. Eventually a sodium-graphite reactor was

US Highway 77

built. It operated for a single full year before "problems" forced the nuclear plant to be permanently shut down. It was reconverted to a conventional coal burning plant.

Three miles (3 miles.)

Princeton. This tiny collection of houses has had a blacksmith for as long as there has been a town here.

Three miles (2 miles.)

*Turn off to the **east** for Hickman, **four miles**. Hickman for years was the traditional campsite for a large band of gypsies who passed through the area from time to time.*

In 1967 one of the worst tornadoes every to hit the area tore through Hickman on June 9th spreading destruction for miles.

***East** of Hickman **three miles** to Wagon Train Lake, a fine recreation area.*

***Three miles south** to Stagecoach Lake Recreation Area. **East** of Stagecoach lake, **three miles** to the tiny town of Holland where the store dates from 1900.*

***East** from Holland, **five miles** to Panama. Just northwest of Panama was a long-time encampment of the Otoe Indians.*

*Turn off to the **west** to Sprague, **two miles**, and Martell, **three miles**.*

***West, two miles** from these villages is Bluestem Lake, another in the Salt Valley Lakes system. These lakes are open to the public for general recreation facilities.*

For years a bench in front of the store in Martell was famous as the meeting place of every good storyteller in the county.

***Seven miles southwest** of Sprague was a traditional camping area for the Pawnee Indians.*

Between here and Lincoln, US Highway 77 passes a small patch of native prairie which has been preserved.

Two miles (2 miles.)

Turn off to Roca which had a limestone quarry used extensively to build many of the buildings in Lincoln.

Two miles (10 miles.)

Near here were the villages of Saltillo (**east, one mile**) and Centerville (**west, one half mile.**)

The highway from here north generally follows the same route as a well-used Indian trail. The Nebraska City Cut-off crossed here, near Saltillo Road, headed east and west. There was a pony mail station about **one mile east** of here in the 1860s.

Ten miles (13 miles.)

Downtown Lincoln. For more information about the Star City, please see entry for US Highway 34.

Thirteen miles (6 miles.)

Ceresco. Ceresco was named after the goddess of corn. It has nearly become a bedroom community for Lincoln, but is still aptly named.

*West of Ceresco **nine miles** via county roads to Valparaiso. Debate still rages on whether to pronounce this town Valpar-EYE-zo, or Valpar-A-zo. Either way, the name is better than the original name for the place: Raccoon Forks.*

Six miles (4 miles.)

Junction with State Highway 63 to Ithaca and Ashland. (See entry for US Highway 6 for information about a famous UFO sighting at Ashland, and other items of interest in this area.)

Just south of this junction, on US 77 the Oxbow Trail crosses the highway. This trail ran from Nebraska City north to the Platte, and then west along the river to join up with the Oregon Trail. The route of the Trail is clearly visible. On the east side of the highway it comes up through a small draw of trees. On the west side of the highway the route up and over a hill is clearly defined by the eroded rut marks of the wagons which passed here more than a century ago.

The route of the Oxbow Trail zig-zags across Saunders County, entering in the southeastern corner and leaving the county approximately where State 92 crosses into Butler County.

Pioneer Wayside Area, just south of here commemorates the Trail.

Four miles (2 miles.)

Wahoo.

There are as many stories to explain the origin of the name of the Saunders County seat as there are citizens in this town on the banks of Wahoo Creek. Common explanations include the story that wahoo was the Otoe name of a berry bush which grew along the creek, another is that it was named after a tree with medicinal properties that was found here in pioneer days.

Other explanations for the name include that Wahoo was the name of an Otoe medicine man, that it was the mispronunciation of an Otoe word meaning "without hills", that it is a word meaning "elm trees."

However, local inhabitants and others not from Wahoo claim that the name was an Indian joke. When the Indians, seeing that the whites were taking their land and building a town on their old burial grounds, suggested the name wahoo, which, instead of any of the above, meant something along the lines of "take it and place it where the great sun spirit will never shine."

In any event, the name er...ah...stuck.

The county courthouse was built on top of an Indian burial ground and as the building was being built workers continually found pottery, bones and other artifacts. The Otoe also frequently camped here and many believe that the combination of the burial ground and the camping area makes Wahoo a particularly holy and spiritual place even to this day.

Many buildings in the town center date from the earliest days of Wahoo's pioneer history.

Wahoo was the home of a handful of famous Nebraskans, the best known was Darryl Zanuck who was one of Hollywood's most famous directors.

Two miles (5 miles.)

Junction with State Highway 109 to Cedar Bluffs. See below.

Five miles (5 miles.)

Junction with State Highway 92 east.

Turn east on State 92 for **six miles, and then north one mile to Yutan.**

A large Otoe village of at least 100 lodges stood here during early pioneer times. The main leader of the large band was named Letan. The pioneer village which replaced the Otoe one is a phonetic spelling of the chief's name. Traces of the Otoe village can still be found in the area. The first church and Sunday school exclusively for Indians was located at this village.

Five miles (6 miles.)

Junction with State Highway 64.

*Go **five miles east** on State 64 to Leshara. Unlike most towns*

40

in the state, Leshara was founded in this century. It was named after a Pawnee Chief, Pita Lesharu who lived in the area with his band of Pawnee over a century before.

Just to the east of the village on the banks of the river is the site of an old village, probably belonging to this same band of Pawnee.

Just north of here a high hill, or pahuk, as the Indians called it, overlooks the Platte. This hill was considered a sacred place by the Indians, and the hill was the locale for many of their religious stories. The word was translated into English and deformed to pohocco which is the name of several local features in the area.

Six miles (1 mile.)

Just south of the bridge across the Platte are markers commemorating the Pawnee Villages which were located on the south Platte River Bluffs at Woodcliff.

Just east of this point is the Pawnee Council Rock. In 1855 Gen. John Thayer held a council with the Pawnee chief Pita Lesharu in order to determine if the Pawnee had been responsible for stealing some cattle. The Chief said that his people were not at fault, and said he personally suspected the Poncas.

Take State Highway 109 west to Cedar Bluffs, so named because of the bluffs covered with cedar in the area.

Two and a half miles north of Cedar Bluffs on a county road to the site of the town of Neapolis.

In January, 1858 the territorial legislature decided to move the territorial capital out of Omaha and to a place "not less than 50 miles west of the Missouri and not more than 6 miles from the Platte River." It was quite a hot topic as to what town would become the capital. Instead of selecting an already existing town, the legislature created a new town on paper and called it Neapolis. Several legislators came to the site and began to discuss the location of various buildings. The tall hill here was selected as the site for the territorial capitol building and was named Capitol Hill.

The early legislature, unlike today's governing body, quarreled and quibbled over mundane and silly issues. One such issue was the location of the capital. There were essentially two sides to this argument, those who wanted the capital to be north of the Platte River (North Platters) and those who wanted it south of the Platte (South Platters).

Although the South Platters outnumbered the North Platters, the session at which Neapolis was created was deemed illegal during the following year and Neapolis never materialized.

One mile (4 miles.)

Fremont.

Junction of US Highway 30. Please see that entry for information about sites along its route.

The surrounding hills and the Elkhorn and Platte Valleys make Fremont one of the more beautiful settings for eastern Nebraska towns. Fremont was a natural stopping point for a journey from Omaha to Kearney and because of this the town prospered in the early days of immigrant trails and military roads which passed through here.

Early maps of the city were irregular because a wet rope was used to measure different lots and inaccuracies resulted.

At one point the Pawnee tried to scare the early settlers out of the area, but a show of force, aided by troops from Omaha, quieted the Pawnee.

Fremont was named for one of the most famous early explorers, John C. Fremont, who had the wanderlust and explored a great deal of the American West.

The Louis May Museum is located in the former residence of the city's first mayor. The home was built in the 1870s. Herein are the collections of the Dodge County Historical Society.

Downtown, the Fremont Opera House, the *Love-Larson*, was built in 1888, was one of the finest in its day. The City of Fremont Performing Arts Center occupies the historic and beautiful building now.

The Oregon Trail marker at the corner of Military and "D" Streets marks the Overland Route, which was also known as the Oxbow Trail, through Fremont to Oregon. In Barnard Park a marker commemorates the Mormon Trail which passed this way from 1847 through the 1870s. This park was once known as "Dead Man's Park" because it was the site of the pioneer cemetery. Many of the graves were unmarked and consequently many of them remain in the park. Legends persist about the pioneer woman, wearing a large old-fashioned bonnet, who can be seen near the edge of the park on many cool, lonely nights. This apparition has been sighted by generations of Fremont citizens. The park is located at Military and Clarkson Streets.

There is nothing in the entire state of Nebraska quite like the Fremont and Elkhorn Valley Railroad. The railroad was started as a scenic tourist oriented venture, and began operation in 1986. The 17 mile run from Fremont to Hooper (there are plans to expand the line

42

for a much greater distance) is made by a 1942 Baldwin steam locomotive. The trip includes a short stopover in Hooper which allows for a tour of the Hooper historical district (see below). On the return voyage the train passes through Nickerson and up out of the Elkhorn drainage and into the Platte River Valley. This is a great way to tour this stretch of Nebraska.

On the northern edge of Fremont is Rawhide Creek. Legend has it that a member of a pioneer wagon train through here was boasting to everyone how he was going to kill the first Indian he saw. One morning as they crossed this creek he spied an Indian and shot and killed him. The dead fellow's friends soon surrounded the wagon train and were about to attack. A truce was initiated and a discussion followed. The Indians agreed they would spare the pioneers if they handed over the man who had killed their friend. The pioneers agreed. The Indians tied the man to a tree near here and skinned him alive. Hence, Rawhide Creek.

Fremont is the location of the well-known summer relaxation and girl/boy watching spot: Fremont Lakes. For a description of this and other areas, also see the entry for US Highway 30.

Four miles (3 miles.)
Trail marker for the Major Long expedition to the Rockies. Long and his party of scientists followed an east-west Indian trail through here in the early summer of 1820.

Three miles (2 1/2 miles.)
Junction with State Highway 91. One mile east on 91 is Nickerson, which was named after its founder, a man who helped to build the railroad which passed through here.

Two and one half miles (2 miles.)
Two miles west of here, on Maple Creek, was the Jalapa Post Office. It was along the creek that soldiers volunteering for the so-called Pawnee War of 1859, assembled.

Two miles (1/2 mile.)
Junction US Highway 275. Please see the entry for this highway for information about sites along its route.

One half mile (9 miles.)
Winslow.
One half mile north and one mile west of Winslow is the

43

US Highway 77

site of Logan Mills on Logan Creek. The mill was first established in 1859.

Nine miles (5 miles.)

Uehling, founded in 1905. Near here, just on the northeast edge of the village is a rare octagonal shaped barn.

Five miles (1 mile.)

Junction with State Highway 32. To the east is Craig and Tekamah. Please see entry for US Highway 73 for information. To the west is West Point. Please see entry for US Highway 275 for information.

One mile (7 miles.)

Oakland.

Oakland holds one of the largest Swedish festivals in the nation in early summer. It is a three day affair and has all of the food, dancing and customs you could ever want. This town is the Swedish center of northern Nebraska and many items from Sweden can be found in the stores.

Seven miles (5 miles.)

Lyons. There is a pleasant campground just west of Lyons.

Five miles (10 miles.)

Junction with State Highway 51. To the east is Decatur. Please see entry for US Highway 73 for information about Decatur.

West on State 51 five miles.

Bancroft.

Bancroft is the Nebraska home of the late poet John G. Neihardt. Neihardt is best remembered, nationally, for Black Elk Speaks, *his report of the life and deeds and words of a Sioux holy man. Neihardt's work however goes far beyond this one book. Many consider his masterpiece to be* The Cycle of the West *an epic poem about the settling of the American west.*

He was a prolific writer. In the early years of this century he and a couple of friends took a long and leisurely boat trip down the Missouri River. While they talked philosophy and recounted stories of the then fairly recent Indian wars, Neihardt scribbled into a notebook. His articles were published in a sporting magazine and later published as the book The River and I. *This book, although hard to find, is still* in print and is one of the great classic river books of modern times. He wrote many other books as well, and many of them are still read and reread by thousands every day.

I had the pleasure to have an acquaintance with Neihardt. Often he would stay with friends in Lincoln, and there, on a number of occasions I visited him.

Neihardt was a short man, with a great head of white hair, and eyebrows which arched above clear cool eyes. There was little small talk with Neihardt. If conversation lagged this man, who had written his first book on the text of an ancient and mystical religious book of India, would sit silently gazing into the air as if into a distant place.

On the other hand, when the conversation moved, as it often did with him, his insightful comments and probing questions drove to the very center of philosophy's great questions.

After my first visit, which was with a group of others, and for not much more of a reason than to have him autograph a few books, I was bound to try and see him again. Some many months later, when I did return he remembered me in an instant. "Oh yes, you were with that group of young people," he said, and then settled into the very conversation which we had started those months before.

One listened to Neihardt. Listened to his crackling voice with the faint far away tinges of an accent from another world, and I don't mean of countries and continents, but of an age long past.

There was always talk of books and religion and the deep sure faith he had that all that happens on this earth is but a shadow to a great spiritual world all around us. "If there were only one road and that a black one, this world would not be much, but there is another road, the good red road of spiritual understanding...This good red road of spiritual understanding goes straight north across the Hoop of the World to the region of white hairs and the cold of death. Where this good red road of spiritual understanding crosses the hard black road of worldly difficulties, that place is holy..." Neihardt spent a good part of his life at that crossroads.

The Neihardt Center is open during the summer on Mondays through Saturdays from 8:00-5:00 and Sundays, 1:30-5:00. During the winter it is opened Monday through Friday from 8:00-5:00 and on Saturdays and Sundays from 1:30-5:00.

The center features many of the Poet Lauretae of Missouri and Nebraska's personal belongings and memorabilia from his life. In addition, the center has a library and serves as the home base of the international Neihardt Foundation.

The special feature of the Center is the Sioux Prayer Garden

US Highway 77

which Neihardt constructed from Black Elk's description of what such a place should look like. The Center is a branch museum of the Nebraksa Historical Society.

North of State Highway 51 is the Omaha Indian Reservation. For more information about the Omaha Indians and this reservation, please see the entry for US Highway 73.

·Ten miles (6 miles.)
Walthill.

The town was named for Walter Hill, son of a railroad man, and not some local hill. This town, while on the Omaha Indian Reservation, is not the home of many Indians.

Walthill is at the junction with State Highway 94. East on 94 to US Highway 73.

Fifteen miles west of Wathill on Nebraska 94: Pender.

Pender is the county seat of Thurston County. Although the Winnebago and Omaha Indian Reservations had been created for the Indians, in 1884 the government opened up some of the reservation for settlement by the whites. Pender was the first town to be formed under this provision, although a part of the buildings in the town had been moved from a place known as Athens, now a ghost town two miles southeast of here.

On August 12, 1977 a man claimed he was abducted by creatures in a UFO just outside of Pender. He lost his memory after seeing a ship land. The next thing he knew he was in a white room with black and white patterns of line on the walls, ceiling and floor. There were no doors or windows. A voice entered his head and began to ask him a series of questions about math and science and religion. Well, that's what he claimed, anyway.

Thirteen miles north to Emerson, the only city located in three counties in the state.

Six miles (3 miles.)
Junction with US Highway 73.

From this point northward to South Sioux City, Highways 77 and 73 follow the same route. For information about Highway 73 south from this point, please see the entry for US Highway 73.

After the Sioux uprising during the American Civil War, the Winnebago were forced into the area from their native Wisconsin.

They were first placed on a reservation on Crow Creek in South Dakota, but could not survive the winter of 1863 and migrated to the Omaha Reservation southeast of here. The Omaha Indians, related by blood to the Winnebago, took the tribe in and helped them adjust to the life of outcasts. Later the Omaha sold 97,000 acres to the Government for a reservation for their homeless brothers and sisters.

Winnebago.

This is the center of the Winnebago Indian reservation.

An early pioneer Alice C. Fletcher wrote a book on her memories of Nebraska. She described her first experience with the music of the Indians of this reservation: "The sound was distressing, and my interest in this music was not aroused until I perceived that this distress was peculiarly my own, everyone else was so enjoying himself (I was the only one of my race present) that I felt sure something was eluding my ears; it was not rational that human beings should scream for hours, looking and acting as did these Indians before me, and the sounds they made not mean something more than mere noise."

Obviously Fletcher never sat on a hot summer evening at the annual Powwow held near the junction of US Highways 77 and 73, and watched from the side of a teepee as the drummers, wrinkles and grey eyes attesting to a kind of wisdom that only comes with age, begin to slowly tap out their rhythm, first one, then another.

She would have watched as one of the drummers begins a low and soft humming, another joins the song. Their voices become a plaintive tremolo, weaving in and out of one another, dropping octaves in long and bittersweet slides. Off in the distance a coyote, or the faint ghost of a timber wolf lifts its ears.

The beat of the drum is insistent now, and firm. Now all of the drummers are singing. This is the Flag Song, or the Friendship Song, or perhaps a war song.

Next the women stand, their shawls and robes about their shoulders to cut the chill that has come on with the dusk. Smoke is in the air. The fires are lit and raging. The women form a wide circle about the drummers, and stand shoulder to shoulder. They begin a slow two-step motion in time to the song. The circle begins to move. The shadows of the women fall upon the stretched skins of the teepees. Children are running about, playing tag, or clinging to their mothers' legs, trying to keep in time to the beat. Everyone, everywhere, is in motion.

Finally, the men start to dance. Slowly they appear, almost

47

out of nowhere and without notice they are in the center of the circle. A knee goes high into the air. Toe down. Heel. Toe down. Heel. Ai-ye-yah-yah-yah. Toe Down. Heel. They spin and twist. Their arms mimic the secret world of eagles, the lonely life of deer, or the power of bear. Room is made for the fellow who has had too much to drink, he is not shunned, nor censored, though there is a bit of kidding as he bumps into a few of the other men.

Now all heads turn. The dancer has entered the circle. He is in full dress: thousands of feathers, all radiating out from center of shiny metal discs adorn his head and his rear. Long strings of them hang from his arms. There are feathers in his headdress: red and grey and white ones. He wears anklets of bells. They jingle, jingle, jingle as he steps, slowly at first, in time to the music. His feet are bare, his face is painted. Even the best of the other men clear a little space for this one. He swirls and weaves and ducks around and amid them, using the seated drummers at the center of the circle as a kind of pivot. The orange of the campfire causes his face to glow. His eyes are impassive, they are looking out beyond this world, out to a place where there is no passing of time, to a place where the winds of the prairies blow forever across open plains.

Then, suddenly, though no one is taken by surprise, the song ends. Where an instant before there was motion, sound and a beat of drums which had entered into the soul of every witness, now there is a hole in the night. The drummers smile, talk softly. The dancers drift back to their places in lounge chairs and take a sip of coffee from thermoses.

Three miles (3 miles.)
This is the Thurston/Dakota County line which also serves as the border of the Winnebago Indian Reservation.

Three miles (8 miles.)
Homer.

One half mile west of Homer is the site of an old Omaha Indian village. The village predates Lewis and Clark, and when those explorers passed this way the village had already been burned to the ground. They estimated it held over 300 huts. The village, believed to have been called Tonwantonga, or Large Village, suffered the white man's invisible first conqueror: smallpox. The disease, previously unknown to the Indians killed over 400 people here. Near here stood Ft. Charles. The state has placed a historical marker for the village two miles north of Homer, but the village actually stood on the side of the *steep hill.*

*East of Homer, **two miles** is Combs School, built in 1857 at a town no longer in existence, named Omadi. This building has moved around the county more than some of its citizens.*

Just to the east of the school is the O'Connor House, a 14 room mansion of brick built between 1865 and 1875 and now a museum. The house is still furnished with many of the original items. Next to the house is the Museum Machinery Building, built by the Historical Society to house some of the many farm implements collected over the years.

*East of the museum **four miles** to an abrupt cliff known as Land's End. Here the Indians came to pray and meditate, to dance and sing. The 500 foot drop to the Missouri River plain affords a dramatic view.*

Along this side of the river were campsites of Lewis and Clark. At one long lost time this entire region—from here south 25 miles along the Missouri river bluffs, was a proposed national park and wildlife refuge. It was proposed that the park would honor Lewis and Clark. The fact that this area was once considered to be National Park material should be enough said for the adventuresome tourist.

Return to US 77.

Eight miles (3 miles.)
   One mile east to Dakota City.
   Dakota City, Nebraska has the oldest church in the state. Emmanuel Lutheran was built in 1860 and cost $2,000...an extremely healthy sum in those days. But this was nothing compared to the $16,000 they dropped into a grand hotel in 1858. The hotel was torn down, the church still stands. Spend a moment in the shade of the cottonwood and elm near by and soak in the peacefulness here.
   Dakota City had one of the widest main streets anywhere as three individual roads were combined to form the street.
   This place was visited by Lewis and Clark on their way to the Pacific. They reached the mouth of the Omaha Creek, just east of here, on August 16, 1804.
   One of their group, Sergeant Charles Floyd, died and was buried near here. Dakota City is the county seat of Dakota County.
   In the days of steamboats, the sternwheeler *Nugget* hit some snags and went down just offshore here. Her cargo was mainly whiskey, and a good many of Dakota City's best labor was to be found helping salvage what they could of the *Nugget*.
   The IBP corporation meat packinghouse in Dakota City was

fined a record $5.7 million for violations of health and safety violations in the late 1980s. The fines, which were handed down by the government's Occupational Safety and Health Administration, were for ignoring the hazards of repetitive motions by the packinghouse workers. Such motions can lead to disabling neuromuscular disorders.

In 1987 government officials said IBP had the most flagrant violations of record keeping about job related injuries it had uncovered in its entire 17 year history.

The $5.7 million was the largest fine OSHA had ever handed down.

The fines were later reduced, and IBP instituted a massive program to reduce the incidents of muscular disorders.

Three miles (0 miles.)
South Sioux City and junction with US Highway 20. For information about South Sioux City and for sites along US Highway 20, please see the US Highway 20 entry.

Zero miles (3 1/2 miles.)
Kansas State Line.

Three and one half miles (3 miles.)
County road to the east leads to Steele City and Endicott. Please see below for a description of the many sites in this area.

51

State Highway 15

Take this county road to the **east** for **one and a half miles**, then **south for two miles**, then west again to return to Highway 15 for one of the most scenic drives in the area.

Three miles (2 miles.)

Intersection with State Highway 8 West.

Two miles west on State Highway 8, then one and a half miles south to a private mausoleum near the banks of Silver Creek.

West on State 8 seven miles to Reynolds. *One and a half miles west* of Reynolds is a marker indicating the site of a very early Jefferson County town called both Mark's Mill and Rose Creek City. It was founded in 1865.

Two miles (1 mile.)

State Highway 8 on the southern edge of Fairbury.

Six miles south on Highway 8 to Endicott.

One and a half miles north and one mile east to John Fremont and Kit Carson Rock at Quivera Park. On a sandstone rock at this place are a few historic words: "John C. Fremont and Kit Carson - 1842".

There is much debate whether these signatures are authentic, although there is evidence that places the names on the rock as least as early as 1890. One misguided early historian deepened the cut of the signatures which made dating even more difficult. In any event, this was certainly one of the inscription rocks along the Oregon Trail.

There is a great deal of difference between those pioneers scratching their names here in hopes that a loved one would come along the trail some time later and know they were alive as far as this point, and the random and egocentric scratchings of modern tourists.

One mile north of Quivera Park to Rock Creek Station State Historical Park. This is a fine state park which offers the visitor many interpretations of this famous site along both the Oregon Trail and the Pony Express route.

Rock Creek Station was a company station founded originally by the Central Overland California and Pike's Peak Company. It was here on July 12, 1861 that Wild Bill Hickok for not much of a reason gunned down David McCanles in cold blood while McCanles' young son watched. Hickok, who killed close to 200 people in his 39 years, started the bloodiest part of his career with this shooting. Hickok's two other victims of this killing spree were once buried near the East Station, but were later interred in Fairbury Cemetery.

This is a fine park and in addition to the ruts from the Oregon Trail which can be seen in the park, replicas of buildings from the Pony Express station and Oregon Trail days are here. This is one of the most significant sites of the Trail in Nebraska, and certainly one of the state's finest historical parks.

Four miles south of Endicott on State Highway 8 is Steele City. The historic district of Steele City contains many fine restored historic buildings, and gives the visitor the feeling of walking down an old western town, which is just what Steele City is. A fine small museum is located here and includes tours of a bank and a blacksmith shop. The stone Baptist Church dates from the 1880s as does the stone blacksmith shop and the stone livery stable.

Three miles east of Steele City, then one quarter mile north. This is one possible site of the famous Fremont Springs.

The Springs were named for the explorer John Fremont who camped here in 1842. There is another, more probable site for these springs, near the Quivera Park monument. In any event, the Oregon Trail crossed from the southeast to the northwest at this point.

Go north to the next county road intersection. Then turn west and go for another half mile. This is the location of the Rock House Pony Express station. This is one of several station sites in Nebraska. The Pony Express was only active for a few years before being replaced by the railroad, however, its history is a very important part of Nebraska since the trail cut across the entire state.

Due east of here ran the Oketo Cutoff, which was a stagecoach line in 1862. The owner, Ben Holladay ,had a dispute with the leaders of Marysville ,Kansas and therefore rerouted his stage road around that town. This was the new route. The controversy was soon settled, and the Oketo Cutoff was only used for a few years.

Two and a half miles to the east was the town of Shea, now nothing but fields mark the place.

One mile (2 1/2 miles.)

Fairbury and the Junction of US Highway 136. For information about this area please see the entry for US Highway 136.

Two and one half miles (1 1/2 miles.)

Two and a half miles north of the intersection with US

State Highway 15

Highway 136 and straight west of the Fairbury Airport, on the west side of State Highway 15 ruts from the Oregon Trail are still visible. Study the land to the west and ask locally in order to best spot the ruts.

One and one half miles (1 mile.)

This is the site of Virginia Station, a Pony Express station and the location of the Whiskey Run marker. This place was unique in that there were soldiers stationed here for a time in order to keep peace between pioneers and Indians.

The story is that the soldiers took the Indians' whiskey and poured it all into a nearby creek which gave it the name Whiskey Run.

In June of 1849 a man from Massachusetts was heading west on the Oregon Trail. He got the fever and soon was delirious. Like many other pioneers, George Winslow died of cholera. What made things different, was that the stone someone finally got to mark his final resting place was rediscovered years later.

Eventually it was placed inside of a larger marker by the state of Nebraska, and by Winslow's sons. The marker and grave is **one and a half miles west** of the Whiskey Run monument. The marker is on private property and if you haven't been given permission to pass through the gate, please don't do so. Trail ruts are visible just southwest of the monument.

One and a half miles west of the Whiskey Run marker, on the west bank of the Little Blue River, was a well-used springs known as Whiskey Springs.

One mile (3 miles.)

There are many interesting places west on this county road. Ask locally for additional information and directions.

Three miles west on this county road is the site of the Little Sandy Stage Station, which dates from the 1860s.

One more mile west is the sleepy town of Powell, and one and a half miles west of Powell is the site of Big Sandy Stage Station, in competition with the Little Sandy Station in the 1860s.

One and a half miles west of Big Sandy Station site, (three miles west of Powell) is an unusual museum dedicated to the District 10 schools which is located on the Oregon Trail and the Pony Express

Trail. This site is eight miles west of State Highway 15 and just south of the Alexander State Recreation Area. It is open Sunday afternoons.

Three miles (6 miles.)

Junction with State Highway 4.

This is the site of the former town of Bower.

Eight and a half miles east of here is the site of the former town of Old Plymouth, and **four miles to the west** of here, the site of the former town of Helvey. Please see entry for State Highway 4 for more information about sites along this road.

Six miles (2 miles.)

West of here is the town of Western. There is a debate whether this town was named because it is western, or after a man named West.

Two miles (4 miles.)

Turn off for State Highway 74.

Eight miles west of here to Tobias.

Tobias was founded in 1884 as a railroad town and to be a market town for an area of the county not easily served by other places.

Tobias was formerly called Castor, but the name change was to avoid confusion with Custer and Closter.

In the early days Main Street had bookstores, hotels and hat stores as well as a race track and roller skating rink.

There are still buildings standing which date to the town's first decade.

Over half of the town was burned to the ground in 1891. The fire was caused by arson.

Alice, a notorious horse, ran in races around here often. Alice was a mare who always seemed to win her races. Sixteen loads of corn were won in a race she once ran. She ran on a lot of tracks in the state, but was most frequently seen here. She died in Utah from eating loco weed.

One story from Tobias' early days was that at a candy and fruit shop three men began to argue over a bunch of bananas which had come in. They decided that they could eat the entire bunch in one sitting. One man ate 20, another 30 and another 34. No report survives about what they did the rest of the day.

The Tobias Cemetery was laid out in 1884. The oldest grave is dated 1883. The site was selected after much debate with a farmer who deeded the land. His concern was that it be placed in such a manner that his family not have to pass a cemetery every time they went to town.

The Community Church, formerly the Baptist Church, was built in 1886.

The bar (called Cookie's in 1984) is a friendly typcial Nebraska bar with stalls along the bar and good food on short order.

Old pioneers say of the area that the Indians didn't give them much trouble, but that they had to beware of the gypsies.

The first appendiectomy in the state was performed in Tobias, in 1896.

Tobias has a nice small museum located in the Tobias print shop. Memorabilia, newspapers, antiques and photographs are all on display here. Volunteer operated, they'd appreciate donations.

Tobias is the home of the 1959 Nebraska High School Basketball champs. (Class E) They beat Wilsonville 45-36.

The historical marker on Highway 74, east of Tobias is for Sgt. Leodegar Schnyder, who served in the Army for 53 years, longer than any other non-commissioned officer. He was stationed for a long while at Ft. Laramie during the peak years of travel over the Oregon Trail., In a way, he was a kind of a landmark for thousands of travelers just as Chimney Rock might have been. He witnessed much of the Old West's famous events, but, unfortunately, he did not keep a diary and he did not like to talk much about his life. He was among 42 people left at the fort after the start of the Indian Wars brought on by the events of the Grattan massacre and the Battle of Blue Water (see entry for US Highway 26). He fought in the Seminole War and other Indian engagements. He was a resident of Tobias.

If there could be anything else you would like to know about Tobias, just ask around.

Four miles (2 miles.)

Junction with State Highway 41 east.

Two miles east on State Highway 41 is Klacel Hall, site of an old dance hall.

Eleven miles east of State Highway 41. Wilber. Wilber is the Czech capital of Nebraska, and celebrates its Czech heritage nearly every day of the year, but especially during the two day long Czech Festival the first weekend in August. There is nothing, absolutely nothing, that can compare with turning the corner on to Third Street and suddenly being swept up in the bright colors, the deep settling smells of Czech foods, and the bright music that clutters the street. The arts and crafts for which the town is noted are on display and the visitor can almost get their year's fill of kolaches, Polish sausage and beer.

Hotel Wilber near Second and Wilson Streets, was built in 1895 and has recently been renovated and features a fine Czechoslovakian cuisine. In the hotel's import shop is a display of heirloom jewels from the old country.

There are many other fine arts and crafts shops in the town. The Czech museum is located at 102 W. 3rd and features doll and quilt collections as well as many other exhibits of early Wilber history. The museum is open in the afternoons from May through November, and at all other times by appointment. Admission is free. The Wilber library was built and given to the city by the Milo Stastny's, an unusual single contribution for a worthy cause. Just north of the city (sniff, sniff) is one of the largest area pork processing plants.

Return to State Highway 15, or continue north on State Highway 103 to Crete and US Highway 6.

Between Crete and Wilber is the Czech Settler's monument, to commemorate Czech settlements in the Blue Valley which date from 1865. The first of these settlers walked here from Nebraska City, following a wagon loaded with supplies.

South of Wilber on State Highway 103 **seven miles** to DeWitt. DeWitt carries the unusual history of having its first church built with money paid in order not to have the new town named Dennison. Dennison was one of the early founders of the town, and when it came time to name the town, many of the locals wanted to name it after this gentleman. He, instead, preferred that the town be named after a minister from his hometown back East, DeWitt Talmage. In order to ensure his anonymity, Dennison paid $500 toward the construction costs of the Congregational Church.

The Methodist church was built in 1873.

Every home handyman or handywoman in the world has a special reason to visit and pay homage to DeWitt, for it was here in 1929, that the Vise-Grip was invented and is still manufactured. The Vise-Grip wrench is a tool so useful, some say, that the object it is used on will often lose its usefulness.

Near here was the location of the once sprawling village of Swan City. Swan City, which covered thirty acres, but probably never *had a population of more than 60, was located on the south bank of Turkey Creek, one mile west of De Witt. For a short while Swan City served as the county seat of Saline County. Until recently pilings, which once supported a mill, could be seen in Turkey Creek. The mill burned to the ground in 1891.*

Two miles (3 miles.)

Junction with State Highway 41 west.

Eight miles wes*t of the intersection and at the junction of Highway 41 and Tobias road: Old Quaker settlement in "early days." It was called Triumph. It was located two miles west of Atlanta Center Cemetery.*

Three miles (7 miles.)

During a blizzard on March 29, 1976, wet snow and high winds brought down hundreds of power lines near here like dominoes, putting power out up to ten days in a 16 county area.

Near here the first brood of pheasant chicks was released in Saline Co. around 1910. If you don't hunt, this information may not be of extreme historical interest to you.

Seven miles (3 miles.)

Junction with US Highway 6, please see the entry for US Highway 6 for more information about sites in this area.

Three miles (5 miles.)

Dorchester. Please see the entry for US Highway 6 for information about Dorchester.

Five miles (5 miles.)

Just after entering Seward County and on the north side of the West Fork of the Blue River, follow county road east to the confluence of the West Fork with the Big Blue. A quiet and beautiful natural spot.

Five miles (4 miles.)

State Highway 15 turns north. Continue east on US Highway 6 in order to go to Milford. See entry for US Highway 6 for information about Milford.

Four miles (5 miles.)

Junction with the Interstate of Nebraska: 80. Please see entry for Interstate 80 for information along its route.

Five miles (5 miles.)
Seward. Please see entry for US Highway 34 for information about Seward.

Five miles (2 miles.)
West 4 miles to Staplehurst.
This town dates from 1873 when the earliest settlers built dug-outs along the banks of Lincoln Creek. The area was settled by Germans, Danish and English. The first Lutheran church in Staplehurst was built in 1882, and was moved south of Seward some years later. It can be seen from the Interstate, just east of the Seward exit.

A dam was built on the Blue River in 1912 to provide electricity for the village and every August since then, the town celebrates the occasion. The Staplehurst Bank has been robbed a number of times. Once so much dynamite was used to blow up the safe that pieces of metal were found two blocks away.

Three and a half miles west of here was a trading post known as Marysville. There was a mill and a post office located there on a well traveled mail route.

Two miles (14 miles.)
Two miles east to Bee.
Bee was founded in the late 1880s with the coming of the railroad. This area was settled by the Irish initially, and later by the Czech and the English.

Fourteen miles (5 miles.)
Junction with State Highway 92.

Five miles (1 3/4 miles.)
David City.
David City is the county seat. The county of Butler was named after the first state governor, David Butler, but inappropriately enough, David City was not named after David Butler, but an early settler.
Butler County is also home to towns with names like Rising City and Surprise.
The Oxbow Trail passed this way. The Oxbow Trail, which connected Nebraska City with the Platte River near Columbus, and eventually the Oregon Trail west of Hastings, passed through what is

State Highway 15

now Butler County. It crosses State 15 about 1 3/4 mile north of David City. It crosses State 64 about 3/4 of a mile before the Polk County line. It crosses State 92 twice, first just as the highway enters Butler County from Saunders, and again, one mile further west.

In general the trail makes a winding route from southeast to northwest through the county. Traces of the route can still be seen in some areas. Ask locally.

One and three fourths mile (3 miles.)

The Oxbow Trail which connected the Missouri River travelers from near Omaha with the Oregon Trail crosses the highway here.

Three miles (6 miles.)

Junction with State Highway 64. On State 64: Bellwood. For information about Bellwood and its unsung hero of Arbor Day, please see the entry for US Highway 81.

Six miles (1 mile.)

Junction with Highway S-12.

Seven miles on S-12 to Linwood. Linwood is located on the banks of Skull Creek, which flows into the Platte. Skull Creek was the location of an old Indian battlefield and burial ground, hence the name.

*The county road to the **west** at this intersection follows the Platte River and makes for a nice and quiet drive.*

One mile (4 miles.)

The Platte River.

Just across the Platte the highway crosses the route of the Mormon Trail which followed the north bank of the river.

Four miles (4 miles.)

Schuyler and the junction with US Highway 30. Please see entry for US Highway 30 for information about Schuyler.

Four miles (18 miles.)

The Benedictine Mission House. The Mission House has been located on this site since 1935. The modern house is built into the side of a hill and looks out over the surrounding hills with a serenity and grace. The Benedictine House coordinates fund raising activities for all Benedictine missions around the world. In the building are displays from the Missions around the world.

Eighteen miles (8 miles.)
Junction with State Highway 91.

Leigh, Clarkston and Howells are three small burgs along the northern edge of Colfax County. All three were founded in 1887. These small communities share many of their activities and yet retain a sense of pride and identity of their own.

Eight miles (12 miles.)
Junction with State Highway 32.

*Take Highway 32 for **eight** miles to junction with State Highway 57, then **north eight miles** to Stanton.*

Stanton. The county seat for Stanton County. Bet you think the town of Stanton was named after the county of Stanton which was named after the Secretary of War in President Abraham Lincoln's administration. Wrong! The city was named after the maiden name of the founder's wife. Not everything is always as it seems it should be. The town was founded by Germans from Wisconsin in 1869.

***Two miles north** of Stanton is the Maskenthine Recreation Area, one of the largest lakes in the area. It was built on the lower Elkhorn system for flood control and recreation. Surrounding the lake is a 300 acre wildlife management area. On the east side of the lake is an arboretum maintained for growing trees, grasses and other natural and indigenous plants of the area. The lake is stocked with a wide variety of fish. Camping is permitted, although no set facilities are available.*

You may return to State Highway 15 the way you came, or take the county road east out of town to Pilger.

Twelve miles (1 mile.)
Pilger. Take the county road **east** of here **nine miles** to Stanton (see above).

***Two miles north** of here is Pilger Recreation Area with a pretty, 40 acre lake.*

One mile (4 miles.)
Junction with US Highway 275. Please see entry for this highway for more information about sites along this route.
For 2 miles State Highway 15 follows US 275.

Four miles (13 miles.)
Since State Highway 15 turned north and broke away from US Highway 275, you have been traveling on the county line between

State Highway 15

Stanton and Cuming Counties. Cuming County, you might like to know, calls itself the livestock capital of Nebraska.

Thirteen miles (10 miles.)

Wayne.

Home of the internationally famous Wayne Chicken Show. Now, this is something to crow about, something that Wayne likes to think makes folks roost here. The event, usually held in mid-summer, has been featured on Johnny Carson's "Tonight" show, on "Good Morning America," in *USA Today* and the *Wall Street Journal*. This is a celebration of the oft-neglected chicken and its talents. SEE the international competitive egg toss! SEE the Chicken Art Show! HEAR the Cluck-Off Competition! TASTE the Chicken Feed! (no, not the feed the chickens eat, but the food we eat made from chickens.) SAVOR the Omlet Feed! All right here in lowly-seeming Wayne, not eggsactly the center of the world.

Wayne State Teacher's College dated back to a Lutheran school started in 1881. The 130 acre campus is now a part of a state arboretum. Wayne is the location of the Wayne County Museum located in a large mansion built in 1901.

Also located here are the Bumble Bee Gardens and Iris Country, two of the largest gardens of perennials in a ten state area. The area is full of nurseries and gardens.

About the turn of the century a boy named George Heady saw a bright star fall from the sky and land somewhere south of town. He went out the next morning and searched the area. What he eventually found was a strange donut shaped circle of burnt grass in the middle of a field. There was a slight depression in the earth. He found a large piece of metal or stone near by and took it back into town. He began telling people that he had found a piece of a star that had fallen to earth. Everyone laughed at him and his story, until finally someone went with him back to the burned field. Slowly the people of Wayne began to believe George's story. He kept the rock all of his life until finally, an old man about to enter a nursing home, he gave the stone to a friend. For a long while the friend kept the rock, but finally the stone—a oval about 17 inches in diameter, was used as a marker to commemorate George Heady. When they tried to carve words of honor to Heady in the stone, all of the tools broke on its incredible hard surface. Instead, they placed a granite stone to mark Heady's passing. The commemorative marker is near the entrance to the Wayne Cemetery on the western edge of the city.

Ten miles (5 miles.)

Junction with State Road 116.

Five miles (3 miles.)

Laurel. This tiny hamlet was the birthplace of a big star, the fine Hollywood actor James Coburn was born here.

Junction with US Highway 20. Please see entry for US Highway 20 for information about sites along this highway.

Three miles (9 miles.)

Junction US Highway 20, State Highway 57 and State Highway 15.

Two miles north *of this intersection on State 57 is the location of the old town of Norris, abandoned after it was bypassed by the railroad.* ***Three miles east*** *of the site of Norris and a quarter mile north is the location of the old Norris Cemetery.*

Please see entry for US Highway 20 for sites along that route in this area.

Nine miles (9 miles.)

Coleridge. Yes, this is named after the man who wrote such lines as "Water, water, everywhere, and not a drop to drink," and who gave us such phrases as having an albatross around one's neck, the poet, Samuel Coleridge

The most famous feature of Coleridge, the town, is the bird zoo. Ask around for its location.

Nine miles (7 miles.)

Hartington.

This is the home of the Cedar County Museum, a fine museum in the old Lammers' home built in 1900. The four story house has 21 rooms and many of the rooms have been turned into display rooms for the museum. The caretakers of the museum live here as well. The museum includes a library, dress shop, military room as well as quilt displays often with members of the local quilting society present to answer questions. The lawn chairs and tables are for your use, feel free to relax at this fine museum for a good long while.

Seven miles (2 miles.)

Junction with the historic State Highway 12. Please see entry for this road for more information about the sites along its route. State Highway 15 ends at this junction, however, continue east on State

State Highway 15

Highway 12 one mile to State Road S-14H.
Turn **north** on State Road S-14H.

Three miles north on State Road S-14H.

One mile west *of here is the brick house of the Lammers. They are the only remaining early-day pioneer family in the county. The house is located on the original homesteading site and is 120 years old. The bricks were made on the property.*

On the southeast corner of this intersection is the St. Helena Catholic Cemetery. It is the 4th oldest cemetery in the state and there are graves which date from the early 1860s. One mile further north on State Road S-14H to St. Helena and the site of the Felber Tavern. For over a century, this was the center for information, comfort, supplies, gossip, cardgames, booze, neighborly conversation and news.

West one quarter mile of St. Helena, then north on graveled road for one and a half miles, then west for two and a half miles. On the northwest corner of this intersection is the site of the Bentz Hill Massacre. Dr. Lorenzo Bentz was killed here by Indians in 1864 as a warning to other settlers who might be so silly as to try and settle in this area.

See entry for State Highway 12 for a map of this area and further information.

Zero miles (10 miles.)

The Kansas border.

Ten miles (1 mile.)

Hebron is just west of the highway. Hebron was founded in 1869 by a group of pioneers associated with the Disciples of Christ. It is the county seat of Thayer County and is built on the banks of the Little Blue River.

Two miles (8 miles.)

At the intersection with this county road is where the Oregon Trail crosses US Highway 81. A marker is on the northeast corner of the intersection. Bear in mind that the trail was not like the straight, narrow roads of today. Instead, in most places, the trail was a general direction with landmarks to keep travelers on course. Don't look for specific routes for many places along the Trail, but remember that the wagons might have been spread out over a half mile either side of this general location.

Three miles west of here on the county road is the site of the Hackney Ranch, an important settled spot on the Oregon Trail. Three miles east on the county road, and then one half mile north to a Oregon Trail marker and the location of Millersville Station on the Pony Express Route. The Pony Express Route generally followed the same route as the Oregon Trail.

Eight miles (16 miles.)

Junction with State Highway 4, west. For information about sites along this road, please see entry for State Highway 4.

Sixteen miles (15 miles.)

Geneva, the county seat of Fillmore County (named for Millard Fillmore), is known for the Girls' Reformatory just west of town. It is somewhat disconcerting to stand at the collection of clean buildings and gaze out on the pastoral setting and realize that this place was founded for the reform of delinquent girls and younger children.

The town was named after Geneva, Switzerland.

Fifteen miles (5 miles.)

McCool Junction...which sounds as if it was named after a failed t.v. show from the early 1960s. The fact of the matter is no one is quite sure how the town got its name. It is located on the cool banks of the west fork of the Big Blue River.

Six miles east and two miles north of here on the banks of the West Blue River is the first frame house built in the county. It was built in 1869 from lumber milled at least three days ride away. The house still stands although it is on private land.

The site of the first homestead in the county is *another five miles east* of this site.

Five miles (1 mile.)

Intersection with Interstate 80. Please see the entry for Interstate 80 for more information about sites along that route.

One mile (2 miles.)

The Nebraska City Cutoff of the Oregon Trail crosses US 81 at this point. This cutoff was a popular alternative route for the westward migration. The Trail passes through the width of York

County. From this point westward the Trail parallels the Interstate. East of here the Trail swings to the southeast toward Beaver Crossing in Seward County.

Two and a half miles east and one mile north is a marker that designates the burial sites of the first two men killed and buried in York County. One of the men, the driver of a stage, was very drunk and threatened the owner of the Stage Station. The air grew quiet, the two men faced off, guns were drawn and in an instant, the stage driver was dead.

The other burial is of a man who was struck and killed by lightening. All he had on his person was $500. To this day he remains unknown. For years ruts from the Trail could be seen in this area.

In 1868 the Pawnee, Omaha, Ponca and Otoes united to fight their common enemy, the Sioux. Although no white settlers were hurt, the warfare made times rough for finding food and raising crops. Luckily that was the same year that a large herd of bufallo wandered into the area, and provided food for the pioneers. That was the last year buffalo appeared in York County.

Two miles (1 mile.)

York. York, the county seat for York county, is the home of York College which was founded in 1890 as a seminary school for the United Brethern in Christ.

York has several fine parks and a golf course.

Shortly after the railroad arrived in town a new community started up on the outskirts of town and was named, logically, New York. New York is now a part of York, that is to say, New York is a part of old York, unless you are talking about the old New York which is in New York, named after York, which is not here at all, but over in England...oh, never mind.

One mile (12 miles.)

Intersection with US Highway 34. Please see that entry for information along this highway.

Twelve miles (7 miles.)

Stromsburg. This town is the boyhood home of C. H. Morrill whose pioneer work in archeology and paleontology played a significant role in the modern theories of those sciences. Morrill Hall, the grand museum at the University of Nebraska in Lincoln was donated to the University by Morrill and is dedicated to his memory. Nebraska writer Loren Eiseley worked for Morrill on several digs in the western part of the state and wrote about Morrill in several of his essays.

Stomsburg was settled by Swedes who found the spot on the banks of the Big Blue appealing. The Big Blue is one of the state's trickiest rivers. It has its headwaters just a mile from the Platte River, west of here in northern Hamilton County, and yet swings a couple of hundred miles to the south before joining up with the waters of the Republican River and eventually the Missouri at Kansas City.

The Blue was an important route for both prehistoric and historic Indians and pioneers, and although few modern roads travel along its banks, traces of those early travelers can still be found in many places. The Blue drainage system flows within 20 miles of Lincoln although many Lincolnites would not be able to trace its course on a map for love or money. As is the case with many other rivers, civilization has turned its back on the Blue, but it just keeps slowly moving along its lazy way to the sea.

Seven miles (9 miles.)

Osceola. At one time Osceola's name was known nation-wide for its fine brooms which were produced from local broom corn, a variety of corn with a stock used in the making of brooms. However, Osceola could not make a clean sweep of the market and consequently was brushed aside by other companies wanting to stand on their own.

The town won the county seat away from nearby Stromsburg by distributing a county map made of cardboard with a pin stuck in Osceola. On the back side were instructions for the finder to place their finger on the pin and see how the entire piece of cardboard balanced perfectly. This proved, the promotion claimed, that Osceola was indeed the center of the county and should therefore be the county seat.

In the grasshopper invasion of 1874 Osceola was particularly hard hit and the local paper reported that it was impossible to step outside for even a brief moment without being hit in the face with several of the pests.

Four miles west on State Highway 92, and then *ten miles north* on State Highway 39:
Polk County's northern border is formed by the Platte River, and along its southern bank is the Oxbow Trail which connected Nebraska City with the Platte and, eventually, the Oregon Trail. The trail can still be seen in selected areas less than a mile south of the river through-out its course through the county.

Nine miles (10 miles.)
When the highway turns north you will be riding down the county line between Butler and Polk Counties.

Ten miles (5 miles.).
Junction with State Highway 64.
Seven miles east on 64 to Bellwood. The founder of this town, Jesse Bell, owned a section of land here and started his own beautification project by planting thousands of trees. His first trees were planted parallel to the roads which surrounded his section, but later he and his family began to plant more and more trees. The folks who lived here since have continued to plant flowers and shrubs and trees. Only Arbor Lodge in Nebraska City has a wider variety of trees in the state. J. Sterling Morton had money and power; while Jesse Bell had simply his love for beautiful trees to sustain his work.

Five miles (1 mile.)
Cross the Platte and then the Loup Rivers, which join just below here.

One mile. (6 miles.)
Columbus.
The Oxbow Trail, which connected Nebraska City with the Platte River near Columbus, and eventually the Oregon Trail west of Hastings, passed here on the north banks of the Loup.
In general the Trail follows the Loup through Platte County. Traces of the route can still be seen in some areas. Ask locally.
For more information about Columbus, please see the entry for US Highway 30.

Six miles (15 miles.)
Junction with State Highway 22. This road parallels the Loup River for 15 lovely miles. For more information about this area, please see the entry for State Highway 14.

Fifteen miles (10 miles.)
Junction with State Highway 91. Please see that entry for information about sites along this route.

Ten miles (14 miles.)
Madison.
This is the county seat for Madison County. Like Norfork, this

town was settled by a colony of Germans in the late 1860s.

After the early settlers returned to their homeland to pack up the rest of their families and belongings, they came back to find that their land had been taken over by another party. Rather than start a fight, they took up the land adjoining and the community began.

An early resident of Madison, Doctor John Quincy Adams Harvey, got his medical degree by self-proclamation. Once, when called on to inspect a pioneer who had frozen to death in his cabin, the good Doctor peeked in the door, jumped back out and told the surrounding people, "He's deader 'n hell."

The windbreaks and trees you see in this area date back to 1881 when local farmers planted thousands of bushes and trees.

Fourteen miles (6 miles.)

Norfolk.

Junction with US Highway 275. Please see entry for US Highway 275 about sites along this route.

A life-long Norfolk resident, Orville Henry Carlisle, was known worldwide for his mastery of fireworks and rocketry. He invented the world's first model rocket for the hobbyist, but lost the patent to a model-rocket company on a technicality. His rockets are on display at the Smithsonian and he held card number one in the National Association of Rocketry.

You need not go to Washington to see his fine works. Carlisle created the only fireworks museum in the world from his vast collection. It is located next to Carlisles shoes in downtown Norfolk.

Norfolk may have more city parks than any other city of its size anywhere. Activities available at these parks include canoeing, archery, go carts and a variety of other recreational wonders.

Norfork is world famous as the home town of Nebraska's most visible citizen, and promoter, Johnny Carson. Carson lived most of his boyhood here and graduated from Norfolk High School. Ask locally for directions to Carson sites.

Norfork was founded by a large colony of Germans who, in 1866, settled the fertile area of this stretch of the Elkhorn River valley. They had selected the name North Fork, but the U.S. Government, in its infinite wisdom, shortened it to Norfork.

If anyone has ever read the pulp novels about "Diamond Dick" published in the early years of this century, this is hallowed ground. Marksman and owner of the first model-T, author Dr. Richard Tanner was a citizen of Norfork.

In 1926 a local boy, Fred Patzel, won the National Hog Calling

Championship. When Fred was asked to reproduce his bellow for the local radio station he blew out the microphone and temporarily put the station off the air.

Six miles (7 miles.)
Junction with State Highway 13.
Nine miles north on Highway 13 to Pierce.
Pierce. This is the seat of Pierce County. The town was named for President Franklin Pierce. Trivia Question: When was he president and what party did he represent? (Answer at end of this description!)
Pierce is also the home of a fine museum complex which includes the Chicago-Northwestern Railroad Station, a school house, blacksmith shop and a building that houses many historical machines. The museum is opened all summer.
The first settlement in this area was made by a man named J.H. Brown who built a sod shanty on the banks of Willow Creek in 1870. Before long his structure not only served as a home, but as a hotel, post office and couthouse as well.
Give up? Franklin Pierce was the 14th president, right between such favorites as Millard Filmore and James Buchanan. Pierce served from 1853-1857. A Democrat from New Hampshire, Pierce, at 48 was the youngest man to serve as president up until that time.

Seven Miles (2 miles.)
Junction with State Highway 98 West. Five miles on 98 to Pierce. For a description of Pierce, see above.

Two miles (9 miles.)
Junction with State Highway 98 East to Wayne. For information about Wayne, please see entry for State Highway 15.

Nine miles (7 miles.)
Junction with US Highway 20. Please see entry for that highway for information about sites along this road.

Seven miles (3 miles.)
Junction with State Highway 59, please see entry for State Highway 14 for information about sites along this road.

Three miles (7 miles.)

US Highway 81

Intersection with county road. Turn east for Coleridge, 10 miles. Please see entry for State Highway 15 for more information.

Seven miles (8 miles.)

Intersection with State Highway 84. West to Bloomfield and the Wild Horse Holding Facility. For more information please see entry for State Highway 14. East to Hartington and the Cedar County Museum. Please see entry for State Highway 15 for more information.

Eight miles (8 miles.)

Junction with State Highway 12, please see that entry for more information about sites along this route.

Eight miles (1 1/2 miles.)

Turn west, follow paved road four miles to a scenic overlook for Gavins Point Dam and Lewis and Clark Lake which is well worth your stop. The dam is the last dam on the Missouri before it reaches the Mississippi. There are several camping and picnicing sites along this lake.

Turn east off of 81 at this same intersection for site of Bentz massacre, Ft. Jackson, St. Helena, Wynot and other sites. For more information please see entry for State Highway 12.

One and a half miles (0 miles.)

The bridge over the Missouri into Yankton, SD.

Zero miles (5 miles.)

Superior. This quaint farming town on the banks of the Republican River is in Nuckolls County.

Five miles (4 miles.)

For the next 4 miles State Highway 14 and US Highway 136 are the same road.

Four miles (4 miles.)

US Highway 136 heads to the east. Continue north on 14.

Four miles (1 mile.)

The small town of Nelson near the divide between the Republican and Blue River drainages.

One mile (8 miles.)

One mile north of Nelson take the county road east ten

State Highway 14

miles to Oak. It is hard to believe that this little town could have as much history as it does, but it is true. Much has happened here. For one thing the Oregon Trail passed right smack-dab through the center of what later became the village. A map to help you get oriented is located in the northeast corner of the city park.

Four and a half miles east of here in 1864 a stagecoach and its nine passengers barely escaped a massacre. The driver saw Indians waiting in ambush in some trees along the Little Blue. He spun the stage around and, under heavy gunfire, sped back to a large wagon train some miles to the east.

One and a half miles east of Oak is the site of the Comstock Ranch massacre. On August 7, 1864 several ranch buildings north of here were raided by warring Sioux and the residents killed. The buildings were destroyed. Also near here was Oak Grove Station, a station on the Pony Express route.

One and a half miles north, then one mile west to the overlook for the Narrows. This place was a bottleneck where wagons, oxen, pioneer and horse had to squeeze between the Little Blue River and a bluff. Near here was the place where 16 year old Laura Roper, a woman named Mrs. Eubanks and her four year old daughter were captured by the Cheyenne. Mrs. Eubanks had taken several children across the river to pick grapes when the Cheyenne attacked their cabin. Mrs. Eubanks pushed the children into a thicket. One of the children cried out when they saw their father being scalped and the Indians found them. Several older children were killed trying to escape and Mrs. Eubanks, the four year old and Laura Roper were captured. Later they were ransomed at Ft. Laramie, Wyoming. In 1929 at age 81 Laura Roper Vance returned here at the invitation of the State Historical Society and, with a crowd of 150 following, identified the spot where the massacre took place.

Just a few hundred yards south of the Roper site is an unmarked grave of a 16 year old boy and a wagonmaster. The boy's job was to keep the oxen prodded and moving. Growing weary, he sat and rested. Unable to rise at the wagonmaster's request, the master took out his rifle and shot the boy. A posse hunted the wagonmaster and hung him at this site. Both were buried on a small hill to the south of the Roper site.

Two hundred yards northwest of this place is the probable location of the Little Blue Station, one of only two stations in the 200 miles between Julesburg, Colorado and Kiowa, Nebraska to have survived the Indian uprisings of 1864.

One mile north and one mile west of Rober/Narrows site:

Just to the south of this point is the grave of Parson Bob, also known as Phill Landon, who was a frontier scout for George Armstrong Custer and later romanced with Calamity Jane. A trail camp also was here known as Camp Kane.

North one half mile and west one mile *to Angus. A reconstructed sod house is in Angus.*

Return nine miles west to State Highway 14.

Eight miles (2 miles.)

The highway crosses the path of the Oregon Trail and the Pony Express route.

Two miles (10 miles.)

West 4 1/4 miles on S-18C *to the intersection with county road on the south. In the southwest corner of this intersection, just north of the town of Deweese, was the Liberty Farm. This station for travelers along the Oregon Trail stood on the small knoll. The trail went in a northwesterly direction, following the north bank of the Little Blue River. This station was destroyed in the Indian wars of 1864.*

Continue west from the Liberty Farm 3/4 mile and then swing south for a quarter mile. Continue west for 4 miles. *Along this stretch you will pass an older cemetery with tombstones dating back to the early pioneer days.* **Turn north and go for three and a half miles** *to the site of Pawnee Ranch. This ranch, or station along the Oregon Trail, replaced Libertry Ranch when it was destroyed by Indians (see above).*

Continue north one half mile. *Turn west. In 3/4 mile the road forks. Straight here one quarter mile, then south across the Little Blue for one half mile. A half of a mile to the west, in this field, is the grave of Elizabeth Taylor, only one of three women to be lynched during the Oregon Trail days. Return to fork in the road. Take northern branch of fork. As soon as the road turns north again, stop.*

One hundred yards to the west *stood the Spring Ranch, a stagecoach station and trading post during the pioneer days. One report has the trading post located at the confluence of the Little Blue with Pawnee Creek, about a mile southeast of here.*

Return to State Highway 14.

Ten miles (4 miles.)

Clay Center.

One system that the railroads employed to name towns was to name them in an alphabetical sequence. Clay County is a good example of this. It has the towns of: Deweese, Edgar, Eldorado, Fairfield, Glenvil, Harvard, Inland and so on.

Clay Center was formed when the usual county dispute on what town should have the county seat was finally settled by deciding to build an entirely new town to serve as the seat of government. They found a spot as near to the center of Clay County and named it, well, yes, Clay Center. The courthouse was built in 1918 at a cost of $100,000.

Five miles west of Clay Center to the US Meat Animal Research Center. Yes, there is such a thing supported by the government with your tax dollars. But heck, wouldn't you rather have more meat on the table and less bull in Washington, anyway?

Four miles (3 miles.)

Intersection with US Highway 136. Please see this entry for more information about sites along US 136.

Three miles (8 miles.)

State Highway 14 leaves US Highway 136 and turns north toward Hamilton County. For more information west and east of here, please see entry for US Highway 136.

Eight miles (8 miles.)

Just before the northern bridge of the Big Blue: near here on the fork of the Blue River, Jarvil Chaffee made the first homestead claim in Hamilton County in May of 1872. The Chaffee family had traveled to Nebraska from Wisconsin (a wise choice) and constructed a 10 X 12 foot dugout in which to live.

Mrs. Chaffee died in 1871, just before their homestead claim became official. The few scattered neighbor women were distraught at the thought of this fine woman being buried in a plain pine box, much less at such a remote place. Before the final words were said over Mrs. Chaffee's remains, the women gathered wild grapes, crushed them and used the dye to stain the box to give it a darker, richer color.

Eight miles (4 miles.)

Read this monument to the Oregon Trail. It may be a bit misleading since the main Oregon Trail was actually about 35 miles south of here. However, in 1861 the Nebraska City/Ft. Kearny cutoff was established in order to save time for travelers and freight from Nebraska City. It is the cutoff which crossed this site.

Seven and one half miles west, and a half mile south of here will take you to the site of the Deepwell Ranch which saw its heyday from 1865-1868. Since a long segment of the Nebraska City Cutoff road had no station, two confederate soldiers, recently freed from a Chicago prison, built a sod house, and dug a 60 ft deep well. It became one of the best known stops on the trail, and many stopped to sip its cool clear waters. The monument is an attempt to reproduce what the well looked like.

P.S. The ranch's well was not made of concrete and stone.
P.P.S. the ranch's well had water in it.

One mile (3 miles.)
Intersection with Interstate 80.

Three miles (5 miles.)
Aurora. For information about this fine and historic community, please see entry under US Highway 34.

Five miles (7 miles.)
Cross the Big Blue River. The headwaters of this river are a few miles to the west in the low bluffs along the Platte River. Although the Blue starts within sight of the Platte, it flows away from the larger river, southward, eventually joining with the Republican and joining the Missouri several hundred miles south of where the Platte joins the mighty Mo at Plattsmouth.

Seven miles (2 miles.)
The Oxbow Trail, which ran from north of Omaha to join up with the Oregon Trail 20 miles west of Hastings, crosses the highway at this point. There isn't anything left to see, but with a good imagination one can still picture the oxen pulling heavily loaded wagons along this pretty stretch of Nebraska.

Two miles (3 miles.)
Before this concrete and steel structure was built a mile long timber, plank and pole bridge once spanned the waters of the wide Platte. The bridge that crosses the Platte was one of the longest wooden bridges in the country.

Three miles (5 miles.)
Central City. A place rich with history and fame. For more information on Central City, please see entry for US Highway 30.

77

State Highway 14

Five miles (12 miles.)

Intersection with State Highway 92.

*Along the western edge of the county, **13 miles west of here**, and paralleling the county line north and south, is a portion of the original Mormon Trail. The Trail wound through here on its way to the Platte, and, eventually, Salt Lake City. Between 1846 and 1861 tens of thousands of persecuted emigrants passed this way. Until the last few years of the exodus most of them carried their belongings in bulky carts pulled by hand.*

Twelve miles (1 mile.)

The Loup River. This river and its many tributaries drains a large portion of the Sandhills region.

One mile (2 miles.)

Junction with State Highway 22 West at Fullerton.

Two miles (6 miles.)

Junction with State Highway 22 East.

*For an interesting sidetrip **Genoa is 14 miles east** on State Highway 22.*

__Genoa.__ Located on the Mormon Trail, Genoa was founded by the Mormons as a trail camp in 1857.

This is the location of the last great concentrations of Pawnee before they were removed by the treaty of 1876. A very large Pawnee village stood one and a half miles west of here at the time the treaty was signed. The village was nearly 250 years old. It was north of the highway about a half a mile, at the highest point of land at the juncture of the Beaver and Loup Valleys. Over 3,000 Pawnee once lived here. In one house 54 bodies were found during an excavation. There is some evidence to suggest that Spanish explorers from the Southwest, searching for the City of Gold, Ciboa, made it as far as this Indian village in the early 1700s.

After the treaty was signed in 1876 the government built the Pawnee Industrial School for Indians, only one of 16 such Indian boarding schools in the nation. The school operated for 50 years, finaly closing in 1934. At its peak over 600 students were enrolled, representing several of the major tribes in the country. The school once sprawled across 160 acres, providing help, as Yellow Knife of the Nez

Perce once said, "to teach us how to cut our Mother the Earth's breast." Today the shop building has been restorted and is open to the public.

Genoa was once site of a large Pawnee Indian Reservation, and the museum in Genoa has once of the largest collections of Pawnee artifacts anywhere in the world.

Six miles (7 miles.)
Junction with State Highway 52.

Seven miles (8 miles.)
Junction with State Highhway 56.
Eight miles west. *Cedar Rapids, Nebraska. Are there rapids here? You'll have to take the side trip to find out!*

Eight miles (9 miles.)
Albion.

In 1872 when this town was first being settled the subject of a name for the burg came up. The two leading contenders were Albion, after the home town of one man—his home town in New York; and the home town of another, Manchester--after the city in Massachuesetts. This disagreement almost came to blows and gunplay, but instead the concerned parties decided to have a game of euchre on it. The town is called Albion for the winner of that famous game, but in the spirit of gentlemanliness, the township is named Manchester.

Albion's fate, like that of a great many towns in Nebraska, rested with the railroad. For a while Albion was the only shipping and supply point for most of the surrounding counties, and the town prospered.

The Methodist Church is one of the oldest structures in the city, it dates from 1878 when it was built for a cost of $1,400.

There is general sentiment around here that the people in Albion are the friendliest in the nation. This fact is little known, but widely appreciated by those who have relied on that good will. Ninety-six per cent of the streets in Albion are paved. The city library is one of the best in the area. And if that's not enough to impress you, check out the Boone County Historical Museum, open year round, but mostly in the summer.

Albion is the county seat of Boone County, and yes folks, it was named after Daniel Boone.

Nine miles (6 miles.)

Just after the road swings to due north, to the west is Beaver Creek. It was at this site where the famous Omaha Indian squaw man, Logan Fontenelle, son of a French fur trader and an Omaha Indian woman, was killed in a battle with the Sioux in 1855. Many people credit Fontenelle with preserving peace between the Indians and the whites as he traveled throughout the area and spoke with the native tribes in their own language, trying to explain why the whites were taking over the land. Others have different opinions about the man. In either case, bow your head a moment here for his ghost surely stalks those fields along the creek.

Six miles (9 miles.)

Petersburg.

The first homesteader in these parts staked a claim in 1871 near the present town of Petersburg. The county has the distinction of being in a kind of transition area, not too sure whether it belongs best to the corn and grain lands of the eastern part of the state, or the cattle and Sandhills of the western.

Nine miles (11 miles.)

Elgin, a small but hardy collection of memories on the edge of Nebraska's least populated area to the west.

Eleven miles (23 miles.)

Neligh, county seat of Antelope County and home of the Neligh Mills. For a description of these and other sites in the area, please see the entry for US Highway 275.

As the road climbs up and out of the Elkhorn River Valley it enters the more orderly fields of the northern half of the county. Look for yucca plants along the roadside for indications of the western feel this county harbors.

Twenty-three miles (11 miles.)

Verdigre. This town's kolaches are so good they even have an entire event set aside to celebrate the fact each summer. If you do not know what a kolache is, immediately turn yourself in to the nearest State Police officer and revoke your Nebraska citizenship.

For an interesting side trip, continue east on State Highway 84 to Bloomfield and on Highway 13 to Bazile Mills.

East 9 miles *on State Highway 84 to Center. The center of the county, and county seat of Knox county. This was a town formed* *because of the dispute over which of the existing towns should be the county seat. After the usual bloodshed and violence, surveyors located the center of the county, bought the cornfield from local farmers and started the town.*

*For a short side trip swing **south on State Highway 13, two miles** east of Center to Bazile Mills. See description below.*

***Seven miles east** on State Highway 84 and five miles west of the town of Bloomfield is the Wild Horse Holding Pens. It is a government run operation that serves as a temporary holding pen and reconditioning center for wild horses taken off range lands. Over 3,000 horses are held here each year before being shipped to adoption centers around the country.*

***East of Bloomfield six miles on 84, then south, seven miles on State Highway 121** to Wausa. A Swedish village with Swedes still making up the majority of the population. Good food and pastries here. Throw the calorie counters away.*

*Return west on 84 to State Highway 13. **South on 13 six miles** to Bazile Mills, so named because of the mills which were once located on Bazile Creek. This included both flour mills and woolen mills.*

Eleven miles (0 miles.)

Niobrara. Please see the entry for State Highway 12 for information about Niobrara and the surrounding area.

Kansas Border (1 mile.)

The sights of Webster County are many, from the rolling land along the divide between the Republican and the Little Blue watersheds, to the quaint country towns like Inavale and Guide Rock, but far and away Webster County is known for the town of Red Cloud, and that town for its most notable citizen, the great writer, Willa Cather.

One mile (4 miles.)

The Willa Cather Memorial Prairie. This 610 acre strip of land has never been broken by a plow. Many native grasses, some found nowhere else for many miles, flourish here. It may be hard for some people to share the excitement of others as they demand the driver of their car stop, and they rush out to smell, taste, feel and inspect the land here, but if you are one of those drivers, please tolerate them and give them as much time as they want in this place. It may be that without people like them the quality of all our lives will suffer. The

Prairie is preserved by the Nature Conservatory.

East of the Memorial Prairie, **4 miles** to site of the Pike Pawnee Village. Zebulon Pike and his 21 men camped on the "commanding hill" in 1803 on their way west. Across the way was a large Pawnee village.

The story is that some weeks before Pike's arrival here the Spanish had arrived at this large Pawnee village and convinced the Indians to fly the Spanish flag. After Pike's arrival he offered the Indians the American flag and they promptly tied it next to the Spanish flag.

Pike spent four days trying to convince the Pawnee leaders that it was pointless to fly two different flags (perhaps the Pawnee were convincing Pike it was pointless to fly even one...). Finally, the story goes, the elders of the village took down the Spanish flag and gave it to Pike, thus ending the brief Spanish domination of Nebraska.

Much archeological work has been done here by professionals and nonprofessionals alike. Remember, it is a crime to violate important historical sites. In short, take nothing but photographs, leave nothing but footprints.

Four miles (1/2 mile.)

The Republican River. This important river traverses the state's southern border and served as an important water source for the Pawnee, Sioux and other tribes of Indians, as well as for the large buffalo herds and Texas cattle drives. Until the 1940s the Republican was a threat to residents because of flooding. A large flood in the mid 1930s killed over 100 people and sent a wall of water down the river valley.

One particularly beautiful description of this river is in Willa Cather's short story, "The Enchanted Bluff" where a handful of children, at the end of a summer vacation, daydream about buried treasure and distant lands while basking in the setting sun of the prairies.

One-half mile (1 mile.)

On the east side of the road, off a bit from the road is the site of the mansion Cather used for the setting of her short novel *A Lost Lady.* The house burned down not long ago.

One mile (21 miles.)

Red Cloud and the junction of US Highway 136. For many

US Highway 281

world citizens, Nebraska's most famous town. For a description of Red Cloud please see entry for US Highway 136.

Twenty one miles (8 miles.)

Blue Hill.

On the high flatlands above the Little Blue drainage, Blue Hill was settled in 1878 by German immigrants. Located here is an early flour mill. It is easy to see how the beauty of this area might have influenced the writer Willa Cather.

Eight miles (1 mile.)

Junction with State Highway 74. Please see entry for State Highway 74 for more information on sites along this road.

One mile (2 miles.)

State Highway 74 continues east, and US Highway 281 turns north.

Two miles (2 miles.)

Cross the Little Blue River. Imagine a blacksmith shop, wells, stores and a couple of saloons. The town of Millington once stood here.

Thirteen miles west of the Millington townsite is the still alive village of Holstein. Ask at Holstein for directions to the Einspahr Sod House Museum, about 4 miles west of the village. This is the only sod house still standing in Adams County. Tours by appointment. See also the entry for US Highway 6 for more information.

Two miles (3 miles.)

One tenth of a mile east: Site of Smith and Simonton Wagon train burial site. Eight men were killed by the Sioux here on a hot, dry Nebraska August day in 1864. They are buried at this place, and were members of a wagon train working its way over the Oregon trail.

A mile to the northwest of here was the frontier town of Brickton. For a delightful side trip into the heart of the Oregon Trail country continue as described below.

Continue east for one mile, then go south for 3/4 mile. Ruts of the Oregon Trail are visible on both sides of the road. They are southeast of a cattle pond.

Continue south 1/4 mile from ruts, turn east, go one mile, turn south, go one mile, turn east and go 1/4th mile. Just to the south, along the north bank of the Little Blue River, was the campsite of John C. Fremont on June 25. 1842. Fremont gave up trying to float the Platte after dragging his boat for miles. He chose the Little Blue instead. Some say that Fremont had to be crazy anyway to want to explore such a wilderness. Fremont was one of the most versatile and well-traveled of the West's early explorers.

Continue east one half mile. The Oregon Trail here crosses the county road. Just to the east of the trial, and to the north of the county road, is the site of Lone Tree Station. This station on the Pony Express line and Oregon Trail took its name from the single lone cottonwood tree which stood on a hill and was visible for miles around. All right, so it wasn't any Chimney Rock, Longs Peak or Scottsbluff, this tree was an important landmark to pioneers moving west. In those days to see a tree anywhere outside of a creek bed was something.

Return to Hiway 281 if you can find your way...only kidding, go west three miles and you are there. If not, boy are you lost!

Three miles (3 miles.)

West 4 miles on gravel road, then south 1/4 mile to the site of 32 Mile Station. This place was so-called by travelers on the Oregon Trail because it was 32 miles SE of Ft. Kearney. The Oregon Trail cuts Adams County diagonally in half going from the southeast to the northwest. The Pony Express route followed the Oregon Trail route in this part of Nebraska.

Three miles (14 miles.)

Junction of US Highway 6. For information about sites along US Highway 6 please see entry for US Highway 6.

Hastings.

Famous Hastings citizens include Barney Pearson, who lived until the early 1940s, was known as "Colonel Idaho Bill" and was a good friend of Buffalo Bill. Colonel Idaho Bill's feature attraction during the performances of the Wild West show was being able to capture a wide variety of strange and wild creatures with his lariat.

Sandy Dennis, Academy Award winning actress was born in Hastings. Other famous Hastings citizens include Carolyn Renfrew, an author, and Adam Breede who was an author, explorer and archeologist. Hastings was the location for the first interstate radio broadcast in the state of Nebraska.

During the 1930s Hastings Municipal Power had the distinction of selling its power at a rate 50% lower than that of the rest of the nation. Hastings has always been a prosperous and pretty Nebraska town, and with the recent improvements to the downtown area i seems to be aware of that distinction. Adams County's first white settlers were Englishmen who came to take advantage of the home steading act. One of them, Walter Micken laid out the town of Hastings in 1872.

Hastings, like many of the towns in Nebraska, was a railroad town, and was named after a man who graded the last section of the St. Joseph and Denver railroad into the townsite. Hastings once boasted three individuals railroad stations. Now Amtrack serves one of the few remaining passenger stations in the state.

There was an early debate over whether Hastings or the town of Juaniata to the west should be the county seat. The issue was settled when a group of men went to Juaniata at night and stole a wagon full of public records and brought them back to town.

Over sixty percent of the bricks used in the state of Nebraska come from Hastings.

Those with a culinary slant should know that the Jerusalem artichoke was developed in the Hastings area. It is today commonly used as a vegetable some parents threaten children with, but at one time it was used not only as food, but as feed and for the manufacture of fuel alcohol as well.

Hastings Museum is at the **intersection of Highway 281 and 14th streets** is a good place to start your tour of Hastings. Built in 1938, the building was constructed of bricks from the old Morton School which once held the museum's collection. The museum encompasses not only local history, but includes such diverse items as the J.M. McDonald Planetarium and the Adams County Historical Society, as well as items of natural science, Indian and pioneer history. This is a good museum, however, be aware that unlike many other museums in the area, the Hastings Museum charges an admission. Hours are from 9-5 Monday through Saturday and 1 to 5 Sundays and holidays.

From the Museum **south on US Highway 281 three blocks**: One of the older cemeteries in the area is located at 13th and Burlington. The Highland Park Cemetery contains the graves of many of the area's first pioneers. East on 14th about 1 mile: The Crosier Monastery Museum at 14th and Pine contains a collection of wood carvings and artifacts from the Asmat people of New Guinea. It is open by appointment only.

The Jacob Fischer Rainbow fountain located **east on 12th to Denver Street** was erected as part of the electrical exposition for the 1932 Adams County Fair. The fountain with eight water jets, twelve lights and the wizardry of 1932, produced various forms for effect.

East on 12th street road, 4 miles. Provancher Cemetery site marker. This was the site of a French Canadian cemetery during the late 1800s.

East on 7th one and a half miles: Hastings College campus. A pretty and quaint campus typical of those state colleges in Nebraska. The oldest building was built in 1883. The college was created by the first meeting of the Synod of Nebraska Presbyterian Church in 1873.

There is a college museum on campus which includes collections of rocks and minerals, animals and paleontological specmins from Nebraska. Before many of these buildings were built, the first airplane to land in the city of Hastings used the fields about the campus as a landing strip.

West on Fifth to Chesnut in Hastings is a relic of the State's intellectual past, a Chautauqua pavilion. Chautauquas once were the major attraction of any town's summer entertainment. The idea of a traveling caravan for intellectual stimulation originated in upstate New York in the early 1800s. At that time the term was used exclusively to denote a series of lectures of a religious nature, but as the phenomenon spread Chautauquas encompassed larger and larger definitions.

By 1907, when this pavilion was built, the events included lectures, discussions, short plays, music and often large picnics. People came from everywhere to participate and to learn. In recent years many states have attempted to revive the Chautauqua by staging traveling events, often sponsored by the state arts and humanities commissions. In recent years a Chautauqua was begun with help from the University of Nebraska. That Chautauqua traveled with a large tent, and used local halls to present its shows.

Intersection of 3rd and St. Joesph Streets is a historical marker denoting the site of Liberal Hall and the Olive Trail.

At 1100 Block of West 2cd Street a marker draws attention to the first well in the Hastings area.

East on Second to Kansas Ave: The first church in Hastings, the First Methodist, was built at this location in 1873.

US Highway 281

At Hastings US Highway 281 and 34 are joined for several miles north, to Grand Island, where they go their separate ways once more.

Fourteen miles (3 miles.)
One half mile east: Doniphan.
***West of here two miles, then north 2 1/2 miles** to Campbell Monument.*

In 1867, during the peak of the Sioux hostilities, a small group of Indians made a raid on the Peter Campbell farm. The adult men were not at home, and the Indians killed a woman and her son, and kidnapped four children, including the Campbell's twin sons. The Indians moved on to a neighboring farm and killed the German farmer who lived there. At a later time the government traded an Indian woman and her child, who had been captured at the battle of Elm Creek for the four children.

Near here was a fine early farm. The legend is that two sons of this farm were pinned together by an arrow as they rode double on a horse, trying to escape an Indian raid.

Three miles (4 miles.)
The Platte River. In 1878 four "tramps" were hung here for no other reason than being on the lam. The Grand Island *Independent* reported "we are opposed to mob violence under all circumstances, still we fear that justice to law abiding citizens may require it." The *Independent,* one of the finest small town daily papers in the nation may no longer be quite so independent, but then their editorials don't speak from both sides of the mouth any longer as this one did.

Four miles (4 miles.)
Down the Tom Osborne Parkway into Grand Island. Three US Highways (281, 34 and 30) come together here, as well as the major State Highway 2. You will find Grand Island sites listed for the entry for US Highway 30. Also see the entries for State Highway 2 and US Highway 30 for information about locations in this area.

Four miles (11 miles.)
Intersection with State Highway 2. Please see this entry for information about sites along this major State Highway.

Eleven miles (2 miles.)

Turn off for St. Libory an earlyday pioneer town. Now mostly memory.

Two miles (9 miles.)
West on State 58 20 miles to Boelus and a small quaint campground near the confluence of the south and middle forks of the Loup.

Nine miles (3 miles.)
St. Paul.

St. Paul is the county seat of Howard County and was founded when James Paul (along with Major Frank North) came up the Loup river and was taken with the beauty and potential of the area around the forks in the river.

Later Paul consulted with his brother, and with leaders in his home country of Denmark, and settlers began to move to the area. The town they founded was originally named Athens, but was later changed to St. Paul. A good part of Howard County was settled by Danes.

The Danish Land and Homestead Colony from Wisconsin was responsible for settling the communities west of St. Paul at Farwell, and Northwest of town at Elba. To the southwest is the small community of Dannebrog, named after the Danish flag, and settled by Danes and Swedes.

The Indian attacks on early settlers, as well as storms and grasshopper plagues kept settlement low. Eventually Ft. Hartsuff, 55 miles upriver, was established to protect homesteaders from the Native Americans and the county's population began to grow. See entry for State Highway 11 for more information about the Fort.

When the railroad reached St. Paul in 1881 the town began to boom since the farmers now had an outlet for their crops. Other Danish communities sprang up including Nysted, west of Dannebrog, and Dannevirke in the northwest part of the county.

At one time the Danish population was 25% of the entire county. It is believed that Howard County has more Danish descendants living in it today than any other area of the state.

Three miles (8 miles.)
Cross the North Loup River at a State Wayside Area.

Eight miles (5 miles.)
Eight miles west of here is the Big Wash. The Big Wash is

a scenic area located on Leonard Well's ranch. It is two miles north and three miles east of the town of Cotesfield. Ask for directions, locally. For information about this unusual accidental man-made canyon, see entry for State Highway 11.

Five miles (3 miles.)

This was the tiny railroad town of Brayton, settled in 1888.

Three miles (4 miles.)

Nine miles west on 22 to Scotia.

For information about Scotia, please see entry for State Highway 11.

Four miles (5 miles.)

Greeley.

One early pioneer woman, who left a beautiful home in Boston, came in sight of the early town of Greeley, mostly tents and lean-tos alongside a barren set of railroad tracks. She turned to her husband and burst into tears. "Is that Greeley?" she screamed.

The town has come along some since those days. The Greeley County Historical Society Museum is located in the County Courthouse and is open 5 days a week.

It seems the more isolated and sparsely populated an area is, the more interest they have in preserving their history, and Greeley is no exception. In 1939 a small history of Greeley County was published, and this book was handsomely reprinted in 1977 by the local historical society.

Greeley was settled in the 1870s largely by the Irish, who were fed up with the British control of their land and immigrated to the United States. Many of the earliest settlers in this area came from Ireland via Boston. The earliest settlers came upon the land by accident. Disgruntled Irish pioneers were about to return to Boston when a surveyor told them of the good land along the creekbeds in an area he had just finished surveying. They inspected the land near here and the first white settlers of the county were soon building their sod houses.

When the railroad reached Greeley it brought a bit of the outside world with it. In the railroad camp just south of town the stable boss got in an argument with the night watchmen who stabbed him in the heart. The watchman was never caught. This was at a time when there were nearly as many saloons as there were people in Greeley. Bank hold-ups and highway robbers were common in those days of the late 1880s.

County couthouses are known for strange characters, and Greeley has had its share. Greeley had one who was known as the eccentric judge. This judge, who presided over the bench at the turn of the century, was never predictable. Once he made a favorable ruling in a lawsuit, and the successful lawyer, knowing the judge's ways, immediately wrote down the words of the decision in the docket so that he would be able to refer to it again should the need arise. Just that very next day a friend stopped by his office. "Heard you lost that case," the friend said, "too bad."

"No," the lawyer said, "I won it."

"Not the way I heard it. The judge was over to the saloon last night and re-tried the entire case. This time he ruled in favor of the defense."

The lawyer rushed to the courthouse and pulled out the docket of the case. The entire page where he had written the judge's words had been torn out.

During a single week in the month of July, 1894 a total of 328 wolf pelts were delivered to the courthouse and the owners were paid the bounty of $3.00 for each pelt. There were no wolves reported in Greeley County much past the turn of the century.

Seven miles west of Greeley on Wallace Creek once stood the town of Horace. Some railroads built small communities to service the line every seven miles. Horace was one such town.

One mile east and one mile south of Greeley is the site of Jacksonville. A small town of a school, saloon, church, blacksmith shop and post office stood here on the banks of the creek in 1878.

Three miles east of Greeley on State Highway 56 and two miles south. Site of O'Connor. The Church of the Visitation is on the National Register of Historic Places.

O'Connor was first laid out as a settlement of the Irish Catholic Colonization Association, which was to be an association of Catholics in the new world.

This town gained a lot of good press, and in the 1880s many hundreds of Bostonians moved here from the east, as well as many others. The Sisters of Mercy opened a school here on the hill near the church. The convent was home to a school, musical academy and retreat house.

During the blizzard of 1888 a snow drift completely covered

a barn near here. The owner cut steps in the drift and then sawed a hole in the roof of his barn in order to feed and water his livestock.

East on State Highway 56 fourteen miles, near the county border. This area is traditionally a cattleman's land, and the cattle industry here dates back to the earliest white settlers in this vicinity, around 1877.

Five miles (5 miles.)

This area was one of the hardest hit areas in the entire country by the deadly blizzard of 1888.

There is a legend here of a ghost dog who still roams the hillsides looking for his master, a seven year old pioneer boy who had been attacked and killed by wolves.

Late at night the lights of cars passing on this isolated stretch of road fall on its ghastly form and the dog's empty eyes glance up in terror and anger.

Five miles (2 miles.)

Turn off for State Highway 91 to Spalding.

To the west here was unclaimed land for a long while. The first homesteaders to claim land in this area did not stake their claims until 1909, and only then did others come to join them. The land, locally known as the "Sandhills" part of the county, or the "Homestead" area, is still sparsely populated.

Ten miles east on State 91.

Spalding. This town almost ceased to exist shortly after it was founded when the Great Grasshopper Invasion of 1874 wiped out every blade of vegetable matter for miles around.

Just west of here a man was captured by the Indians in 1877 when he and his two companions were attacked by Indians while hunting along Cedar River. He was buried two miles west of here.

Just south of Spalding, across the Cedar River, was the site of a large, temporary Pawnee village in 1880. Several hundred teepees were pitched in a circle on a bank above the river. The site covers 35 acres and artifacts from the location can still be found.

The Sisters of Mercy, who had already started a school in O'Connor (see above) started a small school in Spalding as well. Spalding was another town founded by the Catholic Colonization Association.

The Union Pacific built a line to Spalding. The hope was that the railroad would build a line further up the river. This was never to be the case.

One of the greatest prairie fires of the history of Greeley County started near here on a July day in 1890 and over the next few days spread as far south as O'Connor and Greeley and beyond, an area 15 miles square was destroyed.

Two miles (2 miles.)

Cedar River. Excellent fishing to be had here, say the local experts. Also a safe and scenic river for canoe trips.

Two miles (2 miles.)

One mile east: *Lake Pibel Recreation Area. The most beautiful lake in miles. Recreation facilities available.*

Two miles (7 miles.)

Junction with State Highway 70 west.

Seven miles (17 miles.)

Bartlett sets out in the sun and the wind and the storms and the snow and seems like a long ways from any other place in the world. There is some truth to this as there isn't much else in the way of what some people would call civilization for a few miles in any direction. A pop machine maybe, maybe a pay telephone, but aside from a few ranch houses, Bartlett is it.

Bartlett is the county seat of Wheeler County which is a county that has places where people live with names such as Gritty Ridge, Headquarters, Buffalo Flats and Dry Cedar Creek.

When the first settlers came to this area the only trees were a few (very few) scattered in the river valleys. Since then much timber has been planted in the river valleys and on the sandhills and despite what it may look like out your window this is much greener than it was when the pioneers settled this area.

Wheeler County has a number of streams passing through the county but out of their valleys the land becomes typical of the sandhills region.

Seventeen miles (8 miles.)

Turn off to the east for the town of Bliss and Goose Lake, a one-time state recreation area which has some of the best fishing in these parts. Inquire locally.

Eight miles (18 miles.)

Junction with State Highway 95.

Twenty two miles to Swan Lake, but look for trout, not Tschaikovsky.

Eighteen miles (27 miles.)

O'Neill and the junction with US Highway 20 and 275. See the entry for US Highway 20 for more information about this area.

Twenty seven miles (9 miles.)

Spencer. Frontier Acres, a museum on the northern edge of town on US 281 houses farm machinery and a complete old post office. It is open seven days a week in the summer months, and not quite as often during the winter.

Junction with State Highway 12. Please see that entry for information about this beautiful and seldom-traveled road.

Nine miles (0 miles.)

South Dakota border.

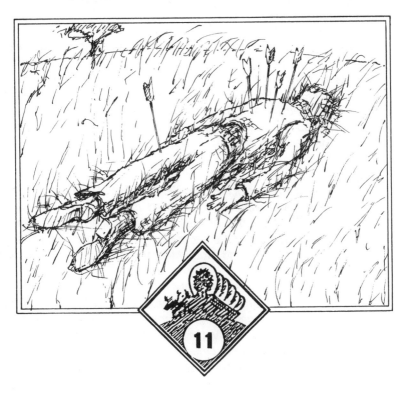

Zero miles (4 miles.)

Intersection with Interstate 80 at Exit 300.

Four miles (1 mile.)

Wood River. State Highway 11 follows US Highway 30 for a mile or so, and then swings north. For information about this location, please see entry for US Highway 30.

One mile north of US 30 (1 mile.)

*Take county road **two miles east** to the bank of the Wood River.*

On a morning in January, 1862 a local farmer by the name of Anderson set out after his neighbor, Smith, who had gone ahead to the Platte to fell trees. Smith had gone out in the early morning with

State Highway 11

Anderson's son, and two of his own sons. Anderson had planned on meeting them at the Platte with another wagon to help load the timber for the return to the farms.

When Anderson reached here he found his neighbor's blood-soaked wagon. The horses were gone. He slowly climbed down off his own wagon and searched among the willows. He soon found Smith's body face-down in the river, clutching the hands of his two sons.

Anderson found his own son a few feet further on. He had been riddled with bullets. The bodies of all four were filled with arrows. The Sioux hostilities were beginning and would last until after the end of the American Civil War.

One mile (4 miles.)

East 4 miles to Schauppsville. The town of Wood River, a few miles distant, was already established in 1874 when Mr. John Schaupp built a flour mill at this site. Its location about midway between Wood River and Alda, and along the Mormon Trail, enticed settlers to move to the land around the mill. Soon a town flourished here.

Schaupp could never quite make things work the way he wanted them to. He wanted to build a canal from the Platte to the Wood River in order to increase the flow of the Wood and to provide more water for local farmers. The voters saw it as a way to increase water power for his mill and denied the funding for the project.

In this river bottom land he next decided to drill a well in order to find coal. The coal in Nebraska would make him rich, he decided. It is an indication of his success to say simply that the town of Schauppsville eventually faded into obscurity.

Four miles (3 miles.)

West two miles to the site of Cameron and Cameron Cemetery.

In 1876, when the post office was started here farms often sold for about $6 per acre. The area had a school, post office, G.A.R. Hall and other niceties. In those days there was a different kind of spirit about things, a kind of community that exists only very rarely these days. Imagine holding a community gathering on Christmas Eve in this day and age of closed-up houses and frightened hearts. In Cameron, Christmas Eve meant coming from miles around to gather in the school house to recite poetry, sing songs, read aloud from the latest novels and watch for Santa Claus' arrival.

Three miles (4 miles.)

One and a quarter miles east to site of Berwick, a small farming community which thrived during the 1880s. Berwick had an interesting social organization in 1886 known as the Berwick Eating Society. The group gathered every few weeks to, well, to eat and enjoy one another's company.

The Berwick cemetery is just west of the town site.

Four miles (5 miles.)

Cairo. Please see entry for State Highway 2 for information about Cairo.

Five miles (12 miles.)

Intersection with State Highway 58.

Five miles west of here, near Boelus is a nice campground at the junction of the South and Middle Forks of the Loup River.

Twelve miles (5 miles.)

Junction with State Highway 92.

Howard County was settled by Danes and is believed to have the highest concentration of Danish descendants of any county in the state.

Five miles (6 miles.)

Elba.

Elba was so named because a bend in the railroad track reminded people of an elbow. There might be sillier reasons to name a town, but if there are, this one would give them stiff competition.

Just north of Elba, on the banks of the North Loup River were several important Indian settlements which dated to pre-Colombian times. North of Elba the highway follows the pretty and lazy Calamus River for the next 45 miles.

Six miles (8 miles.)

Cotesfield.

Two miles north and threee miles east of Cotesfield is the Big Wash, on private land.

The Big Wash was created overnight when a farmer made a drain from a table-land lake into the Calamus River drainage. Over night a canyon one hundred feet deep and over a mile long was created by his mistake.

Today Mother Nature has patched things up a bit and the

*canyon is full of vegetation and it is a haven for wild birds and animals
In the spring the hills are covered with blue bells and other wild flowers*

The Big Wash runs through large rolling hills with oak and cedar trees on the fringes. Ask for directions and permission to visit the Big Wash locally.

Eight miles (1 miles.)

To the west of the highway and below the hill known as Happy Jack Peak is a chalk mine.

The state bought the land, sealed the mine and placed a few picnic tables here for a wayside area. The mine opened in 1887 and the chalk was used in building construction and in the manufacturing of paints.

Happy Jack Peak was named for an Indian scout who climbed the hill to watch for pioneers moving up the valley. When he spied some he would climb down and give them food. The peak offers a wonderful view of the valley and is worth every calorie-burning step up.

One mile (2 miles.)

Junction with State Highway 22.

One mile east to Scotia.

Scotia, by many accounts, should be the county seat of Greeley County, instead of Greeley. The reason it is not the county seat becomes one of those fine Nebraska county seat war stories.

Seems that Scotia won the election to become county seat fair and square. However, as the ballot boxes were being transported from one place to another, 61 additional ballots were added which swung the vote in favor of Greeley. Since the election had taken place just days after the great blizzard of 1888, lawyers for the town of Scotia had trouble reaching the trial of the two men who were supposed to have been responsible for protection of the ballots. Eventually a judge ruled that there was no proof that the ballots had been tampered with and the new vote, that of Greeley as the county seat, was officially adapted.

Later court cases revealed that a mysterious stranger "riding in the direction of Scotia" had altered the ballots in favor of Scotia. By the time the case was settled enough suspicion and doubt existed between the two towns that gunfire and fisticuffs broke out. Eventually an armored wagon pulled up to the temporary courthouse in Scotia and the armed men loaded up the county records and moved them to Greeley under heavy guard where they remain to this day.

The Chalk Building on the east side of Main Street near the lumber yard is the only remaining chalk building in the state.

On November 3, 1958 ten year old Roger Groetzinger was milking his family's cows on a farm at Scotia when he noticed an object circling near his barn. It was an oval-shaped object, flying low and giving off a humming noise. He wanted to stand, but to his horror discovered he was paralyzed. The object slowly moved up and away from the barn, and as it did Roger found that he could move again. There was a funny smell in the air.

When his mother returned an hour later Roger was nearly out of his wits. She believed his story.

Two miles (14 miles.)

North Loup. This, dear reader, is the popcorn capital of the world. The village of North Loup has attested to this fact every year since 1902 by celebrating Popcorn Days.

Those factory buildings are for processing popcorn. As they say here, thanks for popping in.

North Loup is near the junction with State Highway 22 west.

Twelve miles west of here State 22 connects with the route outlined in the entry for State Highway 10.

Fourteen miles (6 miles.)

Ord.

Ord, built on the south banks of the Loup, is the county seat of Valley County. It was named after a general who at the time of the town's founding, in 1874, was commander of the military department of the Platte. There is a small campground here on the north bank of the river. See also the entry for State Highway 10.

Six miles (9 miles.)

Turn-off to Fort Hartsuff State Historical Park. On the north bank of Loup River, just on the Valley/Garfiled County line, is Ft. Hartsuff State Historical Park.

Ft. Hartsuff was in operation from 1876 to 1881 when it was closed and replaced by Ft. Valentine. This fort was instrumental in the settlement of the state, as soldiers from here protected the pioneers from the native population who had roamed Valley County for thousands of years.

A fine state historical park is located here and many of the original buildings have been restored.

State Highway 11

Nine miles (28 miles.)

Burwell.. Burwell is the county seat of Garfield County and is one of the prettiest but least visited county seats in the state. Careful planning has made this town of over a thousand an attractive and comfortable place.

For a long while Burwell has served as an important market and shipping center for the Sandhill region. Cattle and crops come through Burwell on their way to and from market. Burwell sits at the edge of the eastern farm lands of Nebraska, and at the start of the isolated and beautiful Sandhill country.

The town boasts a good number of authentic cowboys and ranchers who may not all wear cowboy hats and spurs, but know their *riatas* from their *remudas*. The junction of the North Loup and the Calamas rivers is here, one of the two most beautiful small rivers in the entire American West.

At the south end of town is Nebraska's Big Rodeo Grounds, a National Historic Site. Each July these grounds are very active with a professional rodeo and the Garfield County Fair.

Several tours of local sites have been designed by residents of Burwell. Ask locally for directions.

For the next fifty miles State Highway 11 passes through the lonely, but beautiful Sandhills region. Make that gas and pop stop now.

Twenty eight miles (4 miles.)

Swan Lake, a natural comfortable lake with good fishing just south of the South Fork of the Elkhorn. Inquire locally.

Four miles (19 miles.)

Turn off for State Highway 95 and the small ranching community of Chambers (**twelve miles east**) This road follows the South Fork of the Elkhorn and connects with US Highway 281.

Nineteen miles (27 miles.)

Junction with US Highway 20/275, at Atkinson. See entry for US Highway 20 for information about this area.

For the next 27 miles the highway zigzags through the northern half of Holt County, entering Boyd County at the Niobrara River.

Twenty seven miles (6 miles.)

At the Niobrara River is the beautiful Kit Wade Canyon. If this isn't "out west" then there is no such place.

Six miles (2 miles.)

Butte. The county seat of Boyd County, Butte was named for the Harvey Buttes just south of town. This makes a nice picnic spot, and, if so inclined, an ideal location for a little roadster romance.

The buttes in this area of the state are of the same formation as the Black Hills in South Dakota. One geological theory is that they were formed by glaciers which deposited a part of their load of rocks as they retreated. The soil on the floor of the valley, and the rock of the buttes are of two distinct origins.

Butte is the location of the junction with State Highway 12. Please see the entry for State Highway 12 for information about sites along this road.

Two miles (5 miles.)

The tiny village of Anoka, which is Sioux for "on both sides." There is nothing here for Anoka to be on both sides of, however.

Five miles (0 miles.)

Just at the South Dakota line is Scalp Creek, named for...well, you figure it out. This is one of the best local fishing spots.

Zero miles (3 miles.)
Kansas border.

Three miles (2 miles.)
East five miles to Lookout Mountain, a limestone hill with a cap. Climb to the top of Lookout Mountain and you will be overlooking an Indian village known as Reams Village. Up until the 1930s several Indian houses still stood at this place and pot sherds and arrowheads were everywhere.

Two miles (2 miles.)
Intersection with county road. This road parallels the south bank of the Republican River for the entire east/west length of Franklin County. It is a treat to drive.

Two miles (14 miles.)
Franklin. For information about Franklin, please see entry in

section on US Highway 136.

Fourteen miles (14 miles.)
Intersection with State Highway 4. Please see that entry for information about sites along State Highway 4.

For the next eight miles State Highway 10 gradually rises as it approaches the headwaters of the Little Blue River.

Fourteen miles (10 miles.)
Minden. Home of the famous Harold Warp Pioneer Museum and much more. For a detailed description of Minden, please see entry for US Highway 6 and 34.·

Ten miles (1 mile.)
Junction to the west with State L 50. Please see entry of US 30 for information about Platte Station, Fort Kearney, "17 Mile Station" the Pony Express and Oregon Trail and other sites along this beautiful road.

One mile (5 miles.)
Platte River. At the Platte is Hook's Ranch, or Dogtown, a stage station and trading post at the junction of the Oregon Trail and the Ft. Kearney Trail from Nebraska City. An early pioneer wrote, "Dogtown is the first settlement west of Marysville and an ugly one at that." This is also the location of Valley Station, a later day stage stop, and Lowell Cemetery an early day cemetery.

Along this stretch of the Platte is the best place in the state to see the migration of the sandhills cranes which might include a sizable number of the 112 or so remaining whooping cranes.

Five miles (1 mile.)
Just south of the intersection with US Highway 30 the Mormon Trail crosses Highway 10.

One mile (7 miles.)
Intersection with US Highway 30.

Seven miles (15 miles.)
Kearney. For information about Kearney and this area, please see entry for US Highway 30. State Highway 10 leaves US 30 at Kearney and heads north.

State Highway 10

Fifteen miles (9 miles.)

Pleasanton. Named after the pleasant view of the valley of the South Loup, known locally for decades as Pleasant Valley.

Nine miles (6 miles.)

Hazzard and the junction with State Highway 2. Please see entry for State Highway 2 for information about this area.

Six miles (12 miles.)

East 8 miles on State 68 and *then south seven miles* on State Highway 58 to a small and beautiful campground at Boelus, near the confluence of the Middle and South Forks of the Loup River.

Twelve miles (10 miles.)

Loup City. This quaint town of over a thousand souls was named because of its location in the Loup River valley.

The Loup River did not get its name because of a misspelling of the word loop, but rather in a round about way from the wolf which once, long ago, roamed its banks. The Pawnee, who lived along the river's edges were known as the Skidi band of Pawnee. Skidi was the Pawnee word for wolf. The French fur trappers, in their attempt to name things so that they might be able to recognize them when they next chanced upon them, called the river where this band of Pawnee lived *Loup,* French for wolf. So the Loup River is the French translation of the Indian translation of the word in English, wolf.

Loup City is known as the Polish capital of Nebraska. Loup City is the county seat of Sherman County. It is the location of Bowman Lake Recreation Area which offers camping and boating facilities.

From Loup City ***seven miles to the northeast*** *is the large Sherman Reservoir and State Recreation Area. This large area encompasses the entire reservoir and offers hiking, fishing, boating and concessions.*

Just northwest of Loup City the hills rise to over half a mile above sea level for the first time in the long ascent to the Rockies. Loup City has a museum which, among other exhibits of local history, houses some items from India and Africa.

At Loup City is the junction with State Highway 92.

West of Loup City five miles *on State 92, just north of the* road to Dead Horse Canyon. The mouth of this pretty canyon is near the road. In 1873 a herd of 28 horses died in this canyon during a blizzard. The horses belonged to scouts for the U.S. Army. The name still has stuck with the canyon.

East of Loup City on 92 17 miles to Farwell. This was the location of the famed Folk School, started by the early pioneers. The Folk School was established in order to lay a foundation for a richer life. The buildings for the school still stand, and are a major part of the structures of this small village.

Continue north on State Highway 10 which is joined at Loup City with State Highway 58.

Ten miles (5 miles.)
Turn off for Arcadia at State Highway 70.
Six miles west to Arcadia "simple pleasure and quiet." Tornadoes have ignored this interpretation of the name and ruined the village three times.
Every fall, well after tornado season, the town celebrates its Fall Festival with talent shows, parades and a rodeo. It is held the first weekend in September.

Five miles (9 miles.)
Junction with State Highway 22 to North Loup and Scotia. See entry for State Highway 11 for further information.

Nine miles (0 miles.)
Ord. A thriving, albeit small, Sandhills community. The North Loup is very pretty here and is well worth a walk. Ord is close to a number of historical and recreation sites.
See State Highway 11 for further information.

Zero miles (7 miles.)
   Kansas border.

Seven miles (21 miles.)
   Alma.

   This is the heart of the great buffalo hunting grounds of the Old West. From here, west to the Rockies, millions of bison roamed the plains. Early settlers were drawn to this area partially because of the great herds.

   The Republican River was known by local Indians and early settlers as the more earthy version of "Manure River" because of the great numbers of buffalo that ate, slept and...er...lived near its banks.

   Alma is located on the shores of the Harlan County Lake, one of the largest man-made lakes in the state. The lake was created when the Republican River was dammed in 1952.

   The dam was conceived after a terrible flood in 1935. An eight foot wall of water moved down the Republican destroying property and taking 104 lives in its path.

On a bluff on the south shore of the lake is a cave where, as legend has it, Buffalo Bill used to camp. He once spent 27 days there after suffering a broken leg. During this stay Sioux Indians found him and took his food, but left him alone.

Alma is one of the oldest towns along the Republican. It was founded in 1871 and is the county seat of Harlan County.

In late 1984 or '85 a citizen of Alma was walking along the south shore of the Harlan County Lake and saw some bones sticking out of a bank. He contacted some officials and then the Kansas University Museum of Natural History, and before anyone could bat an eye, the scientists from the neighboring state had arrived and carefully removed the remains of a "30 foot reptilan creature." The museum has nicknamed the creature, which lived at least 63 million years ago, the Kimono Dragon.

In 1871 Buffalo Bill Cody ran for state representative for the 26 district which included Harlan County. He filed as a Democrat in the predominantly Republican district. However, the Buffalo Bill name and fame went a long way and he was apparently elected by the narrow margin of 44 votes.

He then added the moniker "The Honorable" to his name, but failed to show up in Lincoln at any time to fulfill his duties as a representative. After all, he had better things to do.

His opponent in the election, shocked that he could be beat, began to investigate the election. As it turned out an error in counting the votes had taken place in Alma. The Harlan County Clerk had goofed and sent his count to Lincoln, rather than to North Platte. The additional vote count swung the election in favor of Cody's opponent by 42 votes.

Cody was informed of this mix-up and went on about his business without much of a change. He hadn't bothered to go to Lincoln anyway, and he never dropped the Honorable from his name after that.

As you travel north out of Alma, toward Holdrege try to imagine the vast herds of buffalo that once grazed these rolling, prairies.

Twenty one miles (16 miles.)
Holdrege.

Sixteen miles (1 mile.)

*Before you reach the Platte river, **turn west and go three miles**. This county road, which parallels the Platte roughly follows the route of the Oregon Trail. In three miles is Sandy Channel Wayside Area along the Platte River. Near here was the westernmost ford of the Platte River which connected the Council Bluffs section of the trail with the St. Joesph Trail. This was also the location of Craig Station of the Pony Express and Oregon Trail routes.*

For more information about sites in this area, see entry for US Highway 30 at Overton.

One mile (2 miles.)

Cross the Platte River. Hard to imagine that this sluggish river, littered with rusted cars and concrete blocks, was so important in American history, isn't it?

Two miles (14 miles.)

Junction with US Highway 30. Elm Creek is one half mile east of here. See entry for US HIghway 30 for more information on this area.

Fourteen miles (7 miles.)

Junction with State Highway 40 at the tiny village of Miller, named after an Omaha businessman who bought land in the area. In the deed to his land, Miller stipulated that if the railroad were to come this way, and if a town was formed, it had to be called Miller. Look around, this is his legacy.

The highway crosses the Wood River.

Seven miles (18 miles.)

The highway crosses the South Loup River, and as it does the land seems to perceptively grow wilder and more remote. Ahead lies the great wilderness of Nebraska, the sparsely settled, and little known Sandhills.

Eighteen miles (9 miles.)

Junction with State Highway 2. Please see the entry for State Highway 2 for more information about sites in this area.

Ansley. This village was first settled in 1886 and was named after a woman who invested in the area.

Nine miles (2 miles)

Westerville. Westervillians argue that their town is the oldest in the county. While Sargent will give them a good fight on this issue, many hints of the town's age still stand.

West of Westerville 12 miles to Broken Bow. Please see the entry for Broken Bow in State Highway 2.

Two miles (8 miles.)

Cross the Clear Creek. This is the site of the most noted feud between ranchers and homesteaders in the state.

In 1878 homesteaders Luther Mitchell and Ami Ketchum were fed up with on-going troubles with cattle rancher Print Olive. His cattle broke into their fenced corn time and again, and his cowboys continually made trouble for the sod-busters.

It was here where a gun battle broke out between the two factions. A brother of rancher Olive was killed. The homesteaders Mitchell and Ketchum were arrested for murder.

On their way to the trial they were ambushed about 10 miles southwest of Broken Bow by Olive and his men. The pioneers were hung and then their bodies were burned. Olive was not arrested.

Eight miles (6 miles.)

Junction s-21 C .

Seven miles east to Comstock. This town started in 1901 and has many rustic buildings still standing. The general store was purchased by the historical society and now serves as a museum. Just south of here is the Dowse sod house, built in 1900. It has been restored.

On the same county road and before reaching the house a marker commemorates the site of Fort Garber. It was built and stationed by local citizens during the Indian scare of the 1880s.

Six miles (1 mile.)

Still visible on a hill about one mile south of Sargent on the west side of the road are the mounds of a mysterious encampment made by some early inhabitants of the area. They were probably Indians as this place was already covered with grass when the first white settlers arrived. The mound has 108 pits, arranged in the shape of a large crescent encompassing 6 acres.

Local legend has it that the Indians buried gold in this area, after having robbed a train carrying gold dust and nuggets. The land is in private ownership and the owners would not appreciate anyone tearing up their property to try and find mythical gold.

Others believe that the shape of the ruins indicates that the Indians were trying to form a large ceremonial hill in the shape of some creature. Some of those believers then speculate that this was in order to communicate with beings from outer space.

One mile (8 miles.)

Sargent. Sargent is the oldest town in Custer County (unless you are from Westerville), it was settled in 1880 by Polish settlers. There are several sod houses in this area and many owners will let you have a look. Ask locally for directions.

Six miles west of Sargent is the site of an old flour mill. Ask locally for directions.

Eight miles (10 miles)

Junction with State Highway 91, and Taylor. Taylor is the county seat of Loup County and was named after a local pioneer. It is located on the southern bank of the North Fork of the Loup River. The population of Taylor, by official statistics, increased by 2 between 1930 and 1980. At this rate, Taylor's population should reach 500 by the year 7490. Keep at it Taylorites!

West of Taylor on State 91, ten miles to Almeria, a town founded in this century. The drive between Taylor and Almeria through Cheesebrough Canyon is considered by many to be the most beautiful place in all of Loup County. Just north of town is the Calamus Reservoir with fishing and sand beaches.

Ten miles (8 miles.)

The highway parallels the beautiful and peaceful Calamus River for a number of miles. There is little traffic here, and every passing car seems to have a driver willing to slowly raise an index finger off the steering wheel as a friendly greeting. Try finding someone who will do that in Omaha or Lincoln!

Eight miles (15 miles.)

On the banks of the Calamus River, just as the highway leaves it to swing more directly north and near the Loup County line, were several Indian villages as recently as a century ago. Remnants of many of these villages can still be easily found. The villages were home to the Pawnee and the Arikari. Fishing along the Calamus is reported to be some of the best river fishing in the state.

Fifteen miles (18 miles.)
Rose, a small, almost blown away building or two.

Eighteen miles (10 miles.)
A county road heads east ten miles to the lake country of Rock County. Pony Lake, Smith Lake and others offer fine fishing and beautiful, isolated scenery. Ask locally for directions and road and fishing conditions.

Ten miles (12 miles.)
Bassett, and junction with US Highway 20.
Bassett, the county seat for Rock County and, as is typical for this part of the state, a center for a large area of sparsely populated ranches. There is no significant population center for another 60 miles south of Bassett. However, the trip south along US 183 is particularly beautiful given its isolated nature.
The highway passes through what many consider to be the most beautiful section of Nebraska's unique sandhill region. There are few trees, but many perfectly rounded hills of grass and yucca.
Bassett was named after an important Nebraskan and local citizen who, in 1871, brought the first herd of cattle into the sandhills and started one of Nebraska's most important financial resources: cattle raising.
Rock County is not without other villages, however, and their names would do justice to a Louis L'Amour novel: Horsefoot, Mariaville, Pony Lake, Skull Creek and Rose.
The long hill which forms the town is one of the attractive features of the community. Bassett is a pretty town which serves as a shipping point for much of the cattle and hay produced in the area.
The downtown area was once the hangout of such Nebraska desperadoes as Doc Middleton and Kid Wade. Wade, who was a rustler, gambler and leader of a notorious gang of outlaws called the Pony Boys, was eventually caught and hanged in 1884 just east of town by a group of vigilantes.

Twelve miles (14 miles.)
US Highway 183 and US Highway 20 are the same road for these 12 miles west of Bassett, for information on this section, please see entry for US Highway 20.

Fourteen miles north of US Highway 20 (3 miles.)
North on US 183 to Devil's Gulch a steep canyon where many

US Highway 183

fossils have been recovered. There were once woolly elephants and camels in Nebraska, and if you believe that you'll believe that Nebraska had a native born son in the White House and addressed as "President."

Three miles (2 miles.)

East and south on county roads to the site of the ghost town of Riverview. This is said by many to be the most beautiful spot in the state, especially in the spring when the area is in full wildflower bloom. The road sits high above the river and provides the inspiration for the claims of beauty.

Two miles (5 miles.)

Springview. This is the county seat of Keya Paha County. The county with the most beautiful name in the state, Keya Paha is a Sioux word meaning Turtle Hill. It was the name the Indians gave to the river, and the whites gave to their county. It probably originated because of the many rounded, turtle-shaped hills in the area.

Springview is the haying and trade center of a wide area. The county has never had a railroad, and may be the only county in the state with such a distinction.

When this town was first formed a spring flowed not far from the central square. Story has it that the founder of Springview, a pioneer with a bad back, actually was hauling buckets of water to the site in order to make settlers believe such a spring existed. Soon after the town was incorporated the spring dried up and the founder's back condition improved vastly.

Springview is at the junction with State Highway 12.

Please see the entry for State Highway 12 for more information about sites west of Springview.

Five miles (7 miles.)

Junction with State Highway 12 east. Please see entry for State Highway 12 for information about sites east of here.

Seven miles (0 miles.)

The border with South Dakota.

Zero miles (13 miles.)
    Kansas Border.

Thirteen miles (12 miles.)
    Beaver City.
    Beaver City is located on Beaver Creek which was named for
the beaver that lived there. It is the county seat of Furnas County.

Twelve miles (20 miles.)
    Arapahoe.
    See entry for US Highway 34.

Twenty miles (6 miles.)
    Elwood, the county seat of Gosper County.

Eight miles (3 miles.)

US Highway 283

Johnson Reservoir, and the popular Johnson Lake State Recreation Area. There are several state wildlife management areas in the vicinity and they make for good, patient bird-watching sites.

Three miles (4 miles.)

Just before the highway swings to the east the Oregon Trail crosses the road. Near here are several important sites of the Oregon Trail. See entry for US Highway 30 for more information about these sites.

Four miles (0 miles.)

Lexington. US Highway 283 ends at Lexington. For information on Lexington, please see entry for US Highway 30.

NEBRASKA
U S
83

Zero miles (14 miles.)

Kansas border.

Ranchers got their start in this area by rounding up stray cattle that roamed from the large herds passing north from Texas on the Texas Cattle Road. That road, which led from Texas to Ogallala and north, passed west of here. Throughout the entire Red Willow County, and especially in these open areas, the Pawnee and the Sioux hunted buffalo. Some of the largest herds were in this section of the state on the southern side of the Platte. The largest oil field in the state was discovered near McCook in the late 1950s.

One mile south of McCook is Barnett Park. Barnett Park was formed after several people cleared tons of debris left here by the flood of 1935.

Fourteen miles (10 miles.)

McCook.

For more information on McCook see entry for US Highway

6.

Ten miles (30 miles.)
      Hugh Butler Lake. A state recreation area formed when Red Willow Creek was dammed.
      Hugh Butler Lake in Frontier County is noted for excellent fishing in a remote, yet accessible spot.

Thirty miles (8 miles.)
      Junction with State Highway 23. A short way down this road is the favorite spot of "Evil Doc" Carver, one of the state's notorious bandits. Near here is also the comfortable Strunk Lake. Depending on your time, a variety of interesting sidetrips are available on this route:

      One mile east of US Highway 83.
      Mayfield. Mayfield is a small community on the way to Hugh Butler Lake and McCook (see below). Mayfield holds an annual event known as The Spring Rights.

      Seven miles east of US 83
      Curtis, at the juncture of State Highways 23 and 235 celebrated its centennial in 1987 and owes its existence to the railroad and the cattle industry.
      A few miles north of here the largest mammoth skeleton on display at Morril Hall at the University of Nebraska was discovered in a canyon of loess and red clay. Ask locally for directions to other places with prehistoric artifacts.
      The area around Curtis and Curtis Creek is known for its wild fruit, and, consequently, some of the kinds of birds not often found in most parts of the state including the magpie and several types of hawks.

      East of Curtis on State Highway 23: (all mileage is from Curtis.) Ten miles:
      Morefield is a small town which boasts both a post office and a grain elevator.

      Twelve miles to the junction of State Highway 47 to Interstate 80 and Gothenburg.

      Twenty miles:
      Eustis. Eustis was one hundred years old in 1987 and was

founded as a result of the railroad which was built through the northern part of Frontier County. It was settled by German pioneers and still has a Wurst Tag Day, or, for you noninformed, a Sausage Day during the late summer.

A silica mine once operated just west of town.

Twenty one miles to the junction with US Highway 283.

South of Curtis on State Highway 235:

Seven miles south of Curtis: Frontier County was founded in 1872 when a pioneer named Henry Clifford raised his Sioux teepee on the banks of Medicine Creek. Clifford and his Sioux wife Eena Teglake, had found the only reliable water between the Platte and the Republican River and made their stand.

Medicine Creek cuts the county diagonally from the north-west to the southeast and since it was such an important water source throughout history, many artifacts can be found along its course. In addition many prehistoric Indian villages were located on the hills along the valley and canyon of Medicine Creek.

Ten miles south of Curtis:
Stockville.

A nearly deserted town (but don't mention this to the 40 remaining residents) but with many of the buildings from more prosperous days still standing. Stockville, which is competing with Brewster in Blaine County for one of the smallest county seats in the nation, has a county courthouse that was built in 1888 and is still in use. The previous building, also made of wood, was built in 1872, and burned to the ground in 1884, along with most of the county records to that time.

This is considered the oldest city in southwestern Nebraska. Stockville lost its luster when the railroad passed it by, in favor of a more northerly route across Frontier County. Frontier County would like you to know that 22 men have been sent to the state legislature from near here.

Three miles south of Stockville, along the road which parallels Medicine Creek:
The favorite spot of Dr. W. F. "Evil Spirit of the Plains" Carver. At the age of 14 Craver lived with the Indians of Minnesota after his father booted him out of his family in Illinois. He left Minnesota and

ended up in this part of the frontier, hunting and trapping as a loner. When the Sioux War started in 1862, Carver was named as a scout for General Henry Sibley.

After the war he came back to this area. One of his favorite camps was this spot on the Medicine. He became known as one of the great buffalo hunters. He also became known as a dentist. The two occupations still seem to have some kind of a relationship.

Carver knew many of the legendary Wild West characters including Buffalo Bill, Wild Bill Hickcok, Texas Jack Ojomondro and Kit Carson.

In May, 1883 Carver and Buffalo Bill jointly opened the Wild West Show. Carver was one of the best rifle shots of his day and held a record for a long while. He managed to shoot at clay balls tossed into the air. Out of 6,000 balls he missed only 650. The first performance was in Omaha.

Carver's main act was known as The Great Rifle Shot and involved him shooting glass balls the size of quarters which had been tossed into the air. A hard enough task, but Carver did it while riding horseback.

On a bad day, when Carver's shot was off, he became disgusted with himself and show business and turned his act over to Buffalo Bill and stormed off. Soon after, the partnership was dissolved. Later Carver started his own rival show, and he and Buffalo Bill became enemies and remained so for the rest of their lives.

Carver's shows toured off and on until his death. His last great act, touring the year he died, was a troupe of diving horses, who would leap from a platform into a large tub of water. Carver's shows never became as popular as his rival's, however. Carver died in 1927 and is buried in Illinois.

Ten miles south of Stockville on Coon Creek two divisions of soldiers camped for the summer of 1872.

Fifteen miles southeast of Stockville is Harry D. Strunk Lake, a fine recreation area created by a dam on the once wild Medicine Creek. You can buy bait, soda pop and treats here and boat, fish and relax.

On the way to this lake, and in the surrounding hillsides, you might get a feel for what this area of the state once was like. Not too long ago this land between the Platte and the Republican Rivers was teeming with wildlife. Buffalo, wolf, fox, wild cat and bear roamed these hills.

Eight miles (6 miles.)

The tiny spot on the road known as Wellfleet, which was named after a "whale fleet." Don't even ask how a town here got named after a fleet of whaling ships...

Six miles (15 miles.)

Junction of State Highway 23. See entry for the highway for sites west of here.

Ten miles (5 miles.)

*Ask locally for directions and road conditions. Take the county road to the **east** for about **four miles** to the 3,200 foot hill known as Sioux Lookout. This hill served as a look-out for the local Indians as they watched for buffalo, and for the whites moving along the Great Platte River Road. From this vantage point the Indians could signal hunting or warriors to attack. A statue of a proud Sioux in a double war bonnet was erected on the top of the hill in 1931, but vandals have destroyed much of the structure. Although the statue stands on public land, most of the routes up the hill are on private land. A move is underway to have the entire hill made into a state historical park.*

Five miles (3 miles.)

Turn-off for Maloney Reservoir, one mile to the west. This state recreation area has fishing and boating for all types of crafts.

Three miles (2 miles.)

Just before the highway becomes a four lane road the Oregon Trail crosses it. Just to the west, about three tenths of a mile down a small road, is the site of the Cold Springs Pony Express and Stage Station. It was of adobe construction and also served as ranch buildings.

Two miles (21 miles.)

North Platte. Please see entry for U.S. Highway 30 for information about North Platte.

For the next 23 miles Highway 83 is joined with State Highway 70. Together they lazily climb into the grassy slopes of the start of the Sandhills. This is beautiful and isolated land. Stop the car a moment, turn off the engine and step outside. The quiet and the beauty here can melt the ice of any sorrow or boredom.

US Highway 83

Twenty one miles (4 miles.)

Junction with State Highways 70 and 92. Highway 70 splits off and continues east of this junction. For information about sites along State Highway 70 please see that entry.

Four miles (18 miles.)

Stapleton.

This is the county seat of Logan County, and like 99.97% of all of the counties of the state, there was a battle to get the courthouse and its fine workers here instead of elsewhere. The most recent elsewhere in contention was the small Logan town of Gandy. This particular battle was settled in the courtroom in the 1930s and Stapleton won.

The small town of Stapleton, hovering around a population of 350 houses, is the only school district in the county. Children are bussed here from all of Logan county and from parts of McPherson and Lincoln Counties as well. Even drawing from this wide area, the district enrolls only 215 students. The mural on the side of the Veteran's Building along State Highway 92 through town was finished in 1976 and depicts scenes from the life of the county.

In the Senior Citizen's building, also along Highway 92, the Logan County Museum is starting to grow. This museum is a new venture and any assistance from the outside visitor to help this community effort would be appreciated.

State Highway 92 leaves U.S. Highway 83 here and heads west. For information about sites along its path see entry for State Highway 92. Many of this county's citizens have roots which extend over 200 years in Logan county.

Two miles southeast of Stapleton.

Gandy. The outlaw Parker was captured here in the late 1880s. Gandy tried to increase its stature by legally attempting to become Logan County's county seat. It lost.

Eighteen miles (3.5 miles)

Thomas County/Logan county border.

The great Prairie Fire of the 1890s, which burned thousands of square miles passed by here, destroying barns and livestock. Other, more recent fires have stopped just short of destroying the National Forest lands. A fire on March 6, 1972 burned 100,000 acres in a path 32 miles long and 12 miles wide. It destroyed many ranches

120

in the county.

Three and a half miles (9 miles.)

The Dismal River which flows through Thomas County is still successfully trapped by local ranchers. Mink, muskrat and beaver still frequent the banks of the river.

In this area in the 1930s a rancher started growing sugar cane and started a molasses plant. It was a sticky business...

During the dry years of the 1930s this area of the Sandhills suffered many natural disasters. The storms that did come were intense lightning storms, and many people lost their lives because of them. When the rivers to the south dried up snakes moved further and further north. Thomas County was plagued by the influx of many varieties of snakes during the drought years. The dust storms crossed the county as well, bringing the earth from hundreds of miles away in tall black clouds and raging winds.

Nine miles (5 miles.)

Four miles west on county and private road. The Pearson sod house and school.

Thomas County, like the rest of this isolated part of the state, had many one room schools. Now that the population has declined, and larger and larger ranches occupy the land, one room schools are nearly extinct. Likewise there are still sod houses, now mostly melting back into the hills, or used as cow sheds and storage barns. One fine example can still be seen here. The only remaining two-story sod house in the county it is now abandoned. It dates from at least 1917, and perhaps earlier. It is on the Pearson ranch and permission is required to view the house.

Five miles (21 miles.)

Junction of State Highway 2. Just to the west of this junction is the county seat, Thedford.

Thedford.

Cattlemen from the Thedford Livestock Association were directly responsible for the last great settlement of the American West. They petitioned the US Congressman to introduce legislation to allow homesteaders to claim up to two sections of land as opposed to the old limit of 160 acres. With the support of the Livestock association, Congressman Moses P. Kinkaid passed the new homesteading law which allowed homesteaders to claim up to one section of land. The Kinkaiders, as this new breed of homesteaders was soon known, settled the last great open areas of the American West.

Thedford, when first founded had no trees. For a long while a lone cottonwood tree, outside a homesteader's house, was the only tree. Later pioneers planted apples and other trees.

The Timbers Claim Act required that each owner plant a certain number of trees on each 160 acres, and the results of this act can be seen all over the county.

One of the most famous stories to come out of Thedford was the story of the missing Haumann girls.

In May of 1891 two young girls, aged eight and four, went for a short walk between their house and another. They left their house just north of Thedford at five and when they had not returned by six, the mother went looking for them.

After nightfall men from the town mounted up and began to look for the girls. By morning the only ones left in town were the postmaster and the depot agent. Finally a faint trail was found. At times the searchers crawled on their hands and knees to try to follow the trail. Usually the two sets of footprints were side-by-side, but often there was only a single set: the older girl was carrying her sister.

On the fourth day of the search one of the girls was found, still alive, although barely. When finally she could speak she told how her sister and she had gotten lost while picking wildflowers to bring to their mother. At nightfall the first night they had heard people calling, but her older sister would not let her go to them for fear it would be Indians.

In a few more days the older child was found near Dunning, Nebraska. She had taken off her coat and spread it on top of some wild rose bushes, and then crawled under the shade to sleep. She never woke up again. It was estimated that they had walked 75 miles. By this time the national press had picked up the story, and the newspapers across the nation carried reports.

After the girls were found letters came from all over the world. They became subjects for poems, stories and remembrances. The girls' father for years afterwards would ride about the county in his wagon and give children rides home, warning them sternly about playing too far from home. Trinkets made from the hair of the dead girl began to appear almost immediately all over the county. Many residents still have locks of hair purported to be from her tiny head.

The post office delivered mail by horse every day for a number of years. The 50 mile trip required three changes in teams.

The Cowpoke Inn is well known around these parts for its food and conversation.

The Thedford Vicinity Womens' Club was organized in 1919 and today serves the area as the main civic organization. In addition to collecting local history, the Club is active in a wide variety of charitable causes.

And it isn't as if there isn't any culture in Thedford. The Thomas County Library, for example, received the national Dorothy Canfield Fisher Award for having made the greatest contribution in library service. In addition, the Thedford Art Guild meets often and offers workshops and art shows. The Thedford Catholic Church was built in 1922 from concrete blocks made on a local ranch.

The Thedford Park was nothing more than a couple of cedar trees until 1951 when a retired rancher made it his personal responsibility. Carl Wiese planted hundreds of trees and shrubs and flowers and hand watered them from several cream cans loaded into his truck, to keep them growing. Through the additional efforts of others the park gained playground equipment, a well and a lighted ball field.

The Hillcrest Cemetery was originally formed when an early pioneer was laid to rest on a hill overlooking the Middle Loup Valley. A sign posted over the grave proclaimed, "this is hallowed ground." Today it is the largest cemetery in the county.

On a February morning in 1934 the Chicago, Burlington and Quincy Depot was robbed on horseback, probably the last robbery performed with such a getaway device in the United States. The robber wore a kerchief over his face and brandished a six shooter. He got $17 and was caught within hours, but not because he used a horse, but because he was a local boy whose voice was easily recognized.

Before 1940 there was no north-south highway and although North Platte is only 70 miles distant, many people never visited the town prior to the completion of US 83.

Twenty one miles (20 miles.)

Five miles to the small burg of Brownlee, near Swan Lake, one of the area's most beautiful natural lakes.

Twenty miles (19 miles.)

Near the roadside picnic area is the site of Simeon which was a post office established at a ranch with the same name.

You are now in the center of Cherry County's vast Lake Group, a part of the Valentine National Migratory Wildlife Refuge, a vast 70,000 acre refuge for a wide variety of wildlife. Within easy reach of here are many lakes with good fishing spots.

US Highway 83

The lakes' names read like a kind of western poem:
>Trout, Red Deer, Hackberry,
>Long, Willow and Dewey.

>Ballard's Marsh
>Marsh Lake.

>Pelican and Dad's Lake.
>Beaver and Big Alkali.

Nineteen miles (5 miles.)
Junction with U.S. Highway 20. Please see entry for US Highway 20 for information about sites along this route.

Five miles (10 miles.)
Valentine. See entry for U.S. Highway 20 for information about the Valentine area.

Ten miles (0 miles.)
South Dakota border. The area between here and Valentine is one of the most productive areas for finding fossil in the nation.

This highway begins at North Platte.

Zero miles (31 miles.)

North Platte. See entry for US Highway 30 for information about North Platte.

Go north on US Highway 83 two miles and then take Highway 97. For the next thirty miles this road winds into the Sandhills of Nebraska and a few lonely looks back at the town of North Platte are invited since for the next several hundred miles the traveler enters one of the most sparsely populated areas of the state.

Thirty one miles (29 miles.)

Tryon.

Tryon, Nebraska is the county seat for the sparsely populated McPherson county. Tryon itself has a continually shrinking population, but manages to hold onto the county seat by virtue of the also shrinking populations of its closest competitors Flats and Ringgold.

This is not to say that the county is uninhabited or that it did not at one time have a larger population. In fact the county has many ghost towns to serve witness to those former residents. Nearby Brighton, for example, was located in the Brighton Valley near Tryon.

In the northeastern part of the county the remnants of the village of Omega can still be found. Omega was so named after the phrase in Revelations "the Alpha and Omega, the beginning and ending." Since the location of this burg was nearer the Omega of everything rather than the Alpha, it was so named.

Speaking of names, one story on how Tryon got its name is still apt today. When selecting a name for the new community, some residents felt that the town itself was not worthy of a name. A local boster kept saying, "Lets keep tryin' to have a town." Tryon is still tryin'.

East of Tryon 11 miles on State Highway 92 to the near ghost town of Ringgold which was moved here from Dawson County and kept its name.

West of Tryon 18 miles on State Highway 92 to the turn off north to the White and Brown Lake vicinity and the south fork of the Dismal River where Buffalo Bill once had a ranch. (see below for details.)

West of Tyron 22 miles on State Highway 92 to turn off to the south for Diamond Bar Lake vicintiy. Good fishing and hunting. Inquire locally. Ten miles southeast of here, accessible on backroads only, was the small town of Forks, located at the forks of the East and West Birdwood Creeks. It had a post office until the early 1920s.

West of Tryon 28 miles to Flats, another near ghost town. Because of an early pioneer named Lombard the area was called Lombard Flats. The US Post Office, in its infinite wisdom cut off the Lombard part because it was too long and simply left Flats.

Twenty nine miles (5 miles.)

Take the narrow paved road leading off to the west. **Down this road 15 miles** to the banks of the North Fork of the Dismal River, cross the river and continue another **eight miles** to the banks of the South Fork and the site of the North and Cody Ranch.

This grassy expanse of hills was once the range of thousands of buffalo, antelope and deer. In 1877 William F. Cody, who would *later become world renowned as Buffalo Bill, along with Major Frank North, purchased a herd of cattle at Ogallala and spent a good part of their summer driving them to this range land. Here the men started a ranch that would become known as the North and Cody Ranch. Not much is known about the success of this ranch, or Buffalo Bill's part in it, but for years the ranch was made welcome to any traveler who happened this way. In later years many dignitaries were entertained here. Today the quiet and peaceful river flows through beautiful country of grasslands and thickets along the banks.*

Five miles (0 miles.)

Mullen.

Junction with State Highway 2 and the end of State Highway 97.

For information about Mullen, see entry for State Highway 2.

*North of Mullen the road continues as county roads into the vast Cherry County. Under most weather conditions the road is passable, although it might be a bit washboardy in spots. In **forty miles** is the Samuel McKelvie National Forest, the hideout spots for the state's most famous outlaw, Doc Middleton, and other interesting sites.*

For a full discussion of the area North of Mullen see the entry for Valentine and US Highway 20.

Zero miles (15 miles.)

Kansas Border.

This moonscape landscape of interesting rock formations and canyons is where hundreds of fossils have been found, including those of many prehistoric turtles.

Fifteen miles (8 miles.)

Trenton.

Supply center for those headed for Swanson Reservoir. Intersection of U.S. Highway 34. For further discussion of Tenton, see entry for U.S. Highway 34.

Eight miles (7 miles.)

Intersection of U.S. Highway 6. See entry for U.S. Highway 6 for a discussion of the sites along this road.

Seven miles (8 miles.)
Junction with 25A (west).
Six miles on 25A to Palisade.
In 1867 George Armstrong Custer went from Ft. McPherson to Kansas in order to take part in the Sioux Indian Wars. Custer, as well as many other famous fighters, crossed Hayes Co. and by their passing, created a much-used military trail. The trail crosses Highway 25A at Palisade, and more or less follows Highway 25 north through the county.
For other items near Palisade, see entry for U.S. Highway 6.

Eight miles (5 miles.)
Hayes Center.
There were many battles around these parts in the pioneer days. The Pawnee and the Sioux fought with the pioneers so much so that the battles became known as the Sioux Wars. In addition, the Pawnee often fought against the Sioux for land possession since it was near here that their homelands overlapped.
Hayes Center was known as the windmill city as each family once had their own windmill and tanks. The public windmill was at the hill on Main Street and was a famous landmark for a long while. This water supply was free to anyone in need of it.
This is the location of the Hayes County Historical Society and their museum is located in the old newspaper building.

Five miles (3 miles.)
From here, stretching 70 or more miles to the west was the front line of probably the greatest prairie fire in recorded history. The fire reached Hayes County on April 1, 1893. The wind was near tornado force, and drove the fire across thousands of square miles of western Nebraska, Colorado and Wyoming. Drifts of ashes piled up like snow against houses and fence posts. The sun was blacked out. It is estimated that this great fire moved at about 15 to 25 miles per hour.
The fire's eastward movement was held near here, but it is not clear how far it moved to the south before it burned itself out. Despite the seriousness of the fire, and its great extent, only two lives were lost.

Three miles (6 miles.)
East of here is Grand Duke Alexis' recreation ground on 140

acres, with a 100 acre lake. The lake is well stocked with fish.

In 1873 Grand Duke Alexis, 22 year old brother of the Czar of Russia, was the main attraction of a hunting party led by Buffalo Bill Cody. Gen. William Sherman went along for the ride, as did several others.

They camped on the Big Blackwood, 8 miles NE of present day Hayes Center. It was at this place that the Sioux Chief Spotted Tail and 100 warriors showed the Indian method of hunting and gave a realistic demonstration of a a war dance.

The Duke killed several buffalo, which wasn't much of an accomplishment since the animals are not very smart and will stand around while others near them are shot down.

The famous campground of this famous hunting party is commemorated by a locally made marker at the spot. Buffalo skulls were found at this site as late as 1973. Ask locally for directions to the site.

Six miles (10 miles.)

Near here the Military Road of 1867 (see above) swings to the east toward Ft. McPherson, 55 miles away. It roughly follows Route 25 south to the Kansas border.

Ten miles (23 miles.)

Intersection of State Highway 23. See entry for State Highway 23 for information about this stretch of road.

For the next 23 miles the road winds through the little traveled stretches of Nebraska ranchland.

Twenty-three miles (0 miles.)

Sutherland. See entry for U.S. Highway 30 for information about Sutherland.

Zero miles (5 miles.)
Kansas border.

Five miles (18 miles.)
Benkelman. See entry for U.S. Highway 34 for information about the sites in Benkelman.

Eighteen miles (8 miles.)
Six miles west on this road to site of Hiawatha. The Society of Friends, or Quakers, organized Hiawatha Academy in 1888 which served as the hub of education in the area for years. Unfortunately the economic crisis and crop failures of the 1890s forced the school, and the town, to close down.

The buildings of the academy stood until the 1920s. Since then a school and the cemetery are all that remain of this once thriving community. The great prairie fire of April 1, 1893 swept past this area fueled by a dry previous summer's worth of grass and a powerful wind.

The fire burned a stretch at least from the South Platte River to the Republican and many believe the area was much more *extensive than that. A widow woman was killed near here when she became curious about the fire and left her dugout to climb a small hill to watch the flames. The wind whipped the fire right across the top of the hill and she was burned to death. Her name, ironically enough, was Burner. She is buried in the old United Presbyterian Church cemetery six miles north of Parks. Another man was saved when he burned a little circle of grass around his wagon and horses when he saw the fire coming. He stood in the burnt circle while the fire swept past him. From that point onward this man was never known to travel without matches in his pocket.*

To the east, on back roads are the spectacular canyonlands of Nebraska. Ask locally for the routes and the conditions of the roads since many of these roads are impassable after rain.

Eight miles (9 miles.)

Enders Reservoir, and along its edge, the tiny Chase County village of Enders.

For the next nine miles State Highway 61 and U.S. Highway 6 are combined.

Nine miles (27 miles.)

State Highway 61 turns north and away from U.S. Highway 6 just east of Imperial. See entry for US Highway 6 for information on Imperial.

For the next fifty miles or so the highway roughly follows the route of the Texas Cattle Road of the 1880s. Along here large herds of cattle were driven north from Texas to be shipped east out of Ogallala. This is the territory Larry McMurtry wrote about in his wonderful novel *Lonesome Dove*.

Twenty seven miles (18 miles.)

Grant. The county seat of Perkins County. This is the location of the Perkins County Museum, located in one of Grant's fine old mansions. If you don't find the museum open, just call the posted phone number and make arrangements to view the many fine exhibits located there.

Eighteen miles (1 mile.)

One mile due south of Ogallala, and just west of the road was Gill's Station a Pony Express and military supply station. Both the Oregon Trail and the Pony Express Trail crossed the road approxi mately one half mile south of the Interstate exchange.

One mile (2 miles.)

Ogallala. See entry for US Highway 30 for information about Ogallala.

Two miles (10 miles.)

Junction with US Highway 26. Please see the entry for that route for sites along US Highway 26.

Ten miles (12 miles.)

The dam. The big one. And behind it the big Mac. Lake C.W. McConaughy. There are camping spots, fishing spots, boating spots, parks, wildlife and just about anything else around here for the tourist.

East eight miles on county road on the north side of the North Platte River to Keystone.

Keystone is known for its unusual church, built in 1908 at a cost of $1,000. This is the only known church built to be used by both the Catholics and Protestants. Special dispensation was given by the Pope himself to allow dual services in the building. The church was used by both faiths, and later also by the Lutherans for a number of years. The Catholic altar is at one end, the Protestant's at the other. The backs of the pews are hinged so that they can flip over and be of service to either faith. The stove, bible and organ date to the dedication. The church is no longer in regular use, but is open to the public Sunday afternoons and by special request.

The road to Keystone from Highway 61 follows the Mormon Trail and traces of the Trail extend eastward from here.

Twelve miles (13 miles.)

Arthur County line. Arthur County was the home of many large cattle camps during the heyday of the cowboys. Buffalo Bill Cody, John Bratt and others drove their cattle up this way to feast on the grass of the Sandhills. There were stores at places with names like Lightning Valley and Lena to serve the handful of early pioneers, and with the coming of the Kinkaid Act Arthur County flourished for a time. In 1913 a large tract of land in the western part of the state, which had been set aside to become a man-made forest preserve, was opened to homesteaders.

The county has had a difficult history of being able to maintain its self-esteem. Several times it has disappeared from the maps of the state, usually being swallowed up by the larger McPherson County to the east. The problem was that Arthur didn't have enough people to organize into a county and make it stick. Finally, by 1920, and thanks to an act by the Legislature, Arthur County became official.

Thirteen miles (10 miles.)

Arthur.

The tiny town of Arthur, with a population of under 175, is the largest metropolis in the county. It is the county seat of Arthur County and was named after Chester Arthur, who was President in 1881.

The smallest courthouse in the United States, built in 191 and used until the early 1960s, is now the county museum. It is indeed small. One hopes that the county government officials got along with one another as it doesn't appear there is much room for disagreement

Arthur is also the home of the only baled hay church in the world. The word "only" is used here in case you think that the good Lord has allowed other churches to be built out of baled hay in other parts of the world. If He has then you may substitute the word "first" for the word "only" and thank the good Lord you are in Arthur, where the first one was built. It looks a bit as if it were made from adobe bricks since the bales have been stacked, and then plastered over inside and out. It was built to be the home of the Pilgrim Holiness Church in 1927. The original insides had hand-made pews and pulpit and metal sheeting which served as the ceiling. In 1967 a new building was hauled in to the area to serve the needs of the people and the baled hay church sat unused until it was purchased and renovated by the Arthur County Historical Society.

Junction with State Highway 92. East of here are several sites of interest. For information, please see entry for State Highway 97 at Tyron.

Ten miles (22 miles.)

There are still log cabins and sod houses in this area. Local friendly residents might be able to steer you toward one or two.

A bounty of $25 per pelt was placed on grey wolves in Arthur County at the turn of the century. Forty seven pelts were collected, the last bounty was paid in 1901 for, presumably, the last grey wolf taken in the state of Nebraska.

Before you leave Arthur County, pause a moment to reflect on what life must be like for the residents of this area. Breath deeply. Smell that clear air, see those gentle hills rising in the distance? There is a kind of love for the land which fewer and fewer of us experience. The folks around here know all about that love, that's why they stay in what others would call a God-forsaken place. They'd tell you that God hasn't forsaken Arthur County.

Eight miles (12 miles.)
Eight miles east of here up Spring Valley and located on the east side of Spring Valley Lake in a grove of trees is a small cemetery. Marked with two headstones are the burials of three children, who died between 1923-1933. This fenceless land held tens of thousands of cattle in earlier years. As large as three wagon outfits worked roundups that roamed this area in the not so distant past.

Twelve miles (12 miles.)
Hyannis. See entry for State Highway 2 for information on Hyannis. It is 67 miles from here to the small town of Merriman in Cherry County. This is one of the most isolated stretches of road in the state. WARNING: Do not travel it unless you seek isolation and beauty.

Twelve miles (55 miles.)
Dr. Plummer's home on the Dumbbell Ranch. Built in 1890s this home was to serve as a maternity hospital. It is hindsight that is 20-20 and so it might be more obvious to today's traveler that the sparsely populated Sandhills would not be the ideal place to build a maternity hospital. The name for the ranch came after the good doctor hit his thumb with a hammer while building the house/hospital. He said, "Only a dumbbell would do something like that."

Dr. A.J. Plummer built this house with six upstairs bedrooms, and four downstairs. The size of the house caused the Plummer spread to serve as a community center for years. The good doctor bought out more and more of his neighbors and the Dumbell Ranch grew to 52,000 acres. This was good for cattle ranching, but bad for ensuring patients for the doctor's practice. He later sold the ranch and moved to Montana. The house was built in the 1910s.

Along this stretch of Highway 61 are many small cemeteries and graves. Five miles west near here is Mother Lake. It was here, after the devastating blizzard of March 13-15, 1913 that 600 dead cattle were found. They had wandered into the lake and had frozen to death.

State Highway 61

Fifty five miles (5 miles.)

Merriman and the intersection of US Highway 20. Please see the entry for USA Highway 20 for information about sites in this area.

Five miles (0 miles.)

South Dakota border.

This state highway begins off U.S. Highway 30, seven miles east of Chappell in Deuel County.

Twenty miles north of the junction with U.S. 30 (2 miles.)

Just south of the North Platte River, in the northwest corner of the junction with the county road immediately south of the river, is the grave of John Hollman, who died on the Oregon Trail in 1901. An old state of Nebraska Trail marker, placed in 1914 still stands.

Two miles (22 miles.)

Oshkosh. See entry for US Highway 26.

Twenty-two miles (25 miles.)

Crescent Lake National Wildlife Refuge. One of the largest refuges in the state, Crescent Lake is home to many species of birds and is the birder's paradise. Crescent Lake is one of the largest natural lakes in the state.

State Highway 27

Twenty five miles (8 miles.)

Junction with State Highway 2. For information about sites along this route, please see entry for State Highway 2.

State Highway 250 goes north from here to Rushville. For a description of sites along that route, please see entry for State Highway 250.

A mile to the east is Lakeside. World War One potash was mined here, making this a temporary boom town.

In June of 1897 three companies of Black enlisted men tried to make their way from Montana to St. Louis on bicycles. They were a special division of the Army calvary, and were being used to try and prove that bicycles would bring the Army into the 20th Century.

Each man had to carry 40 pounds or more of supplies. Once they reached the Sandhills they could not move, not even over the faint lines of wagon roads. The sand bogged them down. At this point they got on the Burlington railroad tracks and bounced their way east. They made a total of 2,000 miles in 41 days, and the worst of those days were right along here.

For the next 8 miles east Highway 27 follows Highway 2.

Eight miles. (3 miles)

Ellsworth. Once the headquarters for the gigantic Spade Ranch. At Ellsworth Highways 27 and 2 divide. Highway 27 continues north out of Ellsworth.

Three miles (5 miles.)

Morgan's Cowpoke Haven Museum and Tack Shop. You are not a true traveler of the wilds if you pass up a place with such a name.

Five miles (17 miles.)

A increasingly rare sight in the modern world: a sod house. This is known as the Hunsicker Sod House.

You are entering Old Jules Country, Mari Sandoz country, land of a kind of beauty which was fortunate enough to find a voice of considerable talent. Best known for the book which told the story of her father, *Old Jules,* Sandoz wrote in a unique and gifted voice of the people of Nebraska. Her works have been read all over the world. Many local bookstores contain a more complete collection of her works than you are likely to find anywhere else. To the east on a dirt road from the sod house is where Mari Sandoz lived while teaching.

Between here and the turn-off for Smith Lake Road Highway 27 passes the turn-off for Spade Ranch, on the National Register of Historic Places.

Seventeen miles (8 miles)
Smith Lake Road.

Just south of Smith Lake Road on the west is the dirt road to the grave of Mari Sandoz. "It had always been that the dead returned to the earth which fed them, as the flowers returned, and the tree and the buffalo and all living things go back."—*The Buffalo Hunters*.

Down below the hill is the ranch of Flora Sandoz, who, if she is free and sees you here at the grave, may stop by for a chat. Old Jules' house is among the ranch buildings.

Smith Lake Road. **Turn west** *on this road for a self-guided tour around the locales from Mari Sandoz's books.*

The trees along this road were planted by the local fans of Nebraska's fine writer.

In **13 miles** *this road intersects with State Highway 250 at Hooper Ranch and Smith Lake. See entry for this highway for more information. Good fishing here, along with a campground and a playground.*

At Highway 250 turn North *to go to Rushville, or South for Lakeside and Alliance.*

Eight miles (5 miles.)
Mari Sandoz Rest Area. A woman at a nearby ranch takes care of this pristine spot. See the descriptions of sites to the south along Highway 27 for more information about this great Nebraska author.

Five miles (12 miles)
Cross the Niobrara River. Many consider this Nebraska's finest river.

Twelve miles (15 miles.)
Gordon. See entry for U.S. Highway 20 for a description of Gordon.

Fifteen miles (0 miles.)
South Dakota border.

The entry for this road begins with the junction with State Highway 2 at Lakeside in Sheridan County.

Zero miles (25 miles.)

Traveling north out of Lakeside off State Highway 2 the traveler soon starts to come to a long string of beautiful Sandhill's lakes. Thompson is first, then others by the hundreds, it seems: Peter Long Lake, Diamond, Albrecht, Twin Lakes, Cravath and countless others offer some great fishing.

Twenty five miles (10 miles.)

Intersection of Smith Lake Road, which goes to the east. East of here is the heart of Mari Sandoz county, one of the state's finest writers. See entry for State Highway 27 for more information about Sandoz sites, and things to see along Smith Lake Road.

Ten miles (12 miles.)

A few miles south of the Niobrara River is the turn off to the west for Old Jules Trail.

Old Jules Trail.

Three and a half miles down this road is the pioneer Swiss Beguin Cemetery in the valley of Oxbow Country. This road was the old freight trail and was traveled many times by Mari Sandoz's father, Old Jules. Continue on this windy road another mile and a half and along the river to the site of many Indian encampments, even in Mari Sandoz's time.

In another 3 miles, just before the road swings to the north, is the site of Old Jule's first homestead. The Catholic Church in another 3/4 miles dates back to pioneer times. Continue another eight to ten miles to Walgren Lake. See entry for U.S. Highway 20 for Hay Springs and a description of Walgren Lake.

Twelve miles (0 miles.)

Rushville. Intersection with US Highway 20.

West on US 20 for **eight miles,** and **then south** on marked road to Walgren Lake, the site of Nebraska's only known water monster. In this lonely and isolated lake numerous people have seen a serpent-like creature rise up above the tranquil waters. Others walking by the shore have heard a gigantic wave, and have turned in time to see a large volume of water splashing up. For a while there was talk of making people pay to see the lake (and maybe the monster) but that attempt failed. The visit is free. Check the camera for film, and don't let the dog or the kids get too close to the water.

For more information about this Nebraska legend, about Rushville, and other sites east and west on US Highway 20, please see the entry for US Highway 20.

NEBRASKA
U S
385

Zero miles (3 miles.)

Sidney.

Please see entry for US Highway 30 for information about Sidney.

For the better part of the distance between here and Bridge-port, the highway follows three significant trails. A cutoff, and less traveled branch of the Oregon Trail, known as the Upper California Crossing is to the east of the highway until the town of Gurley, and then it crosses to the west. The Deadwood/Sidney Trail and the Pony Express route are just to the west of the present road.

Three miles (8 miles.)

Old district 77 school house. This school was built in 1916 and is still in use today.

Eight miles (6 miles.)

142

A marker commemorates the first oil well in the area, drilled in 1949.

Six miles (5 miles.)

Dalton. Located here is the well-known Prairie Schooner Museum, a quaint but interesting spot.

Two miles due west of here is Yellowstone Cliff, a famous local landmark. (They are yellow cliffs, made of stone.)

Two miles north of Dalton is the Morrill County line.

Five miles (14 miles.)

Go west on the county road, one mile, and then turn right, to the site of Mud Springs, an old stage station on the Deadwood/Sidney trail. There wasn't much of a springs here, just buffalo wallows which were usually muddy. In 1865 the Sioux attacked the station and everyone at the place was killed. This was also the stomping grounds of Nebraska's most famous outlaw "Doc" Middleton (see description for Gordon in entry for US Highway 20 for details about this notorious outlaw).

Fourteen miles (8 miles.)

Just a quarter mile after the highway swings west in order to begin to parallel the North Platte River, and an eighth of a mile to the north of the road is the site of Amanda Lamin's grave. Two miles to the west are the famous Oregon Trail landmarks of Jail Rock and Courthouse Rock. See description of US Highway 20 at Bridgeport for more information.

Eight miles (35 miles.)

Bridgeport. See entry for US Highway 26.

Thirty five miles (16 miles.)

Alliance.

In 1987, in what was once an unassuming wheat field outside of town, a man named James Reinders made national news by placing old automobiles to look like Stonehenge. Reinders arranged trucks, cars, used appliances and other artifacts of the 20th century in the exact same configuration as the ancient stone monument in England.

Reinders said that his monument "is something to gaze at. It

US Highway 385

is a very intriguing monument. Hopefully someday it will have some kind of historic value."

Some people of the area have other opinions. To judge for yourself just ask anyone in town how to find Carhenge.

Junction with State Highway 2. See entry for that highway for information concerning sites in the area.

Sixteen miles (17 miles.)

Junction with State Highway 87.

*On State Highway 87 **sixteen miles north** of the junction of US 385 and State 87 (13 miles south of Hays Springs) on State Highway 87 the highway crosses the Niobrara River. This was the location of a large fossil quarry excavated by the American Museum of Natural History in New York back in the 1920s.*

Thirteen miles. (11 miles) *Hays Springs. See Entry for US Highway 20.*

From here east to Rushville the highway is combined with U.S. Highway 20. See entry for US Highway 20 for information along this section.

Eleven miles. *Rushville. (see entry for U.S. Highway 20 for further information on Rushville.)*

Twenty miles (Three miles south of the South Dakota line.) *State Highway 87 turns north and leaves U.S. 20 just west of Rushville.*

Twenty miles north, *just before Highway 87 crosses Patton Creek, about 3 miles south of White Clay is the site of the last known Sioux Sundance, 1881. For a description of the Sundance see the entry for U.S. Highway 20 in Dawes County just west of Chadron. This route can connect with the tour north out of Hay Springs. See entry for Hay Springs on US Highway 20.*

End of State Highway 87.

Seventeen miles (16 miles.)

Road to Dunlap. A ghost town in the best sense. Spirits are said to linger here in the old buildings and haunt the banks of the river. The mill was built in 1884 and a few years later a man was shot near

144

its paddle wheel by a jealous husband. Although the town of Dunlap grew up, expanded, and then finally died when the highway passed it by, many a lonesome traveler has reported hearing the moans of a man coming from the weeds and brush along the river's banks.

Sixteen miles (15 miles.)

Chadron State Park. Fine camp grounds, horseback riding, and recreation area. Included on the grounds is a lake, and trapper demonstrations by the park personnel. This is Nebraska's oldest state park, established in 1921.

Ten miles (5 miles.)

Dawes County Museum. For the entry of this fine museum and several nearby sites, please see the entry for US Highway 20 at Chadon. The Dawes County Museum which is run by the efficient and well-organized Dawes County Historical Society is located just off 385. It is open every day during the summer months, and many weekdays during winter.

Down (north) Chadron Creek from the Dawes County Museum one half mile is the site where the great Sioux Chief Red Cloud was captured in his camp on October 23, 1876. He was later killed. This is also the location where the Cheyenne Indians under Dull Knife fought with the army, and then surrendered in 1878. Later this was the site of a ranch and another town with the name of Chadron.

To the west of the golf course is the military road. (see entry for Chadron State College)

Just beyond the city of Chadron reservoirs, to the southeast was the site of Chartran's Trading Post. The reservoirs are located on the site of the cabin of Hurbert Rouleau who was a trapper mentioned by Francis Parkman in 1846.

Directly north of here just where the highway crosses the valley, is the location of Quick Bear's Brule Sioux camp which was captured by Pawnee scouts on October 23, 1876, the day that the Army fought and captured Red Cloud.

This area was the location of an elaborate plan to form a monument to the great Sioux Nation. Sculptor Gutzon Borglum's plan was to create an entire tribe of Indians using the natural rock buttes in the distance, as well as the boulders from Mount Rushmore. "We'll make them 14 to 16 feet tall and reproduce them as our forefather's saw them...wild and carefree." He planned to have additional statues at various important Indian sites through out the region. Borglum's plan gathered much support throughout the region as well as the nation. His death in 1941, however, stilled the idea.

The dirt road that takes off to the east is the old King's Canyon Trail, a beautiful, but nearly impassable route. It connects with the Bordeaux Road.

Five miles (2 miles.)

Just to the east on US Highway 20 is Chadron. Please see entry for US Highway 20 for more information.

Two miles (15 miles.)

Location of the original town of Chadron, before the railroad came in 1884 and convinced the town to move to its present location.

Fifteen miles (0 miles.)

Take the county road west. In about a mile you will see a pile of concrete sitting in the middle of a field. This pile, once a bank vault, is about all that is left of the once thriving community of Wayside. The highway you just left bypassed Wayside and one by one the residents moved. The bank vault, long since empty, was left behind.

Ten miles west of the site of Wayside, in 1892 a find that was to shock the scientific world was discovered. Bill Rossiter and his two sons unearthed a "petrified man" from the badlands of this area. The man was anatomically correct and was exhibited for a while in Chadron where the Rossiters began to gain a bit of fame and wealth from their find. Bill then decided to take it to the Chicago World's Fair for exhibition. Bill eventually sold the petrified man to a local Doctor who then took the man on a tour of eastern Nebraska, Iowa and Kansas. He too got people to pay for the wonder of seeing what a man frozen in the limestone of ancient Chadron may have looked like. Eventually someone noticed a bit of wire and plaster of Paris showing through one of the petrified man's kneecaps. The Rossiter boys smiled sheepishly and shrugged. No one knows what happened to the petrified man after that.

Zero miles (15 miles.)
　　Colorado border.

Fifteen miles (12 miles.)
　　Kimball. For information about Kimball, please see entry for US Highway 30. See also entry for Interstate 80.

Twelve miles (13 miles.)
　　Banner/Kimball County line.
　　Banner County was named by someone who believed it would one day be the "banner of the state of Nebraska," and the "brightest star in the constellation of Nebraska counties." Today Banner County has only a single town, Harrisburg, in the entire county. But don't let these facts steer you away from the place. First of all, although perpetually in running for the least populated county in the state (in 1980 it had 1,000 people...down from 2,500 in 1890),

State Highway 71

Banner's thousand people are some of the friendliest, and most good natured folks alive. What's more, many believe this place is in the running for the most beautiful county in the state.

Banner County was once peppered with sod houses at every section and quarter section. This was partly due to the fact that there was speculation that a railroad was to be built through the county. The railroad never happened and the banner of Banner ceased to flap so hopefully in the high prairie wind. However, there were some benefits to the place. What cattle and summer-fallow wheat didn't bring in, the more than 200 oil wells which still dot the countryside, did.

Two miles (8 miles.)

At the top of a hill 12 miles to the west of here is what many claim to be the highest spot in the state. No one ever wants to call this a mountain, because there aren't supposed to be mountains in Nebraska, but if someone from, say, Connecticut, were to learn that there is a place in Nebraska 5,430 feet above sea level they would call it a mountain.

Eight miles (2 miles.)

Near here to the west is Lover's Leap. Legend has it that this was the place where a beautiful Indian princess, a daughter of a Sioux Chief, jumped to her death. She was upset over the pending marriage her father had arranged with a man from the Ogallala tribe, and wanting to remain faithful to the mysterious man she loved, took a hike, and then a jump.

Two miles (1 mile).

Harrisburg Turnoff.

Foor miles west, Harrisburg.

Brochures from Harrisburg boast that the town is unincorporated, has no mercantile, no restaurant, no major highway, no newspaper and no t.v. or radio stations. But don't let that stop you. If you've come this far, you MUST stop and see this town. Harrisburg's modern courthouse is all paid for, and the town does have churches, schools, a fire department and one of the best museums in the western Nebraska, if not the entire state. The Banner County Historical Society and Museum complex includes several buildings which contain a vast collection of professionally displayed exhibits and exquisite restorations. The museum has pioneer artifacts, cattle brands, Indian artifacts, and other items. The museum can boast one

148

of the few operating (and they fire the baby up once a year, so they know it is working) Case steam threshers. An entire building houses this monster and several other machines. In addition the grounds contain a log school house, a sod house, a pioneer church, a log house and a picnic shelter for you to spend a moment or three in the shade. One block south of the museum is the old Banner County Bank building, established in 1889.

One mile (9 miles.)
Junction with State Highway 88:

In the distance, southeast of the Junction of Highway 88 is Big Horn Mountain, 4,713 feet, called He Sha (White mountain) by the Cheyenne. There once were big horn sheep here, in case you couldn't figure it out from the name.

In 35 miles Highway 88 leads to Courthouse and Jailhouse Rocks, important sites along the Oregon Trail. For a description of these and other sites in that area please see the entry for US Highway 26.

Nine miles (3 miles.)
Wildcat Hills State Park.

This is a lovely area that makes you realize what a wonder the American West is. The State Game Reserve includes a herd of buffalo, elk and deer. It provides the traveler with fine picnic and camping facilities.

Three miles (5 miles.)
*At the first four-way intersection north of Wildcat Hills, **turn west.** Go **one mile and then turn south. Continue one mile** to the site of Fort John. This was not really a fort at all, but a trading post to service first the America Fur Company, and later the gold rush prospectors and the pioneers. There is a small monument 200 feet west of the road, directly under the power lines. There are several unmarked graves around here, including that of a famous French trapper, Pierre Papin who died here in 1853.*

Five miles (6 miles.)
Gering and Scottsbluff.

Here are several sites of historical importance, and several modern-day entertainments and sights. Please see the entry for US Highway 26 at Scottsbluff for further information about this rich area.

State Highway 71

Six miles (7 miles.)

Turn off for Minatare lake. (10 miles east). A fine lake with plenty of good fishing and swimming.

Seven miles (47 miles.)

Before the ranchers were here, this was the land of the Sioux. In 1878 four outfitters got their start in this county and became the first ranchers for a good long ways. On an early scouting trip through the area to find the best land one of these men reported that he had ridden on horseback for six weeks without seeing another human being. Not much different from today an Easterner might say.

Some of the early ranches were actually part of Texas ranches. The ranchers of Texas would send cattle up this way, fatten them on the sweet grass of Sioux County, and then sell them to the Indians and soldiers in South Dakota.

Cattle ranching the old way: round 'em up in the spring and in the fall, brand 'em, sort 'em, ship 'em or turn them loose to fatten up for the next round up. One of the most famous cattle ranches in the county was the N Bar Ranch which lost about 8,000 cattle in an 1879 blizzard. Other big ranch operations were the Bar T, the TOT, the TAN and the Anglo-American Cattle Company, which purchased the other three to form the largest single operation in the state. The operation ranged nearly 50,000 head of cattle over a good part of Sioux County.

The glory days of the big ranches declined as the price of cattle dropped and modernization, railroads and other markets began to take their toll. The last of the great roundups was in the spring of 1898. At least 10,000 cattle were herded in one bunch after a sweep of the area by cowboys from Sioux county.

The highway winds 47 miles through the heart of the Sandhills to the junction with State Highway 2. Turn north on State Highways 71 and 2, nine miles to Marshland, and Crawford via the old Deadwood Trail. For more information about sites along this route, please see entry for State Highway 2.

Forty-seven miles (0 miles.)

Junction with State Highway 2. For a continuation, please see the entry for State Highway 2 at the junction with State Highway 71.

This route begins at Mitchell in Scotts Bluff County and goes north to the South Dakota border.

Ghost towns are abundant in Sioux County as the once prosperous ranching and pioneer towns faded away to the speedy, and efficient modern ranches. Glen, Andrews and Montrose are three such towns.

Zero miles (38 miles.)

Mitchell. For information, please see entry for US Highway 26.

Thirty eight miles (22 miles.)

Agate Fossil Beds National Monument. Fossils, agates,

State Highway 29

ancient mammals, tiny rhinoceros, and other strange creatures from a time long before mankind have been found here. Helpful rangers and amazing exhibits make this worth your journey.

Twenty two miles (0 miles.)
Harrison.

Harrison has a swimming pool at the Grade School Park, and nothing is sweeter than jumping head first into its waters on a hot summer afternoon. On Main Street is the Sioux County Museum which will orient the traveler to Sioux County and its heritage. The Sioux County Fair is the first weekend in August and boasts a rodeo and a fine county fair.

North out of Harrison on county road:

Five miles to Gilbert Baker Recreation and Wildlife Area.

This area encompasses the headwaters of Monroe Creek, one of the finest small creeks in the state. Its waters support one of the few naturally reproducing trout populations in Nebraska. Monroe Canyon offers a view of unique geological features. From the ridge of Monroe Canyon one can look to the north for a view of the Black Hills, if one is so inclined to look into a vastly inferior state.

Beyond the Recreation Area, by about **three and a half miles,** *just as the road takes a sharp curve to the east the Old Fort Robinson Military road crosses the blacktop.*

If you continue on this road for **another 17 miles** *you will reach the ghost town of Montrose, after passing through the Ogalala National Grassland. At Montrose old settlers' fortifications are easily visible in the grass around the site. Just to the northeast of Montrose on the east bank of the creek is where Buffalo Bill had a fight with the Sioux Chief Yellow Hand in July, 1876 during what became known as the Warbonnet Battle. He claims to have scalped Yellow Hand and proclaimed it was "the first scalp for Custer," who had been massacred just weeks before. This is before Bill became a legend in his own time. Just north of the church on a small cone-shaped hill is a monument to Colonel Wesley Merritt and the troups of the 5th Calvary. They stood here and fought off a band of 800 Cheyenne. The Cheyenne were attempting to join up with the large band of Indians that had fought Custer at Little Big Horn and were then encamped in northeast Wyoming. An eyewitness account of this skirmish, along with the part Buffalo Bill played in this era of Nebraska history, can be found in* Campaigning with Crook *by Charles King.*

152

This same hill was used as a "fort" by the citizens of Montrose to "protect themselves" from the possible attack by the Indians of the Ghost Dance cult at Wounded Knee. Turns out there was nothing left of the Indian Wars anywhere in America after that.

Montrose is a T intersection in the road, either turn north to head into South Dakota (who would want to do that?) or turn south for a circle back to Harrison.

Zero miles (5 miles.)

Missouri Border.

Rulo.

Rulo was named after the wife of Charles Rouleau on whose land the town was built. Sorry, but as usual, history has not deemed it necessary to give any credit to this woman other than being Charles Rouleau's wife. Charles was a Frenchman who came west with John Fremont's expedition, married an Indian (Mrs. Rouleau) and took up land on what was then known as the "Half-Breed Treaty."

People who were children of French and Indian parents were not allowed the protection of laws of the Frenchmen, but on the other hand the laws governing the Indians could not be applied to them either. As a consequence, all of the land west of the Missouri, from Rulo to the Nemaha, was deemed "Half Breed Tract" by the government and Indians alike. Half-breeds were allowed to settle here. Rulo, thanks to Mrs. Rouleau, a half breed, sprang forth on the edge of this tract. This half-breed reservation was the only one of its kind in the nation.

Lewis and Clark Trail passes near by to Rulo, the route the explorers took on their way west and their way back east.

In August, 1985 police found the grave of a five year old boy and an older man who had been mutilated. As the search for the killer or killers continued, a bizarre story unfolded that involved a survivalist cult and their charismatic leader who claimed that God spoke to him, and that a birth at the commune was from an immaculate conception.

Before the story left the nation's headlines stories of the cult's strange acts and beatings were splashed over newspapers from coast to coast.

South of Rulo one mile on county roads. Near here was a large Indian Village still in existence in historic times. A small town of pioneers once also stood near here.

South of Rulo three miles to the northern edge of the Iowa Indian Reservation, which borders the Sac and Fox Reservation to the west. You are now very close to the lowest elevation in the state of Nebraska.

On the banks of the Missouri River just east of here you are at a mere 850 feet above sea level, or roughly 4,600 feet lower than a spot in the panhandle which is the highest point in the state.

If you are the odd sort who wants to be one of the few people who have stood in the precise southeast corner of the state, follow this road for another mile. There you will find the Iron Monument, which represents the first surveyor's stake planted to mark the boundary between Nebraska and Kansas, at 40 degrees latitude. This was done in 1854.

Five miles (3 miles.)

A small road leads south two miles to a tiny village. When this town was founded it was called Bluffton and then Sac, in honor of the Sac Indians of the area. Later a pioneer suggested the town's name be changed to Preston to honor his home town in England. Guess who won.

The Sac and Fox Indian Reservation is one of Nebraska's six Indian reservations, although a large portion of this reservation is in Kansas where this tribe once roamed. The other reservations are: the Iowa, just east of here; the Winnebago and the Omaha, both in Thurston County, 70 miles north of Omaha; the Santee in Knox County and a small piece of the Pine Ridge reservation in north central

Nebraska.

Three miles (0 miles.)

Falls City. US 159 joins US 73 here and swings south into Kansas. For information about Falls City, or sites along US 73, please see entry for US Highway 73.

West *of Falls City,* ***three miles.*** *Just to the south of the road is the site of the first oil well ever dug in the state of Nebraska.*

NEBRASKA
U S
136

Zero miles (9 miles.)

Nemaha County.

If there were a single county which offered everything from one of the oldest communities along the Missouri, to what many consider to be the state's finest state park, to one of the most beautiful and yet undiscovered villages in the world, to a steaming, puffing steamboat, to a steaming, puffing nuclear power plant, it would have to be Nemaha County. The county was named after the Otoe Ni Maha, or muddy river.

Brownville.

Brownville may be Nebraska's richest historical location. Though crumbling in recent years, many of the town's residents still recognize the area's unique and important place in the settlement of the American West.

Before the Whites came, the Otoe Indians held these lands. They surrendered the lands in a treaty in 1854. The reservations of the small Indian tribes of the Fox, the Iowa and the Sauk at one time extended to near here. These tribes which were brought to Nebraska by the government resettlement plan, are still located in the extreme southeastern corner of the state.

Brownville had high hopes in its early years. Founded by Richard Brown and Joel Wood who crossed the Missouri in a canoe, the settlement began and the first Christian Church in the state of Nebraska was organized in 1854. It quickly became the main shipping point for trade up and down the Missouri and steamboats docked on the banks of the Missouri and travelers bustled about the town of 5,000's busy Main Street.

Brown started to operate a flatboat ferry across the Missouri, the Nemaha County and soon a road stretched between Brownville and the Marshall's Trading Post near present-day Beatrice. During a single week in 1855 50 families crossed the river to settle here. The boom was on.

One of the state's earliest, and most influential newspapers The Nebraska *Advertiser* was started at Brownville in 1856.

The first telegraph line in the state, from St. Joseph, Missouri to Brownville was strung in August of 1860. *The New York Times* announced that the telegraph now reached "the half peopled wilds of Nebraska." The first message sent out on the line was addressed to the "States of the Union."

A small college, Brownville College, existed here for a short while.

By the mid 1860s at least a half dozen ferries were operating on this stretch of the River, ferrying pioneers and settlers to Brownville. One, the Belle of Brownville, was large enough to carry 22 wagons and their teams.

Importantly, a brewery was begun and over 3,000 barrels of beer a year were made, most of which were consumed by the citizens of Brownville. The remnants of the brewery cave can still be seen at the end of Main Street.

The town became the county seat of the newly formed

US Highway 136

Nemaha County and had high hopes of becoming not only the largest and most prosperous city in the territory, but the capital of the new state as well.

Then came the railroad, passing up Brownville for other cities. Those cities began to grow and to attract the river traffic which had made Brownville bloom. By the mid 1880s the decline of this once thriving metropolis was on, and by the economic woes of the 1890s Brownville had dwindled to a single block of ragtag businesses.

But the town was far from dead. Although it floundered for a long while as a tourist curiosity, Brownville today is home for over 200. The town's historic atmosphere has attracted arts and crafts people and has given the location the cultural feel of a town a hundred times larger.

The *Meriwether Lewis* is a sidewheeler steam boat that has been converted into the Museum of Missouri River History and is run by the State Historical Society. In addition to being located on a steam boat, the museum features exhibits which highlight the historical significance of the Missouri River. The museum is open seven days a week April 1 through November 15.

The Brownville Museum was organized in 1956 by the Brownville Historical Society and has permanent exhibits in the Bailey House, the Carson House, the Dentist Office, the Railroad Station and the Main Street Museum. The museum also operates other historic buildings and homes. The museum facilities are open all afternoons in summer and on weekends and selected other days during the winter months.

The Brownville Village Theater is a repertory theater which offers fine productions during the summer months.

Cruises of the Missouri River on board the *Spirit of Brownville* are available through a local private company.

Many of the fine old houses are made of native brick which was made at Brownville's brickyards.

The Methodist Church, once used to house part of Brownville College, was built in 1859 and is the oldest continuously used church in the state.

Walnut Grove Cemetery, up Cock Robin Hollow to the forks, then left, is one of the oldest cemeteries in the state. It is the final resting place of Civil War soldiers, Indians, pioneers, river boat people and Governer Robert Furnas who founded both the state board of Agriculture and the Nebraska Historical Society. The tombstones here date back at least to the 1850s.

East from the cemetery to a high hill known as Lookout Point, once an Indian lookout which gives a fine view of the surrounding area.

Perhaps many area residents remember the height of the Old Time Fiddlers contests held in Brownville during the mid to late 1960s. Brownville had gained a considerable reputation as having one of the best and most authentic Old Time Fiddlers gatherings in the country. On a warm afternoon the streets of the sleepy village would be packed with cars and people and dogs and music. Music was everywhere. To walk down Main Street was to experience a constantly changing menu of great music. Banjos, guitars, autoharps and, of course, fiddles were brought out of cases and men and women who had been complete strangers moments before now sat or stood in circles grinning and laughing and sharing their lives with music. The entire life of true folk music got its blood and its soul from places like Brownville and the thousand people who gathered there as a single family to share the universal language: music.

The tradition of that festival has made a strong comeback in the fine Brownville Old Time Music Contest which is held in late August usually on the banks of Whiskey Run Creek.

Just south of town, along the Missouri River is one of two Nebraska Nuclear Power Plants. The Cooper Plant, built during the early 1970s at a cost of nearly a half of a billion dollars, went "on line" in 1974. The boom in nuclear power plants has largely faded due to the increased costs of building and financing the construction, as well as the fall-out from such disasters as Three Mile Island and Chernobyl. The plant is run by the Nebraska Public Power District.

The land south of Brownville, from here to the extreme southeast corner of the state was designated a half-breed reservation in 1880. For more details on this, please see the entry for US Highway 73.

What many consider is Nebraska's prettiest state park is just a few short miles south of Brownsville and the most beautiful city in the state, Peru, just a few miles north on these side trips:

Four miles south of Brownville on State 67, *Nemaha City.*

Nemaha City is near the mouth of the pretty Little Nemaha River. The town was formed in 1855.

Five miles south of Nemaha City, *then* **five miles east** *on S-64E to Indian Caves State Park.*

Indian Caves State Park.

This 3,000 acre State Park is considered the favorite state park by many lifelong residents of Nebraska, and it is easy to see why. The park gets its name from the huge sandstone embankment at the southern end of the park which houses the only particular petroglyphs of this kind in the entire state. The origin of the glyphs, ancient Indian paintings etched into the walls, are still a mystery to archeologists. The pictures depict the animals of importance to the Indians who left these signs, but many are of unknown creatures and shapes. Unfortunately many of the pictures have been obscured by modern vandals who believe their names and current loves warrant as much importance as these mysterious and beautiful ancient drawings. Please discourage anyone from defacing the sandstone.

At the other end of the park the state has reconstructed a portion of a river settlement known as St. Deroin. It was named after an Otoe half-breed whose father was French, and whose mother was an Otoe woman who owned the land where the town stood. The park maintains a small reconstructed log cabin at the old town site and rangers there can tell you more about Joseph Deroin, the town's founder, who among other things, it is said, was buried sitting on top of his horse in the town cemetery. A great flood in 1911 washed most of the town away, except for a few buildings.

The park also offers 20 miles of trails for backpackers, cross country skiiers, horseback riders and just plain walkers. Bank fishing in the Missouri is available for those who believe there is no danger in taking fish from 6 miles below a nuclear power plant outlet. The catfish taken from the bank in the park have been pretty large, however. . .

An interpretive program about the area is presented every Friday and Saturday night during the summer. There is plenty of camping for groups, trailers, and backpackers.

The park is home to a wide variety of animals and plants. It is located on the Central Flyway for migrating birds which include the bald eagle. Even turkey vultures, which are somewhat rare in Nebraska, have been seen at the park. In addition there are coyotes, foxes, turtles, wild turkey and flying squirrels. There is quite a debate about which season is the best for visiting the park. Some say spring when all of the many wildflowers are in bloom, while others swear by autumn when the foliage is a rainbow of color. In any event Indian Cave State Park is a prize for the state and deserves to be treated as such.

Take the paved State Highway 67 north, just east of Brownville for the winding and beautiful drive, 10 miles to Peru.

Peru is perhaps the most beautiful village in the entire state of Nebraska. Its brick, tree-lined streets, sleepy downtown and quaint college atmosphere make it the most underrated, undiscovered jewel around. It was founded in 1857 on the banks of the Missouri and soon the Nemaha Valley Seminary and Normal Institute was founded in 1860. It was the forerunner of Peru State College.

The campus, the oldest school still operating in the state, is known as the Campus of the Thousand Oaks and is the alma mater for thousands of graduates. On campus is a glacial boulder which was found south of town and brought to campus in the 1920s. It was deposited by the ice sheets which once covered Nebraska (No, not last winter...!)

Just west of Bluff Road is a hill known as, and I'm not kidding, Nebraska's Pike's Peak. The slopes of this hill are steep, sure, but whoever gave this hill such a name may not have seen the real Pike's Peak in a long while and had forgotten what a peak was all about. In any event, since we are in Peru and not Colorado Springs (one thing to be thankful for) try to climb up to the top of this Pike's Peak. It was used as a lookout by the Indians, and local legend has it that the trail up the hill was the Indian's route as well.

Just northwest of the Peak is the site of several Indian houses, probably dating back to historic times.

Just south of the Peak, at the school site, is the location of an Indian Burial ground. For some reason the original settlers chose the burial ground as the place to start the communtiy. They may have been on o something as the peaceful and special atmosphere of Peru may be because of the spirits of those long ago Indians.

The town has a hiking and nature trail and a viewpoint of a four state area of the Missouri River Valley.

Take some time here, it will be a town that you will dream about retiring to.

Because of a change in the river's course a teardrop shaped part of Nebraska is across the Missouri directly northeast of Peru. It is completely surrounded by Missouri, but is a part of Nebraska.

Nine miles (10 miles.)
Auburn.
For a description of the sites in and around Auburn, please see the entry for US Highways 73 and 75.

Ten miles (10 miles.)
Just north at the junction of State Highway 105 is the town of Johnson founded when a homesteader named Johnson used a part of his land to start a town. It is located in the pretty rolling hills between Auburn and Tecumseh.
For a lovely private park north on State Highway 105, please see the entry for US 73/75.

Ten miles (15 miles.)
Tecumseh.
Tecumseh, the county seat of Johnson County is also the home of the Johnson County Museum at 3rd and Lincoln Streets. It is open most days of the week during the summer and autumn months. An old church, a country school and the town's jail are all a part of the museum.
The courthouse is on the National Register of Historic Places and many of the town's old and historic buildings are still in use.

The town was named after the Shawnee Indian who never set foot in Nebraska.

The ABC TV mini-series "Amerika", which attempted to show what the country would be like under Soviet domination, was filmed in and around Tecumseh.

Fifteen miles (7 miles.)

Just off US 136 is Crab Orchard. The name no longer applies, if it ever did. There may be some crabs here, but there are few orchards.

Seven miles (4 miles.)

Filley.

Two miles south of here via county roads is the Filley Stone Barn, which was built in August of 1874. Since the farmer was fed up with grasshoppers, he wanted to build a barn that would not only keep the pests out, but would hold the produce of the good seasons, once the plague had moved on. The barn is three stories tall, and built against a bank. It was made from local limestone and rock, and the plank floors came from Nebraska City. When they finished work in November, folks from as far away as fifty miles came to the big dance in the barn. The petition to place the barn on the National Register of Historic Places read in part: "This is one of the most magnificent barns in the state, and the largest known limestone structure."

Four miles (8 miles.)

Rockford, a once thriving town, nearly blown away by neglect, has begun to come out from a long sleep due to the state recreation area just **three miles south** of US Highway 136. The area has a man-made lake good for fishing, camping, swimming and picnicing.

Eight miles (19 miles.)

Beatrice.

Whether you are *not* from around here and call it Be-IT, or know better and call it Be-AT, this small city has much to offer.

Beatrice *is* indeed the original home of the nationally known Beatrice Foods, just in case you weren't sure.

Its location on a ford of the Blue River, and its proximity to the Oregon Trail were the features which originally caused people to settle here.

Beatrice still has a fine park named for its use as the site of the old traveling education and entertainment programs: Chautauquas. This park started as a place to train Sunday School teachers. Its original tabernacle and gatehouse have been preserved on the park grounds. Also in the park is a log cabin, originally located on south Fifth Street in the city. The park is located on the southern edge of the city off Sixth Street.

The Paddock House at 1401 N. 10th was built in 1870 and looks pretty much as it always has. It is named after Algernon Paddock, one-time senator of the state from 1875-1881, who lived here. This is a private residence and is not open to the public.

The Gage County Historical Museum is located at Second and Court. It displays the historic artifacts from all towns in the county, as well as displays on rural life, and a part of the old train depot. It is open afternoons and is free.

Sixth and Grant. Gage County Courthouse. This building was built in 1890 and is on the National Register of Historic Places.

The Martin Luther home at 804 S. 12th is one of the best care centers for folks with developmental disabilities. It was established in 1925 and has since gained a national reputation for its programs for children and adults.

Homestead National Monument: 4 1/2 miles NW of Beatrice on State Highway 4.
This National Monument was created to serve as a memorial to the hardships of the pioneers who cultivated the civilization of the American West. At this spot Daniel Freeman made the first claim to a homesteading site under the provisions of the original Homesteading Act of 1863. Although in recent years there has been some controversy whether he was indeed the first, all loyal Nebraskans have no doubt that he was. The property remained in the Freeman family until the Government purchased the homestead and created this Monument.

There is a fine display in the center, and a short self-guided walking tour of the monument.

Across from the Homestead Monument is the brick Freeman School which was built in 1871 and used continuously as a school until

1968.

Nineteen miles (3 miles.)

Jansen.

There are many points of historical interest in this area. The Oregon Trail passed through Jefferson County and is one of the few areas in the eastern part of the state where sections of the original ruts can still be seen.

In addition, this area is where such legendary western men as Wild Bill Hickcock and Kit Carson roamed.

For information about the specific location of these sites please see the entry for State Highway 15.

Three miles (3 miles.)

Oregon Trail markers are in the school yard of the District 39 school house. There are ruts still visible to the west of this school. The school was built in 1904.

Three miles (22 miles.)

Fairbury.

Junction with State Highway 15. There are many interesting sites north and south of town on 15 including areas where the visitor can see the ruts of the Oregon Trail which passed through here. For more information, please see the entry for State Highway 15.

Fairbury was built on the site of an Indian trail. An Otoe Reservation was once east of town.

The Jefferson County Courthouse on the south side of the square was built of native limestone and is on the National Register of Historic Places. Inside are six ceramic tiled fireplaces and many of the antique furnishings are from its earliest days.

The town was founded in 1869 and named after a town in Illinois which was the former home of one of the early pioneers. Like many towns in the state, Fairbury owes its existence to the railroad which came up the river in 1872.

Russian settlers came to this area and established a colony on 27,000 acres near here. Many of the descendants of those settlers still populate the town of Fairbury.

The fine museum in this town is on the west side of the town square. It is open Mondays, Wednesdays and Fridays in the afternoons.

An old log cabin, originally built on a homestead of the 1860s, is preserved in Fairbury's Park.

The town had mostly brick sidewalks until as late as 1981.

On April 4, 1933 Ma Barker and her gang robbed the First National Bank. The outlaws were posted all around the outside of the bank with machine guns. Traffic was stopped while the robbery was in progress. The employees and customers were told to lie on the floor and the inside of the building was riddled with bullets. A deputy sheriff and others were injured during the stick up.

The gang took two women as hostages and they were later released unharmed. As they made their getaway the gang littered the highway with carpet tacks so that the cars that chased them out of town soon all had flats.

Fairbury was the home of the Campbell Brothers Circus which performed over the middle west in the 1890s. The circus consisted mostly of human acrobats.

Take the River Road northwest to the restored Smith Limekiln and house built in the early 1870s. The limekiln was built in order to fire limestone until it became lime. The lime was then used as mortar and sold to places as far away as Denver and Kansas City. The house of the original owner still stands and contains displays about this little-known industry. This kiln was not the only kiln in the area, as there were others who tried to make a living from the booming of far away cities. However, the Smith kiln is the only survivor from that era. Such burning of lime is still practiced, however more efficient kilns are in operation at many cement plants and sugar plants. The limestone exposed in many parts of Jefferson County contains many sea fossils. The museum is run by the local historical society and is open Sunday afternoons, or by appointment.

Five miles east of Fairbury to Rock Creek Station on the Oregon Trail (see entry for State Highway 15 for more information).

Twenty two miles (1 mile.)
Junction with US Highway 81.
North, one mile to Hebron. The Oregon Trail crossed

Thayer county north of here, and there are many sites in the area connected with that route. For more information on the Oregon Trail and other sites in this area, please see the entry for US Highway 81.

One mile (7 miles.)
Junction with US 81 south. Please see entry for US Highway 81 for information about the sites in this area.

Seven miles (7 miles.)
Junction with State Highway 5.

Five miles north on 5 to the Little Blue River. Just on the north side of the bridge, diagonally across the "T" intersection, some ruts from the Oregon Trail are visible. The Trail followed the Little Blue to near Hastings where it crossed a small divide to the Platte.

Continue north 1/2 mile from the bridge. Turn **west**. and go **one mile**. Turn north and go 1/2 mile. Turn **west** again and go 1/2 **mile**. Here, on the north side of the road is the location for the Kiowa Station which survived a series of violent Indian raids in 1864.

Continue west 3 miles, a quarter mile past the Oregon Trail marker just west of the Thayer County line in Nuckolls County. This is the Emery Trail marker which commemorates an incident in 1864 when a number of Indians tried to ambush a stagecoach. The driver spotted the Indians at this point, turned his rig around, and outran them.

Continue west 1/2 mile to "T" intersection, then south for 1/2 mile, then west for 1/2 mile to the site of the Bowie ranch where a rancher and his wife were not as lucky as the stagecoach driver. They were killed the day before the stagecoach incident by raiding Indians.

Continue west and take the first left turn. Turn left and go 3/4 mile to the site of the Comstock ranch which was attacked and burned to the ground by the Cheyenne during the August raids in 1864.

Continue west to Oak. Oak is a delightful town rich with history. For a more complete description of the many additional sites in this area, please see the entry for State Highway 14.

US Highway 136

You may retrace your steps, or continue west from Oak to State Highway 14, and then south, four miles to US Highway 136.

Seven miles (11 miles.)
Ruskin. **North** of here, **six miles** to Oak and many historic sites. For more information about this area, see above and also the entry for State Highway 14.

Eleven miles (4 miles.)
Junction with State Highway 14. For more information about sites in this area, please see entry for State Highway 14.

North here five miles, and then west eleven miles to Oak. Oak is a small town with a lot of history. The Oregon Trail brought both the pioneers and the Indians. Buffalo roamed these parts in gigantic herds. You may visit Oak and then continue east 9 miles to State Highway 5, and then return to US 136 by driving south on 4 for a nice loop trip of this area (see above).

For more Information about this wonderful location, please see entry under State Highway 14

Four miles (6 miles.)
Junction with State Highway 14, south to Superior. Please see entry for State Highway 14 for more information.

Six miles (8 miles.)
Take this county road south to cross the Republican River and then continue west on county roads that parallel the river for a delightful break from the hot asphalt. Return to US 136 via State Highway 78 in eight miles.

Eight miles (10 miles.)
One mile south of State Highway 78 is Guide Rock. The town has preserved a stockade from earlier days before expensive county jails were the thing to do. Guide Rock is so named for the rocky hill southeast of town which served as a landmark for centuries. This place was a holy spot for the Pawnee Indians. It was one of several places where the earth was connected to the sky...a place where the great spirits who watch over all, and the great mother the earth, were connected. It is possible, for those non-Pawnee who are very still and very devout, to feel the holiness of this place. There are not many such

places left in the world. Say a prayer just for that.

Continue south on State 78 across the Republican River *and take the first county road east for a delightful detour off of the hot US 136 along the banks of the Republican River. In eight miles turn north across the river and return to US 136. (see above.)*

Ten miles (5 miles.)
Red Cloud.

An article in an April, 1985 *New York Times* said, "the marvelous thing about Red Cloud is that it has preserved itself utterly unspoiled, hardly changed since the early days of about 100 years ago...here is a place with the charm unbroken, the spell still upon it..."

What draws people from cosmopolitan New York, Chicago, London and Paris to this small town is the writings of Willa Cather, Nebraska's best known and most widely read author.

Cather was not a native of Nebraska, but was born in Virginia where she lived for the first six years of her life. Then, in 1884, her family moved to the open prairies of southern Nebraska. Although Cather was only to live here from then until 1890, she returned to the area for the rest of her life, and, as readers of her works know, the open prairies, and the prairie spirit is what makes her books so timeless.

Cather said of that period, "the years from eight to fifteen are the formative period in a writer's life, when he unconsciously gathers basic materials. He may acquire a great many interesting and vivid impressions in his mature years, but his thematic material he acquires under fifteen years of age."

Cather's appeal has never faded from view, and in recent years she has gained in significance if one can judge by the number of scholarly and popular biographies that have appeared. Cather's modern lifestyle, strangely blanketed with an old-fashioned restraint, is subject of scrutiny these days, but what remains pure and wonderful are her books.

If you have never read Willa Cather's *O Pioneers,* or *My Antonia* you have missed a very wonderful part of American literature, a very wonderful part of being able to read. These two books most clearly capture the essence of the prairie life and times. For Cather, unlike most writers, was able to let the land itself--the very place-- become a dominant character in her work. The open plains, the prairies and fields of her homeland rise up out of the pages of her books and come alive.

Others of her books are also set in Nebraska, and except for one or two books, all of her 12 novels are near masterpieces. Her best of many beautiful works may be a short novel called *The Professor's House*. Citizens of New Mexico still line up at bookstores to buy copies of her historical novel of the Southwest *Death Comes for the Archbishop*. People still weep at the close of *A Lost Lady*.

Willa Cather died in 1949 and is buried in New Hampshire, a distant and foreign landscape from the land she brought to life in words.

Red Cloud and Webster County have preserved many of the sites mentioned in Cather's books, or important in her life.

The Farmers' and Merchants' Bank, which was also known as the Garber Bank, was built in 1888. The founder of this bank, Silas Garber, appears as a fictional character in several of Cather's works, most notably as Captain Forrester in *A Lost Lady.* The bank now houses the museum and interpretive center as well as a fairly substantial archival collection of materials on Cather. Begin your visit in Red Cloud at this special and unique Nebraska State Historical Society Museum.

The entire downtown area of Red Cloud is divided into historic districts. The Main Street district has been preserved because so many of Cather's stories and novels have significant scenes which occur here.

The Seward Street District with its churches and courthouse, also figures in many of her works.

The Elm Street area is significant because in Cather's day this area was the "wrong side of the tracks" of Red Cloud and less fortunate folks lived here. Cather wrote with an awareness and sensitivity about such people, and the area serves as a setting in her works.

The Railroad Addition District is significant not only in Cather's works, but to an entire group of towns whose very existence is owed to the railroads.

In addition to the museum, The Willa Cather Pioneer Memorial and Educational Foundation has a book store and art gallery on

Main Street, and offers guided tours of the surrounding countryside and the sites Cather portrayed in her books.

The Cather childhood home (338 N. Webster) was built around 1879 and the Cather family rented the home from 1884 until 1904. This is the home where Cather grew up, and where she gathered many of the materials for her later fiction. The house is open for tours seven days a week during the spring and summer months, and five days a week during the winter.

The Burlington Depot was built in 1897, and moved to its present location in 1966. The railroad played an important role in Cather's life and in her writings, as it did for so many of the towns in the midwest.

St. Juliana Falconieri Catholic Church was built in 1883 and figures in *My Antonia, Song of the Lark* and other works. Grace Episcopal Church (it is now the Church of Christ) was a frame church built in 1884, although a brick veneer was later added to the structure. Cather was raised a Baptist and became a member of this church in 1922.

Spend some time in this delightful town and you will certainly begin to feel Cather's power and insight come alive all around you.

Five miles (7 miles.)
The Narrows. The Republican River squeezes through a couple of bluffs and creates quite a pleasing view in this pretty county.

Seven miles (16 miles.)
Inavale. Inavale suffered greatly when the Republican River flooded in 1935. Today Inavale is a sleepy, quaint midwestern town. Inavale was long noted for its excellent cheese factory.

On February 6, way back in 1897, a group of people returning from a prayer meeting in Inavale, saw something they could not explain. They looked up into the night sky and saw a bright light directly overhead. They said it was an airship, a cone 50 feet in length with two sets of wings on each side. A few days earlier hundreds of people in Omaha watched as a bright light flew over the city. The Omaha UFO was described as resembling a canoe. No explanation for this rash of sightings was ever found.

US Highway 136

North of here *eight or so miles on the divide lands between the Platte and the Republican River watersheds is the land that Willa Cather wrote about in many of her novels. Catherton, a small ghost town founded by her relatives, is here, as are many of the farms and farmhouses, some still standing, which she included in* O Pioneers, My Antonia *and other works.*

Tours of the countryside Cather made famous are organized in Red Cloud. See above entry for Red Cloud for more information.

Sixteen miles (5 miles.)

Franklin. Yes, named for Benjamin Franklin, this quaint town was once called Franklin City. For a while Franklin was home to a small college founded by the Congregational Church. It lasted from 1881 until 1922 when it closed due to lack of enrollment. The area was made into the city park.

A fine, well maintained road follows the banks of the Republican River on the south side of the river, so get off the lazy and boring US Highway 136 and try it out.

Junction with State Highway 10. For sites along this route, please see entry for State Highway 10.

Five miles (18 miles.)

Bloomington. Here you can find a long-abandoned cemetery, old land office from the 1880s and a mill built in 1882. Ask locally for directions.

Eighteen miles (6 miles.)

Alma. Junction with US Highway 183.

Alma is headquarters for the vast Harlan County Lake, built as a flood control project after the devestating Republican River flood.

For more information about the lake and the area, please see entry for US Highway 183.

Six miles (12 miles.)

Orleans.

Orleans was settled as a part of the Catholic Colonization Association in 1872.

Just south of Orleans the Sappa Creek enters the Republican River. It was here, in 1869, that the Republican Sioux attacked a party of surveyors and killed them all. This massacre led to a series of battles with the Sioux that are known as a part of the Nebraska Sioux Wars.

On August 1, 1955, several people in Oxford saw a formation of a dozen white lights in the sky. This phenomenon, still unexplained, was also observed at Oxford and Arapahoe at the same time.

Twelve miles (8 miles.)

Oxford. Oxford on the Furnas/Harlan County line goes hand in hand with another Furnas town named Cambridge. However a ford of the Republican River near here was locally called Ox Ford, and that is the likely derivation of the town's name.

On August 1, 1955, several people in Oxford saw a formation of a dozen white lights in the sky. This phenomenon, still unexplained, was also observed at Orleans and Arapahoe at the same time.

Eight miles (2 miles.)

Edison. No, not after Thomas, but after a local rancher with the first name of Eddie.

Two miles (0 miles.)

Junction with US Highways 6 and 34. US Highway 136 ends here and the route west is taken over by these two other great American roads. Please see the entry for US Highway 6 for information about the route west of here.

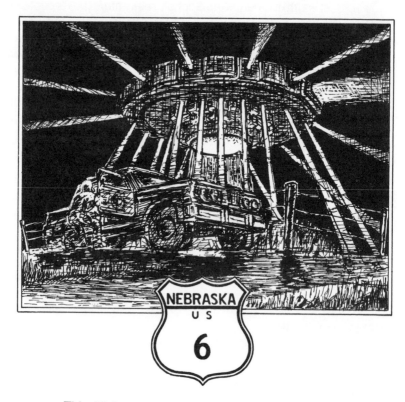

This Highway enters the state at the Missouri River in downtown Omaha and travels the entire length, leaving the state on the high plains of Colorado.

Zero miles (13 miles.)
Omaha. For a description of the many sites in Nebraska's largest community, please see the entry for US Highway 75.

Thirteen miles (14 miles.)
Boys Town. For a description of Boys Town, please see the entry for Omaha on US Highway 75.

Fourteen miles (6 miles.)
Gretna. A beautiful small city overlooked by many who perfer the sightless Interstate for their travel between Omaha and Lincoln.

176

Six miles (1 mile.)
Linoma Beach on the east bank of the wide Platte River.

Hard to believe this was once the most popular recreation spot in the eastern part of the state. Here, before the days of television and state recreation areas, thousands from Omaha and Lincoln would gather to celebrate and cool down in the summer months. Those were the days when the waters of the Platte flowed a bit clearer. There are still those who spend time here and the quiet spot makes for a nice break.

Southwest of here five miles to the Platte River State Park.

One mile (2 miles.)
Just across the Platte River is the junction of US Highway 6 and State Highway 63.

There is a kind of quiet and solemn feel about this area, wouldn't you agree? Now that the Interstate has taken so much of the traffic away from this once busy road, the distance between Omaha and Lincoln seems to have once again returned to the isolated lonely countryside it once was.

There may be more than just a strange feeling about this spot, for this is the location of one of the most famous UFO incidents ever reported. The story has been retold around the world because of the way it has a particular validity.

For one thing, it happened to a police officer.

In the early hours of December 3, 1967 Herbert Schirmer drove past a barn on Highway 63, near the intersection with US 6. Outside the barn in a corral a bull was kicking and throwing himself against the fence. Schirmer stopped to make sure the fence would hold.

Once outside, he noticed that the cows in the barn were kicking at their stalls and brawling.

After making sure things were secure he got back into the patrol car.

He drove toward the intersection.

At first he thought it was a truck. A row of blinking lights were shining in the road about a quarter of a mile ahead of him, but as he watched, the lights began to flash very quickly and then rose straight into the air.

The story is that Schirmer returned to the station and filed a report. In the log he wrote: "Saw a flying saucer at junction of 63 and 6. Believe it or not!" This was what the newspaper picked up on in the next few days. As he entered this information in the log he noticed that it was 3 a.m., much later than he thought it should be. It was this nagging fact that led investigators to convince him to undergo hypnosis.

Some weeks later Schirmer was hypnotised. He was taken back to that dark night at this very spot. What his conscious mind had kept hidden from him was laid open under the influence of the reserachers.

Schirmer began to tell the rest of the story.

After the football-shaped object rose into the air he drove further on toward the intersection and watched as it moved toward a mud field.

He turned the patrol car up the mud road to the field.

The lights were very bright. They were flashing above him in the field. He reached for the radio to make a call for help, but the radio was dead and the car had stopped.

The object hung over the field. It had a silver glow all about it, and the lights continued to flash rapidly.

As he watched tripod legs extended from the craft and it settled to the ground.

He tried to get out of the car, but something was preventing him. Something in his mind kept him from moving, although he tried to fight against it.

As he watched, a form came out of the craft and moved toward the patrol car. He tried to reach for his revolver, but again, he couldn't move. The being drew out some object, pointed it at the car and a green gas soon filled the air. There was a sudden bright flash of lights and he passed out.

What seemed like an eternity later he woke up and rolled down the window.

Now there were several beings about the car. In Schirmer's own words, "he had a very high forehead and a long nose. His eyes were like ours, round, but they were sunken in. Their pupils were not round, but sort of like a cat's: like the small letter a. Their complexion was grey. The mouth was a sort of slit."

The creature reached through the open window and touched him on the neck. He felt an intense, deep pain, and the creature withdrew.

Although the creatures did not speak, Shirmer "heard" their words in his head.

"Are you the watchman of this place?" they asked.

He said that he was.

"Watchman, come with me."

He could not resist. They took him toward the craft, all of the while asking him questions about the surroundings. They asked about the Platte River water supply, and about the Lincoln Electric generator near Ashland.

He was taken inside the craft where it was explained to him that they get energy for powering their craft by reversing electrical and magnetic power. In order to keep going, he was told, they take electrical power from power plants and electrical lines. He was told they draw power from water as well.

After a while longer he was told that he was to report only that he saw a UFO and watched it take off from the highway, and nothing more.

He was taken outside again and from his patrol car watched as the craft's legs were withdrawn, a humming noise began and an orange light was added to the bright and flashing lights. In an instant the craft shot straight into the black sky.

Fantasy?

Maybe so, but Herbert Schirmer was evaluated physically and mentally and his friends and family all checked out. He was a flawless witness: honest, dedicated, straight forward and not the kind to come up with such a story.

Schirmer claimed the beings told him that they would return twice more. One year later, to the day a family from Lincoln was passing by Ashland on Interstate 80 and reported seeing a "beacon that was hovering about 200 feet above the ground. It was shaped like a flat oval. It made no sound."

Yes, maybe a fantasy. You judge for yourself, as you sit here near the very spot Schirmer saw the craft land.

Two miles (13 miles.)

Ashland.

Thirteen miles (9 miles.)

Waverly.

The original Burlington Depot still stands in town.

A log cabin that for years stood here was recently moved to

US Highway 6

a farm six miles west of Lincoln on A Street.

The Old Mormon Trail, an alternate route west for Mormons coming through Nebraska City, passed two miles south of Waverly. Ruts from this trail are still visible at that spot. Ask locally.

One half mile west on US Highway 6, and one miles south to two cedar trees with a boulder between them which marks the old freight trail that passed through here in the 1860s.

Nine miles (8 miles.)

Lincoln. For a description of the sites in Lincoln, please see entry for U.S. Highway 34.

Eight miles (3 miles.)
Emerald.

Near here in 1902 a Burlington train was held up. The robbers got $32,000.

Five miles to the south is Conestoga Lake, one of the several recreational lakes in the Salt Valley system. Four miles beyond Conestoga to the south is another lake, Yankee Hill. Both are open to the public.

Seven miles south of here to Denton. Southwest of Denton the ruts from the Nebraska City Cutoff to the Oregon Trail are still visible. They are three miles south and one and a half miles west of the village. Ask locally for directions.

Two miles northeast of Denton, just northwest of the school, was a well used encampment for the early Indians in the area. Children attending the school in the early years would walk along the creek bed in order to avoid being seen by the Indians.

Denton was located on an old cattle trail which brought cattle up from Texas around 1871. Near here as well was the last open range in Lancaster County. The last open range closed in 1879.

It was near there that three early-day pioneers chased three Indians they claimed had stolen a cow. A fight followed on a hillside near Emerald. One Indian was killed while a pioneer, Jeremiah Garret was hit in the ribs by an arrow. Garret pulled the arrow out with his own hands and then collapsed.

Three miles (2 miles.)

One half mile south of here is the Burd School, a small school which has served the area for over a century in the same building. There are children attending this school whose great, great grandparents sat in the same room to learn their three Rs.

Two miles (9 miles.)

Pleasant Dale.

On October 14, 1959, two people driving down the road late at night saw a UFO here. It made a siren-like sound and the bright light traveled in an arch to the horizon.

Nine miles (8 miles.)

Milford.

The Milford Rest Home, east of town was built in 1888 as an Industrial Home. The first automobile highway west from Omaha, then known as the Omaha-Denver Road, went through Milford.

The Ponca Indians camped here after they surrendered their homeland and were being forced to march to the reservation in Oklahoma. The daughter of the Ponca Chief Standing Bear, Prairie Flower, is believed to have died here of a broken heart and is buried somewhere in the area.

The Shogo Litha Springs produced bubbling natural water (California had nothing on Milford!) which was shipped to Lincoln and bottled as Shogo Soda Pop. The Community College is built near the site of the springs.

The Amish-Mennonite Church was here from 1878 on, and a sizable Mennonite population still inhabits the area.

Milford wanted the county seat so badly that the argument between Milford, Camden (a ghost town north of here) and Seward became heated enough to produce physical violence. Seward won, at least for the time being.

Eight miles (1 mile.) ·

Just north of the bridge across the West Fork of the Blue River take county roads east to the confluence of the Fork and the Big Blue River. Many consider this to be the prettiest place two rivers come together in the state. Ask locally for directions.

One mile (3 miles.)

Blue River Recreation grounds. The timber here is native and nature-planted.

Three miles (9 miles.)

Dorchester.

This is the location of the Saline County Museum which has thousands of exhibits in nine buildings including an old school, a train depot and a post office. It is open Sunday afternoons, or by appointment. The secretary of the historical society is there every day, weather permitting since she walks the six blocks every day to the museum.

Just west of Dorchester is the site of West Mills, built in 1859, and Pleasant Hill, the location of Saline County's first county seat. Inquire at the museum for directions to these locations.

Seven miles east of Dorchester on State Highway 33 to Crete.

Crete.

Near an exquisite older mansion, known locally as "The Maples" is the first cabin built in Crete. It was constructed in 1864. Both places are open to the public the third Sunday of the month, or by appointment.

Tuxedo Park was the home of the first Chautauqua Park in the state. The Chautauqua was a traveling event which featured cultural and religious lectures and demonstrations and was popular at the turn of the century.

Doanne College in Crete is the first liberal arts college in the state. It was established in 1872. Doanne is known for its excellent English as a Second Language program.

Crete received a tiny bit of national fame in the late 1960s, at least with the young. In a popular song called "Tarkio Road" by a couple of Missouri boys named Brewer and Shipley the opening lines mentioned "riding into Crete, Nebraska..."

Nine miles (3 miles.)

Friend. What can be said about a town with the name of Friend?

Three miles (5 miles.)
North on S-76 A four miles to Cordova. Cordova's most famous landmark, the windmill at the center of town, has stood since 1916 and for many years was the main source of water for all the inhabitants.

Five miles (8 miles.)
Exeter. An alphabetical name assigned by the railroad.

Eight miles (1 mile.)
Fairmont, founded in 1871. As was the case in this area many towns were named by the railroad. The railroad had a simple solution as to what to name the towns that sprang up along their routes. They simply selected a batch of names, put them in alphabetical order and started with the A's. This spot was the sixth town to be named. It was first named Hesperia, which was sixth on the list. The citizens changed the name to the more localized Fairmont.

Many scholars believe that Fairmont is the setting for Stephen Cranes masterful short story, "The Blue Hotel."

One mile (14 miles.)
Junction with US Highway 81. Please see entry for that highway for information about sites along its route.

Fourteen miles (11 miles.)
Sutton.
Dating to 1880, Sutton is the oldest settlement in Clay County. The area was originally settled by Russian and Germans.

Eight miles (3 miles.)
Junction with State Highway 14, north. Please see entry for that road for information about locations along its route.

Three miles (3 miles.)
Junction with State Highway 14 south. Four miles south on State 14 to Clay Center.
See entry for State Highway 14 for information about Clay Center and other sites along Highway 14.

Three miles (16 miles.)

Just north of here is Harvard. Don't laugh, Nebraska also has a Cambridge and an Oxford.

Sixteen miles (6 miles.)

Hastings.

Junction of US Highway 281, for information on Hastings and along US 281, please see the entry for that highway.

Junction with US Highway 34. For information about sites along this road, east, please see entry for US Highway 34. Highway 34 joins Highway 6 for the next 135 miles until west of McCook.

Six miles (2 1/2 miles.)

Junction to Juaniata, which is 2 miles north. Juaniata is the oldest town in the area. Named for the Juaniata River in Pennsylvania. The first court house in Adams County was located at 9th Street, it was used from 1871 until 1878.

The park at 8th and 9th Streets was the site of the GAR Hall.

Until the 1950s Juaniata still had a public well, surrounded by a bandstand, in the center of town.

At 4 miles west of town where the road crosses Muddy Creek was the Muddy Creek Stage Station on the Oregon Trail and Pony Express route.

At Highway 6 and Juaniata Junction, go 2 miles south on county road to an Oregon Trail marker.

Two and a half miles (5 miles.)

At the intersection of the highway and county road the route of the Oregon Trail crosses here.

Five miles (1/2 mile.)

Turn south, to get to the village of Holstien and the Einspahr Sod House Museum. See below, for directions and further information.

One half mile (2 miles.)

Turn off to Kenesaw on S-1A.

One and a half miles north: location of a Pony Express station which was mostly a dug out, and rose only a few sod feet above the earth. There was a springs here as well. The place was called Summit Station. The station master here was almost lynched because local settlers thought he had stolen their horses.

One and a half miles more to Kenesaw. Many people envy Coloradans who can find the elevation of their towns listed instead of populations as you enter the town. For those of you longing for the Rockies, Kenesaw is at 2,051 feet above sea level.

Kenesaw has the Edward Ziebarth Museum which contains collections of fossils, pioneer artifacts and other items of interest. While it is open by appointment only, a trip into Kenesaw is worth your effort, as someone is usually around to open the place up.

For an interesting side trip into the past follow this route out of Kenesaw:

Go north one mile at the northern edge of Kenesaw, then go west 3.5 miles, turn north one mile. Turn east, go one mile where a knoll overlooking the Platte Valley is the site of the Susan Hail grave marker.

Susan Hail, traveling along the Oregon Trail in 1852 with her husband and other pioneers drank water from a well supposedly poisoned by the Indians, and died here. She was buried in a coffin her husband put together from the lumber of his wagon. He left the other pioneers and went to Omaha, where he purchased a granite marker. He returned to this site carrying the stone in a wheelbarrow. This is not the original stone, which has long since lbeen ooted by nameless tourists. No one knows the location of her husband's grave.

Return to US 6.

Two miles (17 miles.)

Just south of here is the Blevins Cemetery, a pioneer burial ground where 40 people found their final rest during the 1870s and 1880s.

Seventeen miles (23 miles.)

Minden and junction with State Highway 10. Also please see entry for State Highway 10.

You can't drive through the state of Nebraska without knowing about Minden's Harold Warp Pioneer Village.

The enormous museum's motto "There is nothing like it anywhere..." is quite accurate. Dozens of buildings and over a half of a million items bombard the visitor's eyes and ears. Everything imaginable, and some items not imaginable, can be found here. An entire building of 100 old auotmobiles, original land office, the Lowell Depot, replicas of sod houses, kitchens (the kitchen from 1950 looks just like the one many still use), and countless other displays are too much to see in a single day.

The museum is one of Nebraska's best known attractions if for no other reason than the large billboards along the Interstate which announce Pioneer Village for a thousand miles in any direction. The museum is not free, and it is not devoid of other tourists, but if you have never seen the place, you owe it to yourself and anyone you can take with you to see it.

The Pioneer Village is not the only attraction in Minden. At Christmas time, for example, the Minden pageant is performed with the cooperation of over a hundred citizens. It is presented the first two Sundays in December and includes the pageant and the lighting of the thousands of lights. The pageant celebrates the city lights commissioner J.W. Haws who, in 1915, decided to surprise the city by lighting the courthouse dome. Every year thereafter until his retirement, Mr. Haws hand-dipped light bulbs and strung them about the city.

The Minden Square, with the Kearney Courthouse, is a landmark visible for miles.

The Kearney County Historical Museum, overlooked by those seeking the flash and glamor of the Pioneer Village, is one of the more interesting local museums in the area. It includes three buildings, including the original school house in Minden. It is located at the corner of Sixth St. and Nebraska Ave. If the museum is closed, local arrangements can be made for a tour.

Twenty three miles (22 miles.)
Holdrege and junction with US Highway 183. Please see information contained in the entry for US 183 for more information.

Twenty two miles (6 miles.)
Arapahoe. Junction with US Highway 283. Please see that entry for information about sites along its route.

Arapahoe is a trading center for this busy highway and rural area.

On August 1, 1955, several people in Oxford saw a formation

of a dozen white lights in the sky. This phenomenon, still unexplained, was also observed at Orleans and Arapahoe at the same time.

South of Arapahoe 12 miles to Beaver City. See entry for US Highway 283.

Six miles (9 miles.)
Holbrook.

A trading post for the Indians once stood on the banks of the Republican here and was named after the local river feature, Burton's Bend. Actually the man who ran the trading post was named Ben Burton, so the full name of the curve in the river is Ben Burton's Bend. Boy!

Nine miles (8 miles.)
Cambridge has been called Pickleville, Northwood and Scratchpot. They settled on the best, don't you think?

Eight miles (6 miles.)
Bartley. Near here is Richmond Canyon where in 1874 a 15 foot wall of water swept down on a wagon train making its way west. One man rescued two of his children, but 17 other pioneers were swept away. Only 5 bodies were ever found, and these are buried in the Cambridge cemetery.

South of Bartley 13 miles to Lebanon. Near here was one of Red Willow County's five flour miles. There are none left in the county.

Six miles (5 miles.)
Indianola. In 1944 Indianola was the site of a German Prisoner of War camp. Over 5,000 prisoners were held here and worked on nearby farms. They painted pictures on the walls of the camp, but all of these have been removed by vandals.

Five miles (5 miles.)
Harry D. Strunk Park for travelers. Often you can find some local folks giving coffee away here.
Five miles (1 mile.)
Karrer Park, under the auspices of McCook. This fine little park was built for the traveler. It features picnic tables, showers, local information and during some summer months local citizens serve as

hosts to the park.

One mile (11 miles.)

McCook.

Junction with US Highway 83. For information about sites along this route, please see entry for US Highway 83.

McCook began life as a small pioneer community on the banks of the Republican River in 1879. The town really started to grow around its third birthday when it became a division point for the railroad. During a single month in 1882 over one hundred buildings were built. Soon a land office opened here and new settlers began to arrive.

During the 1920s McCook was one of the fastest growing communities in the country. Its population increased over 50 percent.

In 1935 the devastating flood on the Republican River destroyed hundreds of homes, and several people from McCook were among those who perished. During the flood a shortage of boats in the McCook area contributed to the loss of life.

McCook is the county seat, and yes, it won the dubious honor in a long fought battle with other towns in the county.

Nebraska's best known and most respected politician, Senator George Norris had his home in McCook. Norris was born in 1861 in Ohio where he became a member of the Ohio bar. He moved to Nebraska in 1885 and entered politics. He served three terms as county judge and then was elected to the House of Representatives in 1902. He was reelected six times and then ran for US Senator. He was reelected to the senate a number of times. Norris was registered as a Repuiblican, but his independent ways earned him the respect of many people.

Although best known as the father of the Tennessee Valley Authority, Norris also wrote the amendment to the Constitution eliminating the lame duck session of Congress, and wrote the amendment to the Nebraska Constitution which created Nebraska's unique unicameral legislature. He was a staunch advocate of public ownership of power companies, and created the Rural Electrification Administration.

The US Senate has called him America's greatest senator. His home is a National Landmark and is open to the public. It is located in the 700 block of Norris Avenue.

The McCook Townhouse on Norris Ave. in downtown McCook is the former Keystone Hotel. This attractive old hotel now serves as the city's Senior Citizen Center.

During World War II an airport serviced B-29s which would leave McCook with their deep droning engines roaring on their way to Japan.

The McCook Community College is the oldest junior college in the state, it was founded in 1926.

McCook is the smallest city in the country to have a complete YMCA facility.

The town was named after a major general who fought for the Union in the Civil War.

If you were trying to get from Omaha to Denver, and somehow found yourself in McCook, you are now halfway there.

The Museum of the High Plains is located on Norris Avenue in the old Carnegie Library building. It is open to the public and offers a fine overview of the history of the area.

Ask at the Museum for directions to a home designed by the famous architect Frank Lloyd Wright. The house was built in 1907 and is one of Wright's few homes west of the Mississippi.

On the upper center islands of Norris Avenue a nine block area becomes Santa Claus Lane during the Christmas season. Life-sized statues inhabit the street and help spark the wonder of the season for the local children, and for children of all ages passing through the town's snow-lined streets.

The McCook Post Office is a fine building built in the 1910s, despite the fact it has virtually no heat or insulation.

One mile south of McCook is Barnett Park. Barnett Park was formed after several people cleared tons of debris left here by the flood of 1935.

Eleven miles (3 miles.)

Culbertson. When the great flood on the Republican happened in May of 1935, the river was two miles wide here.

For a long while this town was the end of the railroad and hence a shipping point for many surrounding areas. The railroad worked its way slowly up what is today US Highway 6 and reached Palisades, 27 miles northwest of here, in 1891.

US Highway 6

Three miles (8 miles.)

Junction with US Highway 34. From here east to Hastings the two routes are together. For a continuation of sites west of here on US 34, please see the entry for US Highway 34.

Eight miles (5 miles.)

When the highway crosses Red Willow Creek: near here on the old Walker ranch, two "claim trees" held the bodies of two Sioux Warriors for years until they were finally buried. A post office was on this farm, called "Thornburg."

Grasshopper plagues were common in this area. The pests not only killed off all of the green and growing items in the area, but covered houses, pets, animals and humans.

Five miles (2 miles.)

On Stinking Water creek the first non-sod school house was built of stone and still stands on the A.J. Irvine ranch. Ask locally for directions and permission to visit.

Two miles (7 miles.)

Palisade. The trail that George Armstrong Custer followed from Ft. McPherson to Kansas in order to take part in the 1867 Sioux Indian Wars, crosses the Highway here. This trail was often used in the years that followed.

Seven miles (1 mile.)

Hamlet. The Texas Cattle Road of 1880s passed through here on its way up the Stinking Water Creek on toward the shipping yards at Ogallala.

Throughout the county are still some sod houses on private ranches and farms.

This area was a part of one of the largest buffalo ranges in the country. Buffalo Bill Cody, Doc Carver and other historic figures hunted buffalo here for the railroad in 1868-69. By the late 1880s there were no buffalo to be found here at all.

Stinking Water Creek, which is just three miles north of Hamlet, got its name from the thousands of buffalo carcasses left to rot on its banks. During 1870s this was a sportsman's paradise for hunting buffalo. Doc Carver claimed that it was in Hayes Co. where he killed his 30,000 buffalo. For more information on Carver,who was one of Nebraska's most interesting historical figures, see entry for State Highway 23.

North of Hamlet is a small pioneer cemetery which is located on a hillside, and is reachable only by a footpath. Ask locally for directions.

One mile (6 miles.)
This canyon was one of the difficult crossings for the Texas Cattle Trail. The cattle had to walk the narrow flatland with canyons to the west and east of them. Once, the story goes, a couple of cowboys had been feuding most of the way up from Texas. One of the two, a black man, brought the cattle too near the western edge of the trail and the other, a white man, thought he was getting them too close to the edge. A fight broke out and the white cowboy killed the black cowboy and his body fell into the canyon.

Six miles (7 miles.)
The legendary cowboy and Texas outlaw Robinhood, Sam Bass, said on his deathbed that he buried $10,000 worth of gold he had taken from a railroad train in a holdup "on the Frenchman River, west of the Falls." No one has found it yet.

The Frenchman River flows alongside of the highway from Hamelt to the Chase County line. The Pawnee called the river the Frenchman after a lone trapper who lived seven miles west of here on what is now the county line between Chase and Hayes counties. The Sioux called the river While Man's River after the same trapper.
The story of the French trapper is a mystery. No one knows much about him except for the amazing number of personal items that have turned up near the site of his cabin. He owned a gun and a rifle. He had no horse, and had to carry everything he used up river from St. Louis, probably by dugout canoe. He was probably killed by Indians during the Sioux War, but perhaps after cutting off the hand of one of his attackers. The bones of a human hand were found in the burned out shell of his cabin in the 1880s.

A half mile to the south of his cabin on the Frenchman was a large Pawnee village of 40 to 50 tepees. This village was probably attacked by the Sioux at the same time the Frenchman lost his life.

Ask locally for directions to the historical marker indicating the approximate location of the cabin.

Seven miles (9 miles.)

Wauneta in the SE corner of Chase County was named after the song Juanita, and given an Anglicized spelling. There's no reason to go to Colorado to find a town that seems to be in the mountains. Wauneta's setting gives one the feeling of being somewhere in the Rockies and without all the tourists from Nebraska!

One block from the center of town is a waterfall--a small but an important historic site as in the early days of settlement several people hid in the rocks of the ledge of the falls from raiding Indians.

The well-known and well-used Texas/Ogallala Cattle Trail split Chase County right in two from the northern edge to the southern. During the 1880s this trail was used by cowboys bringing cattle up from Texas to the railheads in Nebraska. Some of the men drove the cattle further and found suitable range in the sandhills and the Dakotas further to the north.

Eight miles (1 mile.)

Junction with State Highway 61, south. Please see that entry for sites along this route.

One mile (8 miles.)

Enders. A tiny community on the edge of the popular recreation lake Enders Reservoir. There's good camping here.

Eight miles (20 miles.)

Imperial. This is the county seat of Chase County. Here is the headquarters of the local historical society, although their museum is in Champion. (see below.)

Junction with State Highway 61, north. Please see entry for State Highway 61 for information about sites along this route.

Eight miles to the SE on state road s15A is Champion. Here are the county's two main attractions for the history buff. Champion Mills was the last water-powered mill in the state. Using the water from the Frenchman River this mill was in operation until recently. Thanks to the State Game and Parks Department, the mill has been turned into a small tourist attraction.

The trip to Champion is made twice as good since the Chase County Historical Society bought a former high school in 1963 and started their museum. They modestly will tell you that the museum consists "mostly of machines." The history of ranching and farming in the southwest corner of the state is spelled out in the steel building which houses a good part of the Society's collection.

Twenty miles (5 miles.)
Lamar, just off the road to the north. Lamar was named for Lucius Quintus Cincinnatus Lamar, Secretary of the Interior under Grover Cleveland. Good thing they stuck just with the last name.

Near Lamar is the home of one of Nebraska's widest read and least known writers. Wayne C. Lee has written dozens of books set in the Old West, full not only of adventure and suspense, but historically accurate and infused with a love of the land that speaks to us all. His books may be a little hard to find, and you may not be used to reading "westerns" but you will not be disappointed in picking up one of Mr. Lee's creations.

Five miles (0 miles.)
Colorado border.

NEBRASKA
U S
34

US Highway 34 enters Nebraska at Plattsmouth. From there until Union it follows the route of US Highways 73 and 75. Please see the entry for US Highways 73 and 75 for information about this section of Highway 34.

Zero miles (4 miles.)
Union. Union is a small town at the "T" intersection of Highway 34 and 73/75.

There are still some small and falling-down traces of the incredible beauty this small burg once had.

When you turn onto Highway 34, heading west, you may not know it, but there are those who claim you are now on the longest road without a turn in the world. You can set your car on automatic pilot and not turn the wheel an inch for the next seventy or more miles.

Another faction claims that this highway is a gigantic sun dial, and that on each summer's and winter's solstice the sun rises and sets at each end of the road.

Four miles (7 miles.)

Turn off for Nehawka, a town of quaint sentimental beauty and wonder.

Seven miles (2 miles.)

Turn off to Weeping Water. Please see entry for State Highway 50 for information about this town rich with history.

Two miles (6 miles.)

Junction with State Highway 50. Please see that entry for information about sites along this route.

Six miles (6 miles.)

Turn off for Elmood, the writer Bess Streeter Aldrich's home. Location of Aldrich Center to commemorate the best-selling author. Aldrich was not born in Nebraska, but spent a number of years here.

Her best known book may be the novel *With a Lantern in Her Hand*. That novel tells the story of three claim jumpers who were caught, hung and buried in a mass grave near here.

Six miles (4 miles.)

Eagle. In 1891 Major Pembleton performed here. The good major was able to play six instruments at once while Indian dancers danced to his music.

You stand in what many consider to be the center of the cornhusker land. Eagle for years held cornhusking contests each fall. The world's record is held by Monroe Barryman, who during an eleven hour period on November 20, 1891 husked 130 bushels. If you have to ask what cornhusking is, go back to New York.

Four miles (2 miles.)

From this hill is a view to the west of Lincoln and the State Capitol Building.

Two miles (6 miles.)

Turn off for Walton, **one mile south.**

Walton is a tiny community about to be swallowed by Lincoln, yet holding onto its own identity. Southwest of Walton is a tiny burial plot containing the remains of one pioneer era family.

*   ***Two miles north*** *of here and a mile east the old stage coach line road crosses the county road. Traces of the road are still visible. Ask locally.*

*   ***Two and a half miles north*** *of here a well-used Pawnee trail crosses the county road.*

Six miles (10 miles.)

Lincoln.

Lincoln is the juncture of US Highways 34 and 77, Interstate 80 and State Highway 2. For more information about sites along those routes, please see the entry for those highways.

Any tour of Lincoln must start at the Capitol Building. This is one of the most beautiful man-made objects you are likely to see.

In 1919 the fourth capitol building was crumbling and the Legislature decided to spend some money amd make a statehouse that would last.

A capitol commission organized a nationwide competition and eventually the design of architect Bertram Grosvenor Goodhue was selected.

Goodhue's design was a unique, and some said outrageous tower that rose from a square base. It looked more like some kind of a monument rather than a building with usable office space.

In 1922 the groundbreaking ceremonies, done with a plow pulled by oxen, signaled the start of construction. The new building was built around the old capitol so that the state government would not have to move to temporary offices. As new offices were completed the workers simply moved out of the old and into the new, and then the old building was demolished.

Ten years after work began the building was finished. The cost was $9,800,440.07. The building was paid for by the time it was completed.

Today, well past the half-century mark, the building shows little signs of wear. The flesh-colored stone walls are thick and stately and rise to a climax on the golden dome visible for miles. A statue of a sower, pointed northwesterly toward the greatest expanse of the state, sows his seeds into the vast expanse of the prairie winds.

On the west side of the building the figure of Abraham Lincoln stands in a pensive pose. The statue was created by Daniel Chester French, who also did the statue of the seated Lincoln which adorns the Lincoln Memorial in Washington D.C. Lincoln's Lincoln predates the construction of the current building.

The north side of the building was once the site of a statue of William Jennings Bryan. The statue had been placed there by the Democrats under protest from the Republicans in the non partisan government of the state. The Democrats kept saying the statue would only be temporary. The "temporary" statue was placed in concrete and stood there for decades. The Republicans finally won out, and the statue now stands at Bryan's Lincoln home, "Fairview" at 4900 Sumner (see below.)

In 1932 the Governor had been successfully petitioned to light the tower at night. Since then, depending on the cost of electricity, and the state's level of environmental awareness verses civic pride, the lights have sometimes been on at night, sometimes not.

A walk through the rotunda and a ride to the observation deck on the 14th floor is the usual tour for most people, but a far better plan is to take the guided tours which are offered almost hourly throughout the year.

The West Chamber is the gathering place of Nebraska's unique, one house, non partisan legislature which was created in 1934. That chamber, along with the governor's offices, the Supreme Court, the Law Library and the Hall of Famous Nebraskans are among the beautiful wonders of this building. In addition the building is like a maze, with little tucked away corners of carved wooden doors, twisting halls and spiral staircases.

The Ferguson House near by at 700 S. 16th is restored to the elegance of the 1915 era. Nearby at 1627 H the Kennard House has been restored as a statehood memorial. It was the home of the Secretary of State when Lincoln became the capital city.

The Harris house at 1630 K Street is open for inspection.

The First Plymouth Congregational Church at 20th and D Streets is second only to the Capitol building as the state's most noted architectural sight. It was designed by H. Van Buren Magonigle and features a 100 foot bell tower and a combination of architectural designs from around the world.

Lincoln was founded by pioneers who discovered salt flats just northwest of the present downtown. They thought these flats indicated large deposits of the precious commodity and began to promote their new town. By the time it was discovered that the salt flats were just the deposit of an occasional flooded creek, the town had already started to grow.

Because of the way it started, Lincoln is one of the few cities in the state not located on a major river course. Tiny Salt Creek is the most major waterway and it barely floats a canoe.

The first non-Indian settlement was at the mouth of Oak Creek where it flows into Salt Creek. That was in 1857. The first Lincoln log cabin, built by Luke Lavender in 1863, was at the intersection of 14th and O Streets. A marker commemorates this site on the southeast corner of the intersection.

The early days of Lincoln were filled, much as they are today, with the political squibbles and squabbles of politics. In 1868, for example, an Iowa postmaster came to town to organize the Democratic party. After announcing his intentions far and wide, only three men showed up. To boost the Presidential campaign of Horatio Seymour they put up a tall pole on Market Square, 9th and O Streets. The trees they lashed together reached 55 feet into the air.

Soon after, the Republicans, not to be outdone, somehow got a 100 foot pine pole at a cost of $300 and had it erected near the Democrats' pole.

During the night someone cut the Republican pole down and whittled it into pieces. A warrant was sworn for a stage driver who was accused of the horrible crime. A gallows was built using, yes, the remains of the Republicans' pole. A judge found the defendant not guilty due to lack of evidence. The stage driver left town shortly thereafter never to be seen in these parts again.

It may not be a coincidence that in addition to such political fights, as late as 1890 the city had to pass an ordinance to remove the hogpens betwen O and P on 14th.

In 1878 the town needed a post office and and courthouse so $200,000 was spent to build the best and newest of facilities. The block on which it was built, between 9th and 10th on O Street, had been the farmers' market. It had an artesian well for years. The building was used for a number of years, then when a new post office was built in 1905, the building was used for city offices. The city remained in the building until the new city complex was built in the late 1960s.

Since that time the building and the block have been sources of much debate and struggle. The fight has surrounded the preservationalists who want to save the building, as well as the old jail to the west, and the second post office just to the north, and the downtown businessmen who claim the city would be better served by using the block to increase retail sales downtown. The issue, and the buildings' fates, has been tossed from city councils, to courts, to the voters and back again. Currently the city leases space to non profit organizations, and the old building still stands.

The hand-hewn limestone of the building is from Nebraska and is typical of early Nebraska limestone construction. The original roof was slate, and the arched windows on either side of the front entrance were once doors. The building was heated by wood, and chimneys once dotted the roofline.

Inside, to the right of the stairs is the old elevator with its ornate ironwork cage. There are Romanesque designs on Corinthian columns in the lobby. The meeting room on the second floor was the original courtroom. The ceiling once extended two floors, but was lowered when the city took over the building. The wood finish through out the building is oak and ash.

The building is also the location for the tourist information center.

Near the old post office in the area around 9th and N were several houses of ill-repute, saloons and two carefully camouflaged opium dens. The former City Mission, which still stands on the east side of 9th between N and O was once one of the houses of pleasure. The madam of the house left it to the city so that "it could still be used by the clients who had used it so well." There are those who want to preserve the old building as a part of the city's history.

The building at 13th and Q Streets which now houses a variety of shops, was the home of Nebraska Buick, which distributed cars to 501 dealers in several states.

The Burlington Northern passenger station at 7th and P was built during the climax days of railroad travel, in 1925. At that same time the state built a mile of track from the railroad yards to the new capitol building to carry building supplies. The old Rock Island station near 20th and O was saved from the wrecker a number of times and is a fine example of the old style stations.

The National Bank of Commerce building at 13th and O Streets was designed by I. M. Pei.

Pershing Municipal Auditorium at 15th and M features a mosaic made from 763,000 tiles, the largest such mosaic in the United States. McKinley High School, the city's first, was built in 1873 where Pershing stands.

Lincoln's first skyscraper, the Burr Block, was built in 1888. It still stands on the northeast corner of 12 and O Streets.

The State Historical Society operates a fine new museum at Centennial Mall (15th Street) and P Streets. The state archives are housed in the Historical Society Building at 15th and R streets.

Lincoln is home to the University of Nebraska, and the location of the main campus just north of downtown keeps the city's downtown area alive and well.

The University was created by a bill passed in 1869 on the same day that the State Asylum was formed. Locals claimed that was a good thing since the asylum would provide teachers for the University, and the University would be needed to provide inmates for the Asylum. Others said that the University was needed to instruct those who thought the state needed an Asylum, and the Asylum was needed for those who believed Nebraska needed a University.

The Asylum became the State Hospital, on west Van Dorn, and the University had its first day of classes with 90 students and five faculty. Today the state's University serves five hundred times that number of students. The original $100,000 budget for the school would not support the recruitment of a single quarterback for Big Red in this day and age.

The football team was called the Rattlesnake Boys, the Antelopes, and best yet, the Bugeaters before a sports editor called them the Cornhuskers in 1900.

Memorial Stadium at 10th and U Streets, was finished in 1928, just a couple of years after the Nebraska team defeated Notre Dame, one of the best remembered games from the old days.

Nebraska's football team was next to the bottom for years before the Bob Devany/Tom Osborne era, but there was another time of high national ranking. From 1929 until 1936 a man by the name of Dana Bible led the Cornhuskers to six Big Six championships in eight seasons. The team even went to the Rose Bowl in 1943 where they were defeated by Stanford 21-13.

The Bob Devany Sports Complex near the Fairgrounds on

north 17th is a 5 acre indoor sports arena that seats 15,000. A special bill had to be passed in the Unicameral to bypass a state law that said no building could be named after a living person. For the uninformed, Bob Devany led the University football team to national importance in the late 1960s and 70s.

The State Museum, Morrill Hall, at 14th and Vine Streets on the University campus is one of the finest museums in the state. It includes Elephant Hall where the remains of the giants which once roamed the state have been reconstructed. A large collection of dinosaurs, and other prehistoric creatures are here, as is a very good children's encounter center where kids of all ages can interact with artifacts from the natural world. The museum also contains the Ralph Mueller Planetarium which gives sky shows throughout the day.

Morrill Hall, while named after the wealthy regent and vast landowner, Charles Morrill, was started by Dr. Erwin Barbour in 1891.

Sheldon Art Gallery on the campus near 12th and R features many collections in a stunning white building.

The Temple Building at 12th and R Streets houses the University's fine drama department. The building was built in 1906 with funds donated by J.D. Rockfeller. There was quite an uproar that his money was "tainted money," and to settle the dispute the regents accepted the money, but built the building "off campus."

In the 1890s the University had a kind of heyday with several soon-to-be notables attending or working on campus. Roscoe Pound, who would become Dean of the Harvard Law School and well known as a football player was a student. Literary giant Willa Cather and writer Dorothy Canfield, who would later come to fame in New England, were friends and students. Pound's sister Louise was already a world-class athlete and would win tennis championships in both the men's and women's divisions.

Architectural Hall on the University campus near 10th and R Streets is the oldest, and one of the most unique buildings on campus. It was the fifth building built for the campus and was constructed in 1895. A vocal fight by architecture students in the early 1970s ensured its survival and placement on the National Register of Historic Places.

The Agricultural School of the University is located several blocks east of the downtown campus at 37th and Holdrege. In 1914 a state referendum was held to decide if the downtown campus should be moved to the Ag Campus site. The act lost in the state-wide election.

Wesleyan University was built as a Methodist College in 1888 in the then fields 3 miles out of town.

The campus, at 50th and Huntington, is the site for one of the most famous ghost stories in America. In 1963 a secretary for Dean Sam Dahl walked into an office in the C.C. White Building. Suddenly all sounds ceased. There was a musty smell in the air. She walked into an adjoining room. A woman with a long, black dress stood at a cabinet. She turned and smiled at the secretary. Outside the window, where there should have been dorms and busy streets, was nothing but open prairie. The secretary had walked back in time. She ran from the room.

The secretary was interviewed by several people about her experience and soon left the city and never returned to the building again.

The Nebraska United Methodists operate a historical center at Wesleyan at 50th & St. Paul Streets as a depository for documents and articles from the church's history in the state.

Union College, at 48th and Stockwell is operated by the Seventh Day Adventists. It was started in 1891.

The now defunct Normal University and its community was at about 56th and South. The town of Normal was there, and that is where William Jennings Bryan lived. The nursing home Madonna at 56th and South Streets was a asylum before it was a nursing home.

William Jennings Bryan came to Lincoln in 1887. He joined the Round Table Discussion Club where political debates between men of honor were held as entertainment and education. Bryan and two partners started a law firm. In 1890 20,000 Populists attended a picnic in Cushman Park, west of town. Their growing numbers sent Bryan to Congress in 1890.

Eventually Bryan became the only man from a major political party in United States' history to lose the race for President three times. He ran twice against McKinley (1896 and 1900) and once against Taft (1908).

Just in case you think this might have been just coincidence, Bryan's brother and advisor, Charles Bryan, was the Vice Presidential candidate on the Democratic ticket in 1924. He too, lost. (But believe it or not, another Lincolnite, Charles Dawes was the vice president for the winning ticket with Calvin Coolidge in the same year.)

Brother Charles Bryan did have some fine ideas. He convinced the city of Lincoln to own and operate a gasoline station. Private gas stations took the city to court, but the Supreme Court said it was all right for a city to operate such a business. Bryan wanted the city to have a city operated, lower-priced grocery store, but alas, that was never to be.

William Jennings Bryan spoke to an overflowing crowd in 1922 at the First Baptist Church at 14th and K where the silver tongued orator told the crowd that the theory of evolution was the greatest menace of the age. Three years later in Tennessee he defended his ideas in a courtroom against Clarence Darrow over whether anything but a biblical view of creation should be taught in schools. Just a few days after the final verdict in the Scopes' trial, he died.

Bryan Memorial Hospital which now nearly surrounds the Bryan home, was started in 1922 after the Bryans gave their home, "Fairview," and ten acres to the Methodist Church.

Bryan's home "Fairview" is located at 4900 Sumner and is open weekend afternoons and by appointment.

The suburb of Bethany was formed as a result of the Cotner College, a Christian Church College that was there until the 1930s.

Havlock, another suburb, was a town that supported the Burlington shops which are located there. This is where boxcars and other trains are built or fixed. Plant tours are available by making special arrangements with the management.

General John J. Pershing lived in Lincoln during the 1890s and taught ROTC at the University. He bought a home at 1748 B street in 1919 after all but one of his children were burned to death in a San Francisco fire. Pershing was America's first six star general. After he was given the honor it was decided that he shouldn't be the only one, so they gave George Washington (who'd been dead for some time) the honor as well.

Charles "Lucky Lindy" Lindbergh learned to fly in Lincoln. The young man from Minnesota who would be the first man to cross the Atlantic solo in an airplane, came to Lincoln on April 1, 1922 and enrolled in a flying school at 24th and O Streets, and first took to the air at a field seven miles south of the Penitentiary.

Lincoln is justified in being proud of its parks.

US Highway 34

In 1928 a New York stockbroker asked if there could be land purchased and developed into a park as a memorial to his parents. Five hundred acres were purchased west of the city, and later 100 more were added. When the park was dedicated in 1930 the stock broker felt it should honor all pioneers and not just his parents and so the name Pioneers' Park came to be.

The park was laid out to feature the skyline of the city in the distance to the east, and the open farmlands to the west. Trees were planted to form openings to feature the best view. An outdoor amphlitheater was added, along with grounds for a small herd of buffalo, a golf course, a nature center and wildlife sanctuary and other features. It soon became the most popular park in the city, and it remains so today.

Family albums around the world have faded photographs of children standing next to the stout buffalo statue that graces the entranceway to the park.

When the U.S. Treasury Building in Washington D.C. was being remodeled four of the building's columns were presented to the city of Lincoln. These columns were where Abraham Lincoln stood to review the troops during the Civil War. The columns have since moved all around the city, from O Street to the grassy slope at Pioneers' Park.

The park can be reached by driving west on either Van Dorn or South Street, it is a mile west of the State Hospital. Just ask anyone for directions.

On the way to Pioneers Park, at 1st and Van Dorn a small, run-down-looking food place called Runza Restaurant offers a unique eating opportunity. In 1950 a few family members started to sell their mother's recipe for a German-Russian sandwich made from ground beef, cabbage, spices and onions and baked inside of bread. Although they sold the trademark to a franchise organization, the family retained this, the original, non-franchised location. To put it another way, it is like you came across the McDonalds' brothers original drive-in.

Yankee Hill Brick, just south of Pioneers Park was founded in 1870 and provided much of the brick for the brick streets that once dominated the city. A few brick streets still remain scattered through out the city.

The beautiful Sunken Gardens at 27th and D were converted from a city dump in the 1920s. The design of this and other Lincoln parks was done by a man named Chet Ager. Ager is commemorated today by the Chet Ager Nature Center at Pioneer Park.

Antelope Park which is near the Sunken Gardens houses the Zoo and the Children's Zoo.

One of the city's newest and most extensive parks is Holmes Lake in the southweastern corner of the city.

The city also has a wilderness park which stretches from 1st and Van Dorn south to Saltillo Road.

Near Wilderness Park, the State Prison, at the junction of US Highway 77 and State Highway 2, has been at that site since 1870, and a few of the buildings date to that time.

On February 11, 1912 the Warden of the Penitentiary was stabbed to death after Sunday chapel. A month later his successor and two other men were killed in a gun battle with some convicts. The convicts escaped and for the next four days they were chased around the county while a vicious blizzard pounded the prairies. When they were at last cornered near Gretna, one convict was killed, another shot himself and the third was returned to the Pen to face a life sentence.

In 1955 prison rioters burned several buildings and the city's citizens spent hours indoors waiting to hear if the streets would be filled with escaping prisoners.

Charles Starkweather was a 19 year old, red-headed punk from Lincoln, his 14 year old girl friend, Caril Ann Fugate, a bored, young girl. Together they roamed the city and Lancaster County for five days killing nearly anyone they met. They killed a young man who tried to help them when their car wouldn't start. They killed a house-wife and her dog. By the time they were captured they had killed ten people and had made national news as the first mass murderers of the post WWII era. Several of the murders were in Lincoln and for those five days in 1958 Lincolnites seldom left their homes, and many refused to answer a knock on their doors.

Starkweather was tried and convicted and sent to the electric chair at the state penitentiary. Fugate served 25 years in prison. Since then novels and movies and songs have retold the horrifying tale of those few days. There is something about the story of a lonely demented kid and the open stretches of prairie that must ring a kind

205

of universal dark truth.

Years later rock 'n' roll giant Bruce Springsteen would record a dark, somber album, call it "Nebraska" and have Starkweather as the central character of its lead song.

During the early 1970s two Lincolnites named Zaiger and Evans had a number one hit world wide with a song about what the future might hold. "In the Year 2525" was the group's only hit, but it was a gigantic one, and became one of the all-time largest selling 45 records.

Lincoln has always prided itself on its fine, extensive and unique music scene. In addition to a symphony orchestra, and the new performing arts theater, Lincoln has always been the home of numbers of fine musicians. Lawrence Welk, who was from North Dakota, got his start playing with his band in Lincoln. Now bluegrass instrumentalists and rock 'n' rollers have continued to refine Lincoln's exciting music scene. One group, *Charlie Burton and the Hiccups,* has recorded four albums and gained national attention. Lincoln's sometimes seedy Zoo Bar has a national reputation as one of the hottest places to see new music in the country.

You owe your hours of brain-numbing music, those happy grocery store tunes of Muzak, to a man from Lincoln. Royal Brewster started the elevator music business in 1930.

The *Back to the Bible* radio program originates in Lincoln. It was started in 1939 and at its peak was heard in dozens of countries.

Radio station KFAB, which started in Lincoln, was one of the first radio stations in the world to broadcast news over the air. This fact survives by being mentioned in dozens of broadcast journalism textbooks, and appearing on hundreds of final exams all across the country.

A man named Clinton Cushman tinkered around with a four-cycle water cooled engine and soon Cushman motors flourished in Lincoln. They built "putt-putt" scooters, golf carts, parking meter police vehicles and lawnmowers. In 1957 they were purchased by Outboard Marine of Illinois.

Smith-Dorsey Pharmaceuticals was founded in Lincoln. Their first lab was at 15th & O and now is east of town on US Highway

6. Millions of cold sufferers have learned the wonders of Dorsey products which were invented by hard-working and fine people right here.

Both United Rent-Alls and the salvation of countless struggling English students: *Cliff Notes,* (which summarize the plot and themes of major books not read for English classes) were started here.

Sherman Field, two blocks west of 1st and South streets, was home to many big leaguers including Ed Cicotte, a pitcher who was ruined with the Chicago Black Sox scandal.

Lincoln is home base for a number of insurance companies and at one time was known as the "Hartford of the West," because of this distinction.

The Nebraska State Fair, always held the first week in September, is in Lincoln. The Fairgrounds are located at 17th and Holdrege.

Lincoln is where you can find the American Historical Society of Germans from Russia, which includes a small museum at 631 D Street.

Lincoln is the home of the National Museum of Roller Skating. Now, don't laugh, for a large number of people went to a lot of trouble to see that the museum, and the Roller Skating Hall of Fame, would be located in Lincoln. In 1992 Roller Skating is an Olympic sport, so the Hall of Fame may well grow. The museum is the definitive source for the history of roller skating. It is located at 7700 A Street and is open during the week.

In late 1957 jets from the Nebraska National Guard scrambled over the city to intercept a UFO that was sighted by the crew of a B-47.
Several of the pilots saw the object and described it as being as large as a hanger. It was a large silvery globe.
On October 1, 1952 two men saw two white-silvery objects fly over downtown Lincoln. They said the objects were 100 feet wide.
Others all around the city saw something that same day. From Waverly on the east, to Pioneers Park on the west reports came of a white object with orange lights.

A Lincoln boy, Eric Salem, recently made the magazine we all really dream of making: *People* magazine. When the 15 year old ran for, and won a seat on the Noxious Weed Control Authority he became, according to the magazine, "possibly the youngest person ever elected to public office in the U.S."

Salem was also on Johnny Carson's Tonight Show and ran a serious campaign.

It is not true, as the locals here might suggest, that no one who remains in Lincoln will become famous. What more fame than *People* magazine is there?

In 1939 five college students from Middlebury College in Vermont were in Lincoln for a covention of their fraternity. The legend has it that two of them found a tin pie plate in a cornfield and began tossing it around. Soon the others joined in. They took their new game back to the college where it spread like wildfire.

The pie tin was from a popular brand of the day, "Frisbie's". When Wham-O Manufacturing Co. got the trademark for the now famous toy, they changed the spelling to Frisbee.

Although there are sculptures and monuments in the East that claim the game was invented at Middlebury, its true origins are here.

Lincoln was the boyhood home of writer Loren Eiseley. Eiseley was an anthropologist and a paleontologist, but gained his fame by writing insightful and thoughtful essays about the nature of humankind. His brooding, beautifully crafted works have been read for 50 years all over the world, and Eiseley has become the subject of scholarly biography and study.

Eiseley often wrote about his boyhood in Lincoln and from those memories he expanded to thoughts about the world. His books are still widely available in most bookstores and libraries. He speaks most eloquently about Lincoln in the opening pages of *The Night Journey*, and throughout his autobiography, *All the Strange Hours—Excavations of a Life.*

Lincoln has a number of fine old mansions offering views of a wide range of architectural styles. Here are a few of them:

—The Lewis-Syford house 700 N. 16th. One of the few remaining houses built in the French Second Empire style. Built in

1878.

—The Clark House, or F Street Castle, 1937 F. One of the better examples of Queen Ann's style this castle has a missmash of window shapes and sizes, chimneys and turrets.

—Phillip's, or D Street Castle, 1845 D. This Romanesque castle contains 40 rooms and 16 fireplaces and cost $60,000 when it was built in 1889.

—Tyler House, 808 D. This Queen Ann's style house was built as a kind of advertisement by the owner of a stone company in 1891.

—Ziemer House, 2030 Euclid. This Romanesque and Shingle style house was built in 1909 from stones transported from Colorado and cut on the site. The shingles, which are made from cedar, were applied wet and then bent to fit the contours of the roof. Rain water is carried by copper gutters to an underground cistern. The porch was designed to be enclosed in the winter and has a hidden water closet.

Ten miles (8 miles.)

Turn off to Malcolm.

North of Malcolm four miles *to Branched Oak Lake, the largest and one of the finer of the many Salt Valley Lakes. South here to Pawnee Lake, another public access lake in the system.*

Eight miles (6 miles.)

North 3 miles to Garland. The Garland Bank, built in 1904 still stands, although it ceased operations during the bank failures of the 1930s. The Folly Movie Theater which was later used as a community hall, now houses grain at the Seward County Co-op.

Six miles (7 miles.)

Seward.

There is something about this town that remains unchanged and unspoiled from an earlier time. Perhaps it's County Courthoues Square, with its large ornate courthouse built in 1905; or the shops clustered around the square and bearing names like the Corner Cafe, Jone's Bank and Books and Brushes. Perhaps it is the Blue River which wraps lazily around three sides of the town. If this were Minnesota there would have been an award winning radio show based on a place like Seward.

Goehner's Grocery, on Seward St., just west of the courthouse, is one of the oldest surviving business buildings in the town. It is next door to the Seward Creamery which dates from an earlier time as well.

At the corner of 8th and South a local bandit named Orlando Cassler was hung in the 1880s. According to local stories, this spot is haunted by the man's ghost, which has most often been seen just at sunset on cool evenings.

Those with metal detectors might prowl around the east block of 7th St. south of South St. since this was the city dump until 1914.

The Cottage Hotel at Highway 15 and Ash, just across the bridge, still stands from an earlier booming time.

A block and a half east on Ash to one of the town's early Burlington Depots.

Seward grew up around the Homesteading Act and the expansion of the railroads. The town boasted quite a boom in business and included bottling plants, mills, egg companies, a pipe organ company and a corn cob pipe factory in its day.

At the north end of 11th St., just at the railroad tracks are the remnants of the old beer vaults from when a fine local beer was produced in Seward.

The Armory, at 10th and Jackson is built on the site of the Chautauqua ground.

One of Seward's largest employers, Hughes Brothers, who make electrical transmission poles and materials, got its start in 1921 after a freak storm destroyed power lines in the area and the electrical company needed replacements.

Columbia Avenue at College Ave. Concordia Teachers' College dates to 1894 when the Lutheran Teachers' Seminary was begun in a single building in Seward with 12 male students. It is a four year coeducational college affiliated with the Lutheran Church. The school includes The Center for Indian Ministries and Studies which attracts many Indian students from all across the nation to gain the education needed to follow the Lutheran ministries.

East of the college at Locust Ave and Moffit is what some believe to be an Indian burial ground. Relics have been found in this area for years.

At the corner of Hillcrest Drive and 10th St. is the beautiful old Hughes home which many claim to be the most beautiful house in this town of many fine old houses.

Follow 3rd St. north to Hillcrest to Seward's most unusual business, museum, farm supply, former mill and home of its most notable citizen. The House of Davisson is the location of numerous enterprises of one Harold Davisson who, among other accomplishments, has created what he claims is the world's largest time capsule (it was built in 1975, to be opened in 2025) containing an entire car, a motorcycle and thousands of other items; the first modern pyramid in the United States (to cover the time capsule); who has written a half dozen books on local history, cooking, the building of the world's largest time capsule, pyramid, etc., and a book of unabashed self-promotion and congratulations; who promoted "the world's longest trip for a high school basketball game" (to Seward Alaska, in 1953, no one seems to remember who won); who built skating rinks, apartment complexes and sculpture for satire, "Utter Futility" to jab at the state's sculpture project along Interstate 80; who saved Seward's old hospital (at 6th and Bradford Streets) and who, it seems, is about as unusual a character as you'll meet in the entire state.

Seven miles (7 miles.)

Tamora, so named because the earliest settlers could not decide on a name, and always talked about coming up with one "tamora'". Now this tiny town is the location of the large, main office of the Tamora-Stapleton Farmers' Co-op. These co-ops are a way for farmers to share the costs of larger, expensive equipment, and to have a business which they own and run. The idea started in the 1920s, although cooperative ventures such as this date back to the earliest pioneer days on the great plains.

Seven miles (13 miles.)

Utica.

Utica's Opera House (1883), City Hall (1912) auditorium (1936, WPA) and many older homes survive from its boom town days.

US Highway 34

Thirteen miles (8 miles.)

York. Junction of US Highway 81. Please see that entry for information about sites in this area.

Eight miles (7 miles.)

Bradshaw.

The area around here was seriously affected by the great grasshopper plague of 1874 as entire farms were wiped out by the infestation. Grasshoppers literally swarmed in great dark clouds which blocked out the sun. They would descend on a field, their humming filling the air, devour every green plant to the ground and then move on. It was impossible to walk outside without crunching 10 or 20 bugs with each and every step.

Seven miles (6 miles.)

Hampton. This town was originally named Plano, but there was another Plano on the Burlington Railroad line, so it was changed to Murray. There was another town on the Burlington line named Murray so it was changed to...well, eventually they decided on Hampton.

Six miles (1 mile.)

Aurora.

Junction of State Highway 14. Please see that entry for more information about sites along that route.

Aurora was founded in 1871 when a bunch of men moved from Iowa (a good idea) and founded the town to make money. They didn't make it, but others did. One of the original men named the town in honor of his wife who had moved from Aurora, Illinois (a good idea, too). The vote to name the town Aurora was 2 to 0, although only one man voted in the election. The politics of the county have improved somewhat since then.

The Hamilton County Fair is the oldest continuous annual county fair in the state. It was started in the fall of 1872 in the then county seat of Orrville, some distance from here. The first fair was centered around the original courthouse, and that area was also used as the race track. Long tables were spread for the communal picnic. It was held at the start of the great grasshopper plague which lasted several years, but still people came to celebrate from all over the area.

An early resident was William Townsley. Townsley 'twas trying the trade of the tiny town's taxidermist. His very peculiar records of early Hamilton County, one might say his "stuff," can be seen at the Plainsman Museum described below.

The Nebraska Youth Leadership Development Center, a 27 acre facility for youth and adult groups, is located on the east edge of the city.

Camp Hamilton, a camp for Company H during training for World War One was located in Streeter Park on the eastern edge of the city

Downtown Aurora still has the feel of an older Nebraska town, not yet inundated with the trappings of a modern fast-food world. Many of the storefronts are buildings which have stood serving the community for decades.

The Hamilton County Courthouse located in the center of town, is one of the most beautiful and unique courthouses in the entire state, and, some would say, the nation. The building was constructed in 1895, and still contains the original tile floors and other architectural wonders. Hard to believe that this stately building, with corner spires and built with red limestone, was built for under $60,000—less than the cost of two legislators' salaries. The grounds are pristine and maintained in a similar fashion to the way they first were groomed. Take time to walk around inside.

The Plainsman Museum, at 210 16th Street is one of the more interesting and exciting museums in the area. The Plainsman contains the consolidated collections of several museums, and has under its roof several complete historic buildings, early farm equipment and a vast doll collection. The new museum, dedicated during the nation's bicentennial, contains murals, exhibits, artifacts tracing the area's history from the Indians, the early Spanish explorers, through the modern day. In addition there is a courteous staff to assist the visitor. Among special treats in the Plainsman Museum is an exhibit on Dr. Harold Edgerton, the inventor of the strobe light, inductee into the National Inventors' Hall of Fame and member of the National Academy of Arts and Sciences. In addition to Dr. Edgerton's many other accomplishments, he helped to develop the underwater photography techniques used by oceanographer Jacques Cousteau.

One mile (14 miles.)

Turn north and go for one mile. Turn west and go for another one and a half miles to the Spafford grave, located in a grove of trees. The inscription once read:

"Rev. S.W. Spafford Died Nov. 9, 1876 Aged 47 years 8 months 11 days.

Farewell my wife my children all
From you a father, Christ doth call,
Mourn not for me, it is in vain,
To call me to your sight again.
—Lincoln Marble Works."

It is not known if the Lincoln Marble Works wrote any other poetry as well.

Fourteen miles (5 miles.)

Just before the highway crosses the Platte River it crosses the route of the Nebraska City Cutoff of the Oregon Trail. This road went from Nebraska City west to the Oregon Trail 20 miles west of here.

Five miles (163 miles.)

Grand Island. Junction of US Highways 30, 34, 281 and State Highway 2.

For information about Grand Island, please see entry for US Highway 30.

US Highway 34 joins US 281 for 17 miles south, and then for another 145 west it joins US 6. For information about sites along 34 until west of McCook, please consult the entry for US Highway 281 and US Highway 6.

For information about State Highway 2, US Highway 30, US Highway 281 or Interstate 80, please see entries for those routes.

US Highway 34 joins US Highway 6 for the next 163 miles. For information about sites for this distance, please see the entry for US Highway 6

One hundred sixty three miles (4 1/2 miles.)

Junction with US Highway 6. From here east to Hastings, US

34 and US 6 are joined. From Hastings to Grand Island US 34 and US 281 are joined. For information about this route, please see entry for US Highway 6 and US Highway 281.

Four and a half miles (4 miles.)

Massacre Canyon. In 1873 the Sioux and the Pawnee, long-time rivals and enemies, had one of the worst, and last of their many battles. The government had designated particular hunting grounds for each tribe, but the designation favored the Pawnee who were more friendly toward the whites. In 1873 the Pawnee were coming up the Republican River on a massive buffalo hunt. Three hundred warriors and 400 women and children were moving into Sioux territory. The warriors noticed spots on a far hillside up the Frenchman River and, at first thinking it was a large herd of buffalo, rode toward it.

As they approached, Sioux and Brule warriors, all wrapped in buffalo robes, threw off their disguises and attacked the Pawnee. The Pawnee were taken completely by surprise. The women and children hid in a ravine and the Pawnee warriors counter attacked. But then additional Sioux appeared and attacked the Pawnee from behind. The lone white witness, a man named Williamson, who had helped to guide the Pawneee on the hunt, raised a white flag and rode toward the Sioux. His horse was shot out from under him.

The Pawnee women, in the ravine, began their death chants. The Pawnee fled back down the Frenchman toward the Republican and it is here, in this narrow canyon, that the bloodiest of the fighting took place.

Soldiers from Ft. McPherson arrived too late to save most of the Pawnee. The Pawnee returned to their government lands north along the Loup and never returned to their traditional lands along the Republican again.

In the cleanup, 65 bodies were buried in one grave alone. This battle ended hostilities and opened the land to cattlemen. The first ranches in Nebraska were in this area. They were started shortly after the graves had been dug.

Four miles (3 miles.)

Trenton. Location of various reunions of survivors of the the battle at Massacre Canyon. In 1925, the 50th anniversary of the battle, many Sioux and Pawnee gathered here for a week of festivities.

Junction with State Highway 25. For more information on this area, please see entry for State Highway 25.

Three miles (19 miles.)

In 1881 trouble was brewing between the cattlemen and the homesteaders. The cattlemen, encouraged by the release of a cowboy in Custer Co. who had killed a homesteader, began to pressure the homesteaders. For their part the homesteaders, used to considering the cattle they found stranded from the cattle drives as their property, were unwilling to give up their habits. A couple of cowboys approached a homesteader near here and demanded the return of a cow. The homesteader refused, but added that he would give it up if the cowboys would go to the justice of the peace near by and get an order from him. The cowboys said "there aint no law in these parts" and said they would be back with a hanging rope. A mob was formed near the mouth of the Stinking Water to teach the homesteaders a lesson. Although the cowboys gave up the idea for a lynching. the hostilities between the two factions grew.

Twenty two miles (3 miles.)

Three miles east of Max was the town of Sandwich, which once was going to be the metropolis of Dundy County, but died when a local rancher would not sell land needed to expand the town. Most every building was moved to a new location, many to Max, and others to local ranches. The town lasted from 1881 until the last building was moved in 1955.

South of here in 1899 a 19 year old transient, seeing himself as a latter day Billy the Kid, killed a local rancher for $20, threw the body in the river and then drove a herd of cattle across everything in order to hide the evidence. The victim's false teeth and broken eye glasses were found, however, and the murderer arrested. He was convicted and sent to prison where he died while attempting to make a break.

Three miles (2 miles.)

Max. The Max Public Park is only a faint reminder of its once grand canopy of trees, most of which have fallen in the years since it was first designated as a park in the 1920s.

When the dust storms rolled through here in the 1930s it was considered a good day if you could eat an entire meal before you were able to write your name in the dust that collected on your plate. Folks cleaned up their houses just enough to make them livable before the next storm came through a few days later.

In 1933, on May 26, a freak storm turned day into night. A thick tornado cloud, combined with a dust storm, passed over this area. However, most people had no phones or radios and were not aware what was causing so strange a phenomenon. It is generally believed that the good Lord hadn't heard from as many Dundy County residents before or since that strange day.

North of here are the deep canyon lands of Nebraska. Inquire locally as to the road conditions in the area.

Two miles (6 miles.)

At this spot, over one hundred years ago something fell from the sky. On the afternoon of June 6, 1884 a cowboy by the name of John Ellis and his boys were working some cattle near here when a strange object came out of the sky and roared over their heads. It hit the ground and skimmed over the prairie for a mile before disappearing into a wash.

The cowboys rode to the wash. There they found metal machinery all over the ground. The metal was hot. The prairie grass was on fire.

A kind of vehicle was burning. It had a long, cylindrical shape. As the cowboys watched its bright light, their faces were scorched red.

The next day people came to the site and the area was combed. The vehicle was gone, but pieces of metal were found and collected. The story was carried in the weekly newspaper in Holdrege and in the Lincoln *Journal* on June 8.

There are, of course, many people who do not believe the story, and others who claim it is yet another UFO story neglected and laughed at by skeptics.

Six miles (10 miles.)

Benkelman.

Junction with State Highway 61. Please see that entry for sites along its route.

Benkelman was originally known as Collinsville and came into being as a railroad town and shipping point for the early cattle business.

Benkelman is the county seat, and at under 1,500 souls, the largest population center between here and McCook. However, Dundy County has seen better days and in 1925 reached its peak in population.

While Hiawatha, Ough and Allston were bickering and fighting over which town was to get the county seat, the citizens of Benkelman quietly built a county courthouse and the commissioners simply moved in. The current courthouse was built in 1918.

Benkelman is home to the active Dundy County Historical Society and their fine Dundy County Museum located in the old Moorehouse Hospital. It includes 13 rooms of exhibits and many area historical items from the pioneer and war years.

North of the business district, near the American Legion building, is a house which once was a fine Hotel known as Scotts. It was built in 1879. The Scotts was known for its lavish parties which included dances often lasting a week.

The Ough Hotel was the first brick hotel, and the first building in Benkelman to have steam heat. It was built in 1908.

A terrible fire of undetermined origin burned half of Benkelman to the ground in 1911.

Benkelman was the birthplace of an actor by the name of Ward Bond who got to know John Wayne before The Duke made it big. When Wayne got to Hollywood, he remembered his friend Bond and got Bond parts in movies. Bond's most famous roles were in *Gone With the Wind,* and as the Wagon Master on the 1960 TV series *Wagon Train.*

Just east of town is the Benkelman Fish Hatchery.

North of town a small lake provides a pleasing atmosphere for locals.

Just south of the town is the confluence of the north and south forks of the Republican River. This place, known for years simply as the Forks, has been an important gathering spot for centuries.

For a long while the Forks was a logical meeting place for tribes of the northern lands to meet and trade with tribes from the south.

In July of 1867 George Armstrong Custer camped at the

Forks when he was attacked by Pawnee Killer's band of Sioux. Later 40 of Custer's troops under the command of a captain named Hamilton pursued the war party northwest for seven miles when they were led into an ambush. Most of the men escaped. Later still, Lt. Kidder was overwhelmed by Pawnee Killer's band near Beaver Creek, ten miles west of here and was killed. The trail through here, which roughly followed the same route as State 61 now follows, was for years known as Custer's Trail, or Buffalo Hunters' Trail.

The Leavenworth/Pike's Peak Stage route came through the forks and then traveled on the south fork of the Republican to Denver.

One of the last Indian raids in this part of the country took place just south of here when the Cheyenne Dull Knife and his followers raided several ranches. Dull Knife was fleeing the Army that was ordered to send him and his band to Oklahoma. Dull Knife camped at the Forks as well.

Ten miles (7 miles.)

Parks. Parks has been a settlement for a long while, starting off in the 1880s as a community and store for local ranchers. It was named after a local cowboy. It grew until the late 1920s when drought, grasshoppers, bad winters and a bad economy stunted and reversed its growth.

North of here on Rock Creek Dundy County's first sheep ranch was started in the summer of 1880. When nearly all of the sheep died in the cold of the first winter the owner left the county on foot, never to return again.

Parks, like so many other towns along the Republican, suffered greatly in the flood of 1935 when a wall of water rushed down the Republican Valley. Children were torn from their parents' arms, houses were swept away and entire towns were destroyed. In Parks the rush of the water could be heard miles away. Some hog barns which were caught up by the flood were found in Cambridge, 70 miles downriver.

Near here is "Tater Hill" a tall hill where cowboys would go to spot stray cattle during the cattle drive days. They roasted potatoes on the hill, hence the name.

Ask locally for directions to the site of the Pikes Peak Stage Coach route and the stations along its way.

Twelve miles north and three miles west of Parks was the town of Lux, not much more than a post office and local stopping place. The post office closed in 1920. In 1934 a couple of local young men stole a car in Colorado and had hidden it in a valley just west of the post office. A neighbor called the sheriff, Chester Crosby, when he noticed that everyone on the ranch was armed. Sheriff Crosby got together a posse, drove out to the ranch and a gun battle erupted. The sheriff was shot in the arm, and in return shot and killed one of the men. The others surrendered and a slice of the Bonnie and Clyde days ended.

Five miles north of the Lux site is the site of the town of Rollwitz, which was named after a pioneer from Germany. This small town was centered around a church and a school. It was born of the Kinkaid era of homesteaders around 1904. In 1943 a hailstorm and tornado destroyed a 25 mile area. The storm, added to the troubled times of the 1930s and just about ended the community. An unmarked cemetery and old buildings, now moved and used as tool sheds, houses and barns on neighboring ranches, are the chief remnants of the town.

Many ranches in this area still have the original sod buildings, and many of them are used as sheds yet today.

Ten miles northwest of Parks is a state fish hatchery which provides trout for many Nebraska streams. Located here is the Rock Creek State Recreation Area which is a fine and comfortable place to give one the feel of this beautiful and seldom visited part of the state.

Several miles south of Parks are the remains of a dugout hole in a cliff known as Horse Thief Cave because the gentlemen who lived there in 1890 were suspected of being horse and cattle thieves. Finally, when it got too hot for them, these gentlemen moved on to the Dakotas.

Seven miles (4 miles.)
The Texas Cattle Trail, a meandering route at best, crossed near here. Some cowboys followed the Beaver River up from the south until it joined with the Republican for one route north.

The first large cattle ranches in Dundy County started in the early 1870s with cattle brought up from Texas on this trail.

Many early day cattlemen, fearing the end of their way of life when the rash of homesteaders began in the 1880s, and later with the Kinkaiders in the early 1910s, had their cowboys stake out homesteads so that their ranch lands would remain open and fenceless. Ranches up to 20,000 acres were secured by these means.

In 1902, while helping to build the road that would one day become US 34, Frank Tecker's plow uncovered two caskets on the downslope of Trail Canyon. One was an adult and the other was a child with "the most beautiful red hair covering his skull. There was a silk string tie with a metal cross, and two China vases about three inches high, one at each shoulder." There was no marker, and to this day those graves remained unmarked and unknown on this hillside.

One mile south in the Trail Canyon was the site of a large Sioux village in 1859.

Near this area were a trading post and the cabin of a herd checker. The herd checker helped to sort out the cattle belonging to other trail drives that had strayed. Later drives would pick up the strays as a courtesy and take them to this\point for sorting.

Four miles (4 miles.)
Haigler.
Just west of town, after crossing the Arikaree River is the approximate site of the dugout and headquarters of Jake Haigler's Three Bar Ranch. He stocked his ranch, opened a post office, organized Dundy County, got a town named after him and eventually moved to Arizona taking 5,000 head of cattle with him to the south, surprising untold numbers of cowboys who were driving their cattle north. When Jake operated the post office, he simply flipped letters into wooden boxes marked with the general directions of the compass. Jake would give the entire box to any rider who happened to stop by and was headed in the right direction.
At this spot a battle took place between the Arapahoe and Sioux. A few hundred yards west is the site of a mass Indian burial, probably dating from that battle.
Before that this was the camping grounds of the prehistoric Yuma Tribe which existed about 10,000 years ago.

McKay's Garage in Haigler was once a livery stable when such conveniences were needed in every town.

The school was built in 1914.

At the junction of Porter Ave. and US 34 the town well once stood for decades, serving the locals with cool and nonalkaline water.

West of Haigler the green croplands attest to the early pioneer's ability to build and maintain a canal irrigation system. In 1917 Colorado sued the founders claiming that water could not be diverted from one state to serve the needs of another. The Supreme Court ruled in favor of the Nebraska pioneers and established an important water rights precedence.

The first Democratic candidate for governor of Nebraska was from Haigler. (He lost.)

Four miles (7 miles.)
Sanborn. An ancient town, now a skeleton of its former glory days. A few old brick buildings in the area date back to the town's founding days.

South of Sanborn on backroads is a marker where Colorado, Kansas and Nebraska come together. You can stand there and then tell people you were in three states at one time, but since you are so close no one will be the wiser if you want to just stay here and claim you were in three at once.

Seven miles (0 miles.)
Colorado border.

Although the Interstate is possibly the state's busiest high-way, the information that follows in this description only sketches about 10 percent of the sights and sounds available within a few miles of its course. The reason for this is that most travelers who chose to go via the Interstate do so for speed. They wish simply to get from here to there. Consequently, the traveler wishing to see the most interesting and beautiful places in the state should get off the Interstate and take some time.

You may locate sites near the Interstate by checking in the entry for the various roads that intersect I-80.

Exit 454A.

Rosenblatt Stadium, home of the College World Series, and Omaha's Triple A team the Royals.

Henry Doorley Zoo. A natural environment zoo with the largest collection of species for many miles.

Interstate 80

A mile beyond this exit is the home of Falstaff Beer north of the Interstate. This is Omaha's local beer, brewed here for a century.

Exit 452.

Omaha.

Nebraska's largest city with many activities for both the small town lover and the urbanite. For more information on Omaha please see entry for US Highway 75.

Junction with US Highways 75, 275 and 6. Please see entries for those highways for further information about sites along their routes.

At the Travel Information Center is one of the unique features of Interstate 80 in Nebraska. The steel-plate sculture, "Praxis," by Dan Peragine is one of several sculptures commissioned for the state's celebration of the national Bicentennial.

The idea was proposed in 1973 and the Nebraska Bicentennial Commission made a $100,000 grant to start the program off. Further funding came from the Nebraska Arts Council and the Nebraska Art Association as well as from the National Endowment for the Arts. Although these grants were generous, a full $350,000 of the eventual $500,000 cost was raised by Nebraska businesses. The sculptures, which number nine, but growing, are all abstract, which still causes quite an uproar by some locals who insist that art should look like something. On the other side there are those who maintain these sculptures do look like something: they look like Art.

Other sculptures are located at:

Eastbound at the Platte River crossing between Lincoln and Omaha; Eastbound at the Blue River Crossing near Milford; Eastbound at the Grand Island Rest Area. This one had the added trouble of being considered too erotic for public display.

Westbound at the rest area near the York exchange; Westbound at the Kearney rest area; Westbound at the Brady rest area; Westbound at the Ogallala rest area; Westbound at the Sidney rest area.

Exit 451.

The stockyards. Omaha was made what it is today by the stockyards where cattle from all over the West are brought for transport to other places. In the old days the cattle were bought and sold here as well. While the stockyards are not as vast as they were in bygone days (some people thank their noses this is so) they are still quite impressive.

Exit 450.

University of Nebraska at Omaha.

The train tracks south of the Interstate carry the numberless coal trains through the state of Nebraska. These trains, usually 60 to 80 cars long, rumble eastward carry coal to the factories in Ohio and Pennsylvania, and westward, and empty, to the coal fields of Wyoming and Montana.

Exit 445.

Junction with Interstate 680, which circles the outside of Omaha. Take this to Boystown. See description for Omaha in the entry for US Highway 75 for more information.

Exit 440.

Papillion is **five miles east**.

Don't for a moment confuse this town as a suburb of nearby Omaha. Papillion not only has its own unique and interesting history but is proud not to even be in the same county as Omaha.

Named for the Papio Creek and the high hill nearby which was first described by an early pioneer. He looked off to the north, where today the look-alike houses of the city of Omaha march ever closer: "As far as the eye could see was a wide expanse of rolling prairie, unmolested by the hand of Man. It lay in silent slumber just as it was left at Creation. No sign of human life was visible. It was still. The same death-like stillness as at the beginning of time."

The present town is a grandchild of the older Papillion City, a site about 2 1/2 miles northeast of here.

The house at 4th and Monroe was the location of the home of the grandson of Papillion's founders, the Beadles.

The building at the southeast corner of 3rd and Jefferson was the Wilcox Hotel, and early landmark dating back to the 1880s.

The railroad station is still standing with little change from the way it looked in its prime, except that the insides have been torn out and it is mainly used for storage today.

The Stautter home is one of the few buildings left from an earlier era with a German influence. The Sarpy County Historical Society has restored the house to its original beauty and it is open to the public. The City Hall building is the original courthouse and many of the old furnishings such as desks, cabinets and counters are still in use.

Papillion was visited by gypsies as well as Indians around the turn of the century. The gypsies would camp outside of town and children were warned not to go near them for they were known for stealing children.

Papillion had a large mill, which for a time was water-powered by the Papio Creek. The creek had power too, it often flooded, causing the dirt streets of the town to turn to quagmires.

A flood in 1903 nearly ruined the town's newspaper which had offices in the basement of the bank. In 1959 a devastating flood put the entire town under water and wiped out the Washington Street bridge.

In 1964 more than 5 inches of rain fell one afternoon on already soaked ground. A wave of water swept through the business district on June 16th. Trees, homes, cars and buildings were swept away and tossed about. Over $5 million of damage was done in the Papio Basin, and several lives were lost. Hailstones fell so thick that they could still be found 24 hours later.

Offut and SAC are **seven miles to the east** of Papillion. Please see the entry for US Highway 75 for more information about other sites in this area. The unusual coffeepot water tower near this exit excites comments from everyone.

Exit 439.

Exit for Bellevue. Please see entry for US Highway 75 for information about this historic Nebraska town.

Crossing the Platte River. Between Exits 432 and 420.

The Platte is the true Nebraska River. It was the path that humankind took westward for centuries. It started with the Indians who used the river as a road west, and then the French fur trappers. The pioneers used the Platte as a constant landmark for the Pony Express, the Oregon and Mormon Trails, all of which follow its banks. The designers of Interstate 80 knew a good thing when they saw it. The Interstate follows the Platte through all of Nebraska. Even many commercial airliners pass across the state in sight of the blue ribbon of the Platte.

The Platte was always referred to as being a mile wide and an inch deep, and at this crossing that is pretty true.

Three miles north of here is where one of the most famous UFO sightings ever took place. A police officer claimed he saw a spacecraft. Under hypnosis he revealed that he had been taken inside the craft and asked a number of questions. For the complete story see entry for US Highway 6.

Eastbound, two miles west of the Platte River.

Platte River Crossing Rest Area.

This rest area contains the sculpture Memorial to the American Bandshell by Richard Field, and is one of several sculptures at rest areas along the Interstate.

The idea for the sculptures was proposed in 1973 and the Nebraska Bicentennial Commission made a $100,000 grant to start the program off. Further funding came from the Nebraska Arts Council and the Nebraska Art Association as well as from the National Endowment for the Arts. Although these grants were generous, a full $350,000 of the eventual $500,000 cost was raised by Nebraska businesses.

The sculptures, which number nine, but growing, are all abstract, which still causes quite an uproar by some locals who insist that art should look like something. On the other side there are those who maintain these sculptures do look like something: they look like Art.

Other sculptures are located at:

The Nebraska/Omaha Travel Information Center near the intersection of I-80 and US Highways 73/75; Eastbound at the Blue River Crossing near Milford; Eastbound at the Grand Island Rest area. This one had the added trouble of being considered too erotic for public display.

Westbound at the rest area near the York exchange; Westbound at the Kearney rest area; Westbound at the Brady rest area; Westbound at the Ogallala rest area; Westbound at the Sidney rest area.

Rest Stops between Omaha and Lincoln.

There was a plan at one time to build a gigantic arch over the Interstate between two rest stops between Omaha and Lincoln. The arch would symbolize the gateway to the West and would contain information about Nebraska and the West. It was going to be the biggest arch ever. Cars would pass under it with their riders in awe. Well, not only the Interstate, but the air above the Interstate is under Federal jurisdiction and they vetoed the idea.

Exit 420.

Take this exit to get to the Platte River State Park. In this area, along Camp Creek and other small streams, the earliest inhabitants of the state, known usually as the Nebraska Culture, camped and built their earth houses. The culture probably flourished about 1,000 years ago. The Nebraska Historical Society has done much research on the culture. Their museum is located in Lincoln.

Exit 405.

Junction with US Highway 77. Please see that entry for sites along this road. Many towns in this area were named by the Union Pacific Railroad as it moved west in the 1870s and 80s. Near here was the town of Arbor, now a ghost town.

The green signs you see all along the Interstate that advertise local attractions were a part of the original plans for the Interstate through Nebraska. The signs are made to look similar to the official roadside signs of the Interstate system. They advertise only a tiny part of the vast attractions available to the traveler along Interstate 80.

Exit 401.

Lincoln. The state capitol and home of the University of Nebraska. Junction with State Highway 2, and US Highways 77, 34 and 6. Please see those entries for more information about sites along their routes.

Exit 388.

This exit is at the top of a hill created by a glacier during the ice age. The sand and boulders along the glacier's edge were deposited behind as it melted leaving this hill.

Exit 382.

The church at the Milford exit is the First Lutheran Church first built in Stapleton in 1882 and later moved to this spot. For more information about sites in this area, please see the entry for State Highway 15.

Eastbound. Rest area between exits 379 and 382.

The Eastbound Rest Area at the Blue River contains one of several sculptures located at rest areas along the Interstate in Nebraska. This sculpture is called "Arrival" and was created by artist Paul Von Ringelheim. The idea for the sculptures was proposed in 1973 and the Nebraska Bicentennial Commission made a $100,000 grant to start the program off. Further funding came from the Nebraska Arts Council and the Nebraska Art Association as well as from the National Endowment for the Arts. Although these grants were generous, a full $350,000 of the eventual $500,000 cost was raised by

Nebraska businesses.

The sculptures, which number nine, but growing, are all abstract, which still causes quite an uproar by some locals who insist that art should look like something. On the other side there are those who maintain these sculptures do look like something: they look like Art.

Other sculptures are located at:

The Nebraska/Omaha Travel Information Center near the intersection of I-80 and US Highways 73/75; Eastbound at the Platte River crossing between Lincoln and Omaha; Eastbound at the Grand Island Rest area. This one had the added trouble of being considered too erotic for public display.

Westbound at the rest area near the York exchange; Westbound at the Kearney rest area; Westbound at the Brady rest area; Westbound at the Ogallala rest area; Westbound at the Sidney rest area.

Exit 379.

Seward County's earliest residents were the prehistoric Indians who predated the Sioux, Otoe, Pawnee and Omaha who lived in the area when the white man finally arrived. Although there is no evidence that the Spanish explorer Coronado ever made it as far north as Nebraska, Seward residents feel they have as much claim to the distinction as anyone. In 1500 Coronado reported a storm that dropped 8 to 10 inches of rain and dropped hailstones "as large as porringers."

Originally the county was named Greene, after a well-known Senator from Missouri, but after the start of the Civil War the name changed to honor the Yankee Secretary of State, William Seward.

Among many other things, Seward is the home of the state's "official" July Fourth celebration.

Junction with State Highway 15. Please see that entry for more information about sites in this area.

Exit 369.

South to Beaver Crossing. Beaver Crossing is located on the Nebraska City Cut Off Trail which led from Nebraska City to join up with the Oregon Trail west of Hastings. This location was a popular camping spot for pioneers moving west along the Trail. The town's name came from the fact that this spot was considered one of the finer places to cross the Blue River. The fishing here is good, ask locally for the best holes.

Interstate 80

An early-day farmer convinced many others to plant lilies and iris and many of those beautiful flowers are still growing wild in the area.

Westbound rest stop between exits 360 and 353.

At the rest area near York is one of several roadside sculptures along Interstate 80.

This impressive stone sculpture, "Crossing the Plains" by Bradford Graves, is arranged along the four points of the compass.

The idea for the sculptures was proposed in 1973 and the Nebraska Bicentennial Commission made a $100,000 grant to start the program off. Further funding came from the Nebraska Arts Council and the Nebraska Art Association as well as from the National Endowment for the Arts. Although these grants were generous, a full $350,000 of the eventual $500,000 cost was raised by Nebraska businesses.

The sculptures, which number nine, but growing, are all abstract, which still causes quite an uproar by some locals who insist that art should look like something. On the other side there are those who maintain these sculptures do look like something: they look like Art.

Other sculptures are at:

The Nebraska/Omaha Travel Information Center near the intersection of I-80 and US Highways 73/75; Eastbound at the Platte River crossing between Lincoln and Omaha; Eastbound at the Blue River Crossing near Milford; Eastbound at the Grand Island Rest area. This one had the added trouble of being considered too erotic for public display.

Westbound at the Kearney rest area; Westbound at the Brady rest area; Westbound at the Ogallala rest area; Westbound at the Sidney rest area.

Also located at this rest area is a time capsule which was buried on October 5, 1977. It is to be opened on the Fourth of July, 2076, and contains local, state and national bicentennial publications and newspapers, and books about York County.

Exit 353.

One mile north *the Nebraska City Cutoff of the Oregon Trail crosses US Highway 81. The Trail was an alternate route west, and serviced pioneers headed west from Missouri. The Cutoff joined the Oregon Trail in central Nebraska. Junction with US Highway 81. See* *that entry for information about sites in this area.*

Anna Bemis Palmer Museum with exhibits on pioneer life is in York. Take exit 353 to 211 E. 7th.

Exit 342.

An alternative route to the Oregon Trail, known by many names including the Nebraska City Cutoff ran through this part of the state. Along its route were many stations which operated like the motels and filling stations of today. The first of these stations to be established in this area was located one and a half miles north of the Henderson exit. Known as Porcupine Ranch, it was started in 1863 by a man named Benjamin Lushbaugh, who was an Indian agent for the Pawnee.

Later the ranch served as a relay station for the Overland Stage route. The buildings were built into sides of hills and made from sod. The ranch provided food for travelers, had some items for sale, and usually could make basic repairs to equipment.

A historical marker designates the location of the Porcupine Ranch.

Exit 332.

Aurora is home of the fine Plainsman Museum, three miles north on State Highway 14. For more information about sites in this area please see the entry for State Highway 14.

Eastbound rest stop between exits 312 and 318.

Erma's Desire, one of several sculptures along the Interstate through the state, is at this cozy rest area.

The project was controversial, but Erma seemed to spark the greatest debate in the state when it was unveiled. Some saw the spires of rusting steel as overly erotic and suggestive. Others saw them simply as rusty steel spires. Still others saw them as a work of art by John Raimondi. The idea for the roadside sculptures was proposed in 1973 and the Nebraska Bicentennial Commission made a $100,000 grant to start the program off. Further funding came from the Nebraska Arts Council and the Nebraska Art Association as well as from the National Endowment for the Arts. Although these grants were generous, a full $350,000 of the eventual $500,000 cost was raised by Nebraska businesses.

The sculptures, which number nine, but growing, are all abstract, which still causes quite an uproar by some locals who insist that art should look like something. On the other side there are those who maintain these sculptures do look like something: they look like Art.

Other sculptures are at:

The Nebraska/Omaha Travel Information Center near the intersection of I-80 and US Highways 73/75; Eastbound at the Platte River crossing between Lincoln and Omaha; Eastbound at the Blue River Crossing near Milford.

Westbound at the rest area near the York exchange; Westbound at the Kearney rest area; Westbound at the Brady rest area; Westbound at the Ogallala rest area; Westbound at the Sidney rest area.

Exit 312.

North: Grand Island. Among the many fine items in this area is the Sturh Museum, one of the finest in the Midwest.

Also Mormon Island State Wayside Area and Crane Habitat Trust for fishing, swimming and watching sandhill cranes migrate.

Please see entries for US Highway 34, 30, and 281 and State Highway 2 for more information about the sites in this area.

South: Hastings. The museum at US Highway 281 and 14th Street is a fine one. Please see the entries for US Highways 34, 6 and 281 for more information about Hastings and the other sites in this area.

Just two miles to the south of the exit, across the Platte River, is Doniphan.

Go west on county road at Doniphan, 1.8 miles, then take a right and go 2.4 miles to the site of the Campbell Graves. Five graves are located within the enclosure, most of them the Campbell family members who died during an Indian raid in July of 1867. The Sioux entered the Campbell home while the father was away, they killed one woman and her son, and kidnapped four children.

Some time later the government exchanged these hostages for $4,000 and a Sioux woman and her child who had been captured at Elm Creek. No one recorded the Sioux grievance which perpetrated the attack. Near here was the site of another Indian raid.

An English farmer, George Martin, displeased with the beetles of Liverpool, came to Nebraska and started a farm. Martin and his two sons were hauling hay one day when the Sioux appeared. They wounded Martin and chased the two boys who were riding on one horse. The Indians fired an arrow which passed through the boy in back, and entered the shoulder of his brother in front. The two boys were pinned together by the arrow. The boys fell from their horse and the horse tumbled over them. The Indians left them for dead, but they were later found and nursed to health by their parents.

Exit 300.

To Wood River. Please see entry for State Highway 11 for sites along that route.

Exit 285.

North to Windmill State Wayside Area with an exhibit of antique wind machines. Cool and shady.

Exit 279.

Minden exit.

You can't have traveled on the Interstate and not seen the signs for the Harold Warp Museum. There's a lot more to see as well. For a description of this and other fine locations in the area, please see the entry for US Highway 6 and State Highway 10.

Every surviving member of the whooping crane family passes through about a 30 mile bottleneck on their way north and south. The highest concentration along that stretch is between this exit and exit 272. One of the best places to view the 120 or so remaining whoopers and their grey sandhill cousins, is one mile south of this exit, across the Platte River.

Exit 272.

Every surviving member of the whooping crane family passes through about a 30 mile bottleneck on their way north and south. The highest concentration along that stretch is between this exit and exit 279.

The Frank House Mansion, built in 1889 and other attractions are in Kearney.

Exit here for Kearney and Ft. Kearny Historical Park. Please see State Highway 10 and US Highway 30 for more information.

Westbound rest stop between exits 272 and 263.

Westbound at the Kearney Rest Area is another of the several sculptures exhibited at various rest areas on Interstate 80 through Nebraska. "The Nebraska Wind Sculpture," by George Baker, gently swirls and turns in the wind. The stainless steel sculpture is the only kinetic one of the many that grace the road's rest areas.

The idea for the sculptures was proposed in 1973 and the

Nebraska Bicentennial Commission made a $100,000 grant to start the program off. Further funding came from the Nebraska Arts Council and the Nebraska Art Association as well as from the National Endowment for the Arts. Although these grants were generous, a full $350,000 of the eventual $500,000 cost was raised by Nebraska businesses.

The sculptures, which number nine, but growing, are all abstract, which still causes quite an uproar by some locals who insist that art should look like something. On the other side there are those who maintain these sculptures do look like something: they look like Art.

Other sculptures are at:

The Nebraska/Omaha Travel Information Center near the intersection of I-80 and US Highways 73/75; Eastbound at the Platte River crossing between Lincoln and Omaha; Eastbound at the Blue River Crossing near Milford; Eastbound at the Grand Island Rest area. This one had the added trouble of being considered too erotic for public display.

Westbound at the rest area near the York exchange; Westbound at the Brady rest area; Westbound at the Ogallala rest area; Westbound at the Sidney rest area.

Exit 257.

US Highway 183. Please see that entry for more information. North at this exit and then take the gravel road one mile east to Chevyland USA, an auto museum.

Exit 248.

The area around here was seriously affected by the great grasshopper plague of 1874 as entire farms were wiped out by the infestation. Grasshoppers literally swarmed in great dark clouds which blocked out the sun. They would descend on a field, their humming filling the air, devour every green plant to the ground and then move on. It was impossible to walk outside without crunching 10 or 20 bugs with each and every step.

The Oregon Trail and the Pony Express route are on the south bank of the Platte River, just south of the Interstate, and the Mormon Trail runs right alongside of the Interstate on the north from here, seven miles to the east.

Exit 237.

Lexington and junction with US Highway 283. One of the

state's largest and finest recreation areas, Johnson Lake is ten miles south. There is much to see in this area. Please see the entries for US Highway 283 and 30 for more information.

Exit 222.

Cozad. One of the state's most interesting places is the Robert Henri Museum and Historical Walkway. Henri was the son of the founder of Cozad, John Cozad. John Cozad was a bit of a gambler and roustabout. His son changed his name to avoid the negative publicity generated by his father, and, as Robert Henri became a well known artist in the early years of this century. He even founded a movement in modern art for his nontraditional realism called "the Ashcan School."

Exit 199.

Brady. One mile south, turn west and follow the exact route of the Oregon Trail by following the country roads as they zigzag westward. Watch for historical markers along the way and signs of the rut marks from the wagons on hillsides. This route will lead you to North Platte and back to the Interstate.

Westbound rest stop between exits 190 and 199.

Westbound at the Rest Area near Brady is "Nebraska Gateway," a stone sculpture by Anthony Padovano. One hundred thousand pounds of granite sit perched in the middle of shade trees. It is one of several sculptures along the Interstate.

The idea for the sculptures was proposed in 1973 and the Nebraska Bicentennial Commission made a $100,000 grant to start the program off. Further funding came from the Nebraska Arts Council and the Nebraska Art Association as well as from the National Endowment for the Arts. Although these grants were generous, a full $350,000 of the eventual $500,000 cost was raised by Nebraska businesses.

The sculptures, which number nine, but growing, are all abstract, which still causes quite an uproar by some locals who insist that art should look like something. On the other side there are those who maintain these sculptures do look like something: they look like Art.

Other sculptures are at:

The Nebraska/Omaha Travel Information Center near the intersection of I-80 and US Highways 73/75; Eastbound at the Platte River crossing between Lincoln and Omaha; Eastbound at the Blue

Interstate 80

River Crossing near Milford; Eastbound at the Grand Island Rest Area. This one had the added trouble of being considered too erotic for public display.

Westbound at the rest area near the York exchange; Westbound at the Kearney rest area;Westbound at the Ogallala rest area; Westbound at the Sidney rest area.

Exit 190.

Maxwell. You are entering the real West now.

To the north are the rugged and isolated sandhills, Nebraska's natural wonder. They cover nearly a third of the state.

Two miles south of the Interstate and then south one and a half miles to Fort McPherson National Cemetery. There seems there could be no more remote, or beautiful site for a cemetery of this vast size. This is one of the most comfortable and interesting places to get off the busy Interstate. Rest in the cool of the big shade trees.

Continue south from the cemetery for 1/2 mile to the site of Cottonwood Springs stage stop and Oregon Trail station. This was one of the most widely used stations on the Oregon Trail. A Fort McPherson once stood here as well.

West of here seven miles to a tall hill known as Sioux Lookout, which affords the best view of a wide area. The top of the hill and the trail up are public property. Ask locally for directions.

Exit 177.

North Platte.

North Platte has a rodeo every night of every summer. See Buffalo Bill Cody Museum for information.

Scouts' Rest Ranch which was built in 1878 by Buffalo Bill Cody is now a 65 acre state historical park. Items are on display from Cody's long life on the frontier as a scout, buffalo hunter and showman. His mansion has been preserved and you can get a glimpse of the hero himself by watching the film made by Thomas Edison of Cody in 1898.

There is a buffalo stew cookout going on most summer evenings, so for a taste of the Old West, the Rest Ranch is the place to be. Also in the summer is the Rough Riders Rodeo near the Ranch. The rodeo is run seven nights a week during summer.

North Platte is home to the gigantic Bailey Yards, the largest rail complex in the United States. The yard was named after the famed Union Pacific President, Edd Bailey, who grew up on a dry-farm homestead in eastern Colorado, got his first railroad job in his early teens and rose to become the president of one of the largest transportation companies in the world. Bailey Yard includes three locomotive repair shops and puts together trains bound for both coasts of America. There is a tour and an observation area.

North Platte is home to several museums including the Railroad Museum and the Western Heritage Museum.

The Lincoln County Historical Museum is located on the way to the Buffalo Bill Ranch off Buffalo Bill Ave. It contains many fine displays and a small library of local books. On the grounds are several buildings including a school, a barn and the first two story log house built in the county South on US Highway 83 one and one half miles.

Just west of here was the Cold Springs Pony Express Station. Continue south three miles to the turn-off for Mahoney Reservoir. Turn east and go five miles, and then north for three to the 3,200 foot hill known as Sioux Lookout (see above). For more information about locations in this area please see the entries for US Highways 83 and 30.

Exit 158.

Sutherland.

The rest areas at Sutherland between North Platte and Ogallala are located near O'Fallon's Bluff, an important site long the Oregon Trail. The Trail had to pass along the side of the bluff because of the small distance between it and the South Platte River.

A stage station was located here, as well as a military post. O'Fallon's Bluff was also an important landmark for the fur trappers headed through this area in the decades before the mass migration of the California Gold Rush, the Mormon migration and the Oregon Trail.

At the eastbound rest area the ruts from the wagon train can be seen about 500 feet behind the area. Wagon tires mark the area of indentation. It is estimated that between 1843 and 1863 250,000 people moved west along the Oregon Trail. Today Interstate 80, as well as the jet planes from California to New York, follow their route.

Please see entry for US Highway 30 for further information about sites in this area.

Exit 145.

Paxton.

Among the many sites in this area is Ole's Big Time Game Lounge in downtown Paxton. A lot of animals that used to be alive are hung up here. See entry for US Highway 30 for more information about sites in this area.

Exit 126.

Ogallala.

One half mile south of the exit are the remnants of the Oregon Trail. Gills Station, a Pony Express station and stage stop stood just west of State Highway 61. For more information about sites in this area please see the entry for State Highway 61.

Ogallala served as the terminus for many Texas cattle drives in the 1870s and 80s. Here the railroad would ship the cattle east, and the cowboys who had been on the trail for weeks would unwind. Once called the "Gomorrah of the Plains", its present-day role as a convenience stop for tourists makes it a show place for travelers through the state.

It is the gateway to Nebraska's largest lake, the gigantic Lake McConaughy a few miles north of town. The lake has over 100 miles of white sand beaches and plenty of good fishing and boating.

At Lewellen, north of Ogallala, Ash Hollow State Historical Park gives a portrait of the human inhabitants of the area for the last 10,000 years. The Ash Hollow Cave, which is here, is a site used by nomadic tribes thousands of years ago. In addition, the ruts of the Oregon Trail are still visible here, preserving the traces of a much later band of nomadic travelers.

Eastbound rest stop between exits 117 and 126.

This is one of the finest rest stops in the country for the tourist. It is here where the tourist can still see the ruts of the early day tourists, the pioneers who headed west over the Oregon Trail. The ruts are clearly marked and interpretive signs help explain the sights.

Also at the rest area for the **eastbound** traveler near Ogallala is one of the several sculptures which grace many of the rest areas along the Interstate in Nebraska.

"Over/Under" by Linda Howard is a nostalgic and graceful arch of suspended I-beams. Its beauty and simple design add delight to a stop here.

The sculptures were controversial, but little of the controversy centered on the fact that of all the sculptures in the project this is the only one by a woman. The idea for the roadside sculptures was proposed in 1973 and the Nebraska Bicentennial Commission made a $100,000 grant to start the program off. Further funding came from the Nebraska Arts Council and the Nebraska Art Association as well as from the National Endowment for the Arts. Although these grants were generous, a full $350,000 of the eventual $500,000 cost was raised by Nebraska businesses.

The sculptures, which number nine, but growing, are all abstract, which still causes quite an uproar by some locals who insist that art should look like something. On the other side there are those who maintain these sculptures do look like something: they look like Art.

Other sculptures are at:

The Nebraska/Omaha Travel Information Center near the intersection of I-80 and US Highways 73/75; Eastbound at the Platte River crossing between Lincoln and Omaha; Eastbound at the Blue River Crossing near Milford; Eastbound at the Grand Island Rest area. This one had the added trouble of being considered too erotic for public display.

Westbound at the rest area near the York exchange; Westbound at the Kearney rest area; Westbound at the Brady rest area; Westbound at the Sidney rest area.

Exit 76.

Lodgepole. Just north of the interchange the access road crosses the Pony Express route. Another half mile north and it crosses the Oregon Trail. Lodgepole has a nice museum.

Lodgepole Wayside area commemorates the contribution of the Union Pacific Railroad. Near here is one of the state's "highest points" this one is south and register's 5,426 feet. At least two other "highest points" exist in the state considered flat by many people. One is near the point where Colorado Wyoming and Nebraska join and another is north of Kimball in Banner County.

Westbound rest stop between exits 69 and 59.

For Westbound travelers the rest area near Sidney features the sculpture "Roadway Confluence" by Hans Van de Bovenkamp. The aluminum structure rises up from the grasslands of western Nebraska and is one of a series of sculptures along the Interrerstate.

The idea for the sculptures was proposed in 1973 and the Nebraska Bicentennial Commission made a $100,000 grant to start the program off. Further funding came from the Nebraska Arts Council and the Nebraska Art Association as well as from the National Endowment for the Arts. Although these grants were generous, a full $350,000 of the eventual $500,000 cost was raised by Nebraska businesses.

The sculptures, which number nine, but growing, are all

abstract, which still causes quite an uproar by some locals who insist that art should look like something. On the other side there are those who maintain these sculptures do look like something: they look like Art.

Other sculptures are at:

The Nebraska/Omaha Travel Information Center near the intersection of I-80 and US Highways 73/75; Eastbound at the Platte River crossing between Lincoln and Omaha; Eastbound at the Blue River Crossing near Milford; Eastbound at the Grand Island Rest area. This one had the added trouble of being considered too erotic for public display. Eastbound at the Ogallala rest area.

Westbound at the rest area near the York exchange; Westbound at the Kearney rest area; Westbound at the Brady rest area.

Exit 59.

Sidney.

For more information about the sites and sights in this area, please see entries for US Highway 30 and 385.

Legion Park is the perfect place for a walk or a nap under shady trees. It includes a public swimming pool, tennis courts and playground equipment. Ft. Sidney was established to protect workers building the Union Pacific railroad westward. With the discovery of gold in the Black Hills the fort expanded and became the starting point of the infamous Deadwood-Sidney Trail.

Ft. Sidney, which many claim is haunted by the spirit of a woman who killed herself, is preserved and offers many exhibits for inspection.

Exit 38.

Potter at Exit 38 features Buffalo Bend, a musical stage show of renown. It is performed every weekend from June through August.

Exit 20.

Kimball.

Those oil wells spotting the horizon help keep this area going, although ranching is still important to the citizens. If you can't see an oil well, you are probably looking at a site of an Intercontinental Ballistic Missile. This area has the highest concentration of ICBMs of anywhere in the world. The Kimball Recreation Area includes a golf course, shuffleboard and tennis.

Stop off here instead of one of those cold rest stops. Oliver Reservoir offers swimming and boating and a cool place to pull off the road before leaving the state for hot and dry Wyoming. Every once in a while folks who live in Nebraska's Panhandle start to talk about how the government way the heck over in Lincoln doesn't pay them much mind. When this kind of talk gets especially loud it leads to the next subject: succession from the state. The Panhandlers often believe they would get better attention from Cheyenne if they were a part of Wyoming, or, the most radical of the talkers will add, their own brand new state.

Exit 1.
Welcome to Nebraska, if you are headed east. Your last chance to get off the Interstate and still be in the fine state of Nebraska, if you are headed west.

Pine Bluffs southwest of here is the point where Colorado, Wyoming and Nebraska join and near there is the highest point in the state at 5,524 feet.

NEBRASKA
U S
30

Zero miles (1 mile.)

US Highway 30 bridge on the Iowa/Nebraska border.

East of Blair on US Highway 30 to the DeSoto National Wildlife Refuge and the steamboat *Bertrand* museum and site. The museum is actually in Iowa, but since the location of the boat itself is in Nebraska, we will allow an entry here from someplace nice, but not quite as nice as Nebraska. The steamboat sank in 1865 loaded with cargo, was rediscovered in the river mud in the early 1970s and excavated. The museum contains items taken from the boat in nearly perfect condition.

One mile (18 miles.)

Blair. Blair is the center for a large area of historic and natural beauty. For more information about sites in this area, please see the entry for US Highway 73.

Eighteen miles (1 1/2 miles.)
    Fremont.
    Junction with US Highway 77.
    There is plenty to see and do in the Fremont area. For more information about Fremont and the surroundings, please see entry for US Highway 77.

One and a half miles (2 miles.)
    South here on Military Avenue to Beebe-McNeal Monument. This monument commemorates the Mormon Trail which passed near here, as well as two pioneer families.

Two miles (4 miles.)
    South one mile to Fremont Lakes State Park.
    You are not a citizen of Eastern Nebraska until you have spent a July afternoon spread-eagle on the beach at Fremont Lakes. The lazy sun beats down on you as you gaze about the scenery, both natural and humankind. When that lazy sun beats a bit too much, you simply plunge into the water for a moment's relief from the heat. Don't bother moving farther than the campgrounds where you can continue to laze away the hours until nightfall. After dark the park becomes a quiet and restful kind of place, a place for dreaming grand dreams of the future, and of an ideal life. There are many thousands of people across the world who do not pass a hot summer without remembering just such days of idle and innocent youth experienced at this very same wonderful spot.

Four miles (1/2 mile.)
    One half mile east of Ames.
    You are now entering the original Lincoln, Nebraska. First named Albion after the ranch and hotel once located here, the name changed to honor Abraham Lincoln. It was called Lincoln when the first post office was located here, around 1862, and later the name changed again to Timberville, after Timberville Lake which was near by. The town died in 1868 after Ames began. Through here passed the Mormon Trail, the Overland Trail, and the military road to Ft. Kearney.

One half mile (8 miles.)
    Ames.
    *Take county road and go **five miles north** out of Ames to the Jamestown site.*

Here was once the town of Jamestown, founded by two men named Jim. The town thrived from 1870-1880. Through here was the Indian trail that Major Stephen Long followed on his exploration voyage of the West. Near here the expedition camped for several nights in the early spring of 1820.

Eight miles (1 mile.)
>North Bend.
>Junction with State Highway 79.
>Settled in the 1850s by Scottish.

Go south here one half mile to the banks of the Platte on State Highway 79. To the west, Indian Peak is visible. Now, for most people that hill is not a peak, but for some local folks, and especially pioneers longing for the mountains of Oregon, that hill and its neighbors became a "peak" and a "range of peaks."

Indian Peak got its name for an incident which happened there long ago. In the early days a group of Indians came up the Platte to hunt for beaver. While at this place the chief's son became sick and died. They buried him on top of Indian Peak. In the spring they returned to take his body back to their homeland near Council Bluffs. For many years thereafter Indians passing this point would pile stones and bring food and water to feed the spirit of the dead boy.

For sites north out of North Bend on State Hiway 79, see entry for sites north out of Fremont on US Highway 77.

One mile (5 miles.)
In 1856 the first pioneers in the area settled near here. From this point to Schuyler (14 miles) the highway parallels both the Mormon and Overland Trails which were just south of the highway.

Five miles (9 miles.)
>*Go **north, five and a half miles.***
>*On this creek bed Major Stephen Long and his expedition camped on their way to the Rockies. Also a post office, with the enticing name of Purple Cane stood here in the 1870s. This was also the route of a well-traveled east-west Indian trail.*

Nine miles (17 miles.)
>Schuyler.
>Schuyler and Colfax County were named for Schuyler Colfax

who was the Vice President of the United States when both the town and the county were formed in 1869.

Schuyler, the county seat, was at one time a ripsnorting cowboy town. This town was the first town on the Union Pacific Railroad from which Texas cattle were shipped east.

The town still carries the predominately Irish and Bohemian make-up it has held since it was founded.

In the 1860s a wagon train moving west over the Mormon Trail through here reported that three or four Indians came riding over a hill, waving their arms and shouting.

The emigrants slowed their teams, but kept moving, their hands tightening on their guns "in case this meant war." It was the first time these travelers had ever seen Indians on their home land, and they were a bit frightened.

The Indians came closer and the whites began to understand what they were shouting was "tobacco." The Indians saw the pioneers and were running low on tobacco, so decided to ask for some.

The travelers told the Indians they didn't have any tobacco, and the Indians rode off. Now why this story survived over 120 years is unknown, but it seemed like an important thing to pass on.

The Old Oak Ballroom, a building some consider to rival the State Capitol for beauty, is located in Schuyler. It was built in 1937 by the WPA program. The gigantic roof-beams were cut from local oak, and native rock was used for the walls. The Ballroom is at the entrance to Community Park, on the Mormon Trail.

The Schuyler Historical Society is here as well as many fine small parks.

Seventeen miles (7 miles.)

Columbus. Junction with US Highway 81.

Columbus is the county seat of Platte County and was first settled by the whites in 1856 by folks from Columbus, Ohio.

The location near the confluence of the Loup and Platte Rivers made the town a natural stopping place for settlers moving west. Ezra Meeker and many Mormons paused here on their way west.

Two prominent Indian fighters from the 1870s were from Columbus—Major Frank North and Captain Luther North.

Columbus is the headquarters of the vast Loup River Public Power District. The dams, canals and electrical plants which cover a 200 mile area were a project of the 1930s. Today these projects provide some of the water recreation in the area.

In Columbus is Glurs Tavern, a National Historic Site. Glurs is believed to be the oldest tavern west of the Missouri River. The tavern has been in existence since 1879, and except for prohibition days, when it still served as an entertainment and social establishment, has been serving the thirsty of Platte County continuously. In 1887 Buffalo Bill strolled into the bar, whipped out a thousand dollar bill, and bought rounds for the house. The place boasts of its small playground for children, who are not required to show i.d. cards in order to have a root beer.

The Platte County Historical Society is centered in Columbus and their museum is at 29th Ave. and 16th Street.

One little-known fact of the area is that Buffalo Bill's Wild West Show held rehearsals for its first show at Columbus. The show was to open after a dress rehearsal near Grand Island, in May of 1883.

At the rehearsals Buffalo Bill insisted on authenticity, which, according to him, meant that the stage had to have half-wild and unbroken team of mules to power it. The hired Pawnees swooped into the arena on cue to "attack" the stagecoach. Onboard was the Mayor of Columbus, Pap Clothier and other dignitaries. The mules bolted at the rifle shots and began to stampede. The Indians, sensing they had some good actors to deal with, intensified their war whoops. Buffalo Bill joined in trying to stop the stage. The mayor, when he finally came out of the shredded stage, had to be restrained from beating Cody to a pulp.

The Mormon Trail followed the Loup River west of Columbus, and the Platte River eastward.

For more information about Columbus and the surrounding area, see entry for US Highway 81.

Seven miles (10 miles.)

Duncan. Small village between here and there.

For the next 22 miles the road closely parallels the Platte River, and offers fine views. Across the river was the Oxbow Trail and its route is still followed by an occasional county road.

Ten miles (14 miles.)

Junction with State Highway 39.

For information to the south, please see entry for US Highway 81.

North on State Highway 39 to the Mormon Trail and Genoa, site of the last great concentration of Pawnee ever held. For more information about this area, please see the entry for State Highway 14.

Fourteen miles (10 miles.)

Junction of State Highway 92.

Take 92 **east, 2 miles**.

Site of Pawnee hunting grounds and burial site. This used to be the banks of the Platte, 130 years ago, and once two Pawnee villages stood here. The dreaded and thoughtless enemy of all this American and Nebraskan history, the Pot Hunter, has been here many times and snuck away with arrowhead, pots and remnants of the once noble villages. It is a crime to remove any archeological artifacts from sites.

Ten miles (9 miles.)

Central City.

Central City was first named Lone Tree after the large cottonwood tree that grew, solitary and brave, on the bank of the Platte. This tree was on the Oxbow Trail, and the Overland Stage Route, which connected people who crossed at Council Bluffs, with the Oregon Trail. The tree died, mainly due to tourists carrying away bits and pieces of the trunk, and the town moved a few miles away to the present location of Central City. A concrete monument of the tree...supposedly designed to look a lot like the original trunk of the tree (all that stood for the last several years of its life) now marks the spot, **three miles** straight south out of Central City.

One of the earliest settlers of this area was the Hard family who originally settled in Virginia in 1654, moved to Wyoming, and finally settled in Merrick County after buying up a good part of the area. Hard's eleven ranches held as many as 50,000 cattle and 90,000 head of sheep. He got a lot of his livestock by sending men down to Mexico where they would procure (we mean "steal") cattle for his ranches. He also owned lumber mills, coal plants and feed outlets in as many as 25 Nebraska towns.

After the old man died, his family donated his 19 room house to the city of Central City for a hospital. The Merrick Manor Retirement Home is now on this site. The home is still there, in fine shape.

Central City was once called the irrigation capital of the world back in the days when people knew what an artesian well was and before they had heard of $30,000 Briggs and Stratton pumps.

The Merrick Museum is in Central City and is located in a fine old Victorian home. Some of the displays in the house are fixed to remind one of a home 100 years ago.

Central City is an important literary town for it is here, and in the area around the town, that America's foremost novelist of the last 30 years, Wright Morris, has set many of his finest novels.

When people who have read his works are talking about him, you are likely to hear things like "why this guy hasn't won a Nobel Prize, I'll never know..." Or, "this guy is the best writer in America, it is a shame he isn't known by everyone.."

One of this master's best novels is a work called, appropriately enough *Ceremony at Lone Tree.* If you are a tourist and haven't read this wonderful work, or any work by Morris, rush to your nearest library or bookstore and get something, anything he has written. If you are a Nebraskan and haven't read Wright Morris, shame on you!!!

Nine miles (14 miles.)

Near here the Mormon Trail rejoined the Platte River for its westward journey. It swung north here to take the easier route down the Loup River, eastward, until it rejoined the Platte near present-day Columbus.

Fourteen miles (2 miles.)

On the county line between Merrick and Hall Counties is a marker commemorating the California Overland Trail. This was also the Mormon Trail. The road was used both by the migrating Mormons, gold seekers and Oregon pioneers.

Three quarters of a mile south of here, and a mile east is the site of a sad battle. In 1868 two men had left their sons on the banks of the Platte in order to proceed to the Loup River to hunt elk. When the men returned a few days later they found that the boys had been killed, and all their supplies had been taken. This was during the Sioux hostilities, when the Sioux were making a last great stand to save their traditional homeland.

Two miles (5 miles.)

Grand Island.

Junction of US Highways 281 and 34 and State Highway 2.

This location was known for a long while for the large island which was formed when the nearby Platte River broke into a couple of channels around a large mass of land.

The fur trappers who wandered this way in the 1700s from Canada, used the island as a well-known site for navigation through the wilds. Members of John Jacob Astors' party reached "an island about seventy miles in length which they presumed to be Grand Isle." This was in 1812. Stephen Long, who explored the western states in

US Highway 30

1820 passed this way as well.

Soon after these early explorers the American fur trappers followed their trails to the fur streams of western Nebraska and Colorado. The famous explorer John Fremont wrote these words on September 19th 1842 while camped about where Grand Island is today: "I can not write because of the mosquitoes..."

Grand Island was formed when a "town company" set out from Iowa to find a spot to build a town that would make them some money. They wanted land to the west of the Missouri, and land that might eventually sit in a good spot for a rail line—the lifeblood of pioneer communities.

A group of settlers came out this way in 1857 and staked homesteading claims and then assigned a part of their claim to the company for a share of the hoped-for profits.

There was a financial panic in 1857 and that, combined with a few other factors, made the original plan fall apart. Still there were now settlers in the area that would one day become known as one of Nebraska's finest cities.

Many of the earliest non-native settlers in this area were Germans who settled on prosperous farms on the good earth of the Platte Valley.

Grand Island, capital of the United States of America. Impossible? Well, that's what a great many people had planned on for a long while. By 1866 the railroad did make it near where the land company had scattered their settlers. By then the idea of a city, located near the center of the United States, which would make travel from each coast an equal burden and would make protection from outsiders an ease, was growing in the minds of a number of enthusiastic settlers. Grand Island, the nation's capital! There was a concentrated effort to lobby the powers in Washington to make just such a change.

The idea may seem absurd to us, but such a move is common even today in countries like Brazil and others. Think of it, think of the possibilities, instead of standing, as you are now, in a pleasant town full of friendly children and reasonable men and women, you could be in the nation's capital! Instead of smelling the faint, earthy odor of the stockyards on the edge of town, you could be watching Congress pass laws! Instead of spending your hard-earned money on a vacation through Nebraska, you could be watching the Pentagon spend it for you! Why, instead of touring the sugar plant where that white, sticky sweet stuff without any nutritional value is manufactured, you could be

touring the President's mansion where...well, nevermind--their plan
fell on the usually deaf ears of the policy makers anyway.

There is much to see in this overllooked city of Nebraska.
Grand Island even has a growing artists' community just to the north
of the railroad tracks near downtown. Yes, there are those writers and
artists who would prefer the quiet streets and friendly faces of the
Midwest to the hustle and bustle of a New York, or the satin and silk
of an L.A.

Stolley State Park is at the southern edge of town, on Stolley
Park Road. The trees that originally defined this park were planted by
William Stolley who built a farm and made a fort here on the banks of
the Platte River in 1857. Remnants of Stolley's efforts at bringing his
kind of civilization to the plains is still evident here. Stolley had worked
for a naturalist before coming west and believed in foresting the plains.
He single-handedly planted 6,000 trees in 1860 alone.
In 1864 the Sioux increased their attacks on pioneers traveling the California trails. Stolley built his own fort, called Fort Independence here. It was made of wood, but surrounded by sod to ward off
flaming arrows. It had a 90 foot long underground stable and was quite
large. The reconstruction was built in 1940.

Grand Island is also the site of one of the state's finest
museums. The Stuhr Museum is dedicated to the memory of the
pioneer and strives to keep that memory alive in its exhibits and rides.
Don't pass up this fine collection. The museum is located on the
southern edge of the city and charges a modest entrance fee.

The great movie actor Henry Fonda was born in Grand Island
in 1905.
During one night in August of 1965, a rash of UFO sightings
were made. Reports came from Air Force bases and weather stations
and individuals from Oklahoma to South Dakota and from several
places in Nebraska. Several people in Grand Island were among
those who saw the strange lights in the sky.

Turn on Blaine Road to the site of Blunk's Mill. This was one
of the larger water powered grist mills in a good distance. It was a mile
long mill race which created a 10 foot drop in the water to create power
to turn the waterwheel. It started operation in 1877 and soon gained
a reputation as one of the best, and cheapest mills around.

US Highway 30

For more information about Grand Island and the sites in this area, please see the entries for US Highway 281 and US 34; Interstate 80, and State Highway 2.

Five miles (8 miles.)

Alda.

In 1883 a school teacher was brought to trial here in 1883 for assault and battery because, it was claimed, he whipped one of his pupils a bit too much. The courtroom was so crowded with the curious that a new room had to be found. During the trial the defendant was out on bail and continued to teach. The case ended in a hung jury. The case gained considerable statewide publicity.

Just south of this village is an historical marker placed to mark the California Overland Road. This road was used by gold seekers and pioneers and connected with the Oregon Trail at Ft. Kearney. A hundred yards or so of the ruts can still be seen stretching southwest of the marker.

From here to Grand Island to the east and Gibbon, 22 miles to the west, the Mormon Trail followed the north bank of the Wood River.

Eight miles (8 miles.)

Wood River.

The town was formed with the coming of the railroad. When the railroad decided to move, the town moved too. The older town site is at the Catholic cemetery.

This was an important town on the road to California gold fields, now generally known as the California Overland Trail. All along the general route of US 30 were also road houses and farmers who enjoyed a brief boom by supplying travelers with fresh eggs and butter.

For more information about this area please see entry for State Highway 11.

Eight miles (6 miles.)

Shelton, on the Hall/Buffalo County line.

Near here passed the Mormon Trail. During the early settlement of Salt Lake City, the Mormons were seldom able to afford oxen to pull their belongings to the promised land. Instead, and at the insistence of the church's leader Bringham Young, the faithful pulled handcarts across the west. These carts were usually pulled by four adults, men and women, while the children and old walked.

The town of Shelton began when some English converts to

Mormonism broke an axle on their handcart. They camped here and soon decided the axle could not be fixed. They built a hut on the banks of Wood River in order to sit out the winter. Instead of returning east, or going on to Salt Lake, they opened a store and settled here.

Except for those stranded in the high passes of the Rockies in winter, few perished as a result of the journey. Part of the reason was that other Mormons operated farms and supply points along the Trail to help those who came along. The first, and most important of these was at Winter Quarters, now Florence (see entry for Omaha). Near here was the site of one such resupply point. The acres of corn and wheat were home to another family who didn't make it to Salt Lake City.

One of the first newspapers printed west of the Missouri, the *Huntsman Echo,* was started here in 1858.

Six miles (2 miles.)
Gibbon.

Free homes sites and reduced railroad ticket fares brought a colony of 61 settlers to this area in 1871. An instant community was born, although many of these colonists lived in railroad cars for a long while. Gibbon Heritage Center located in the old Baptist church is a museum containing artifacts of local history.

One item of local history of interest is that the television host and writer Dick Cavett was born here in 1936. Cavett's subtle humor and wit and his intelligent insights make him a rare talent in modern entertainment.

Two miles (4 miles.)
Near here was the home of James E. Boyd who was the governor of the state from 1891-92. Also near here was a brewery which sold its kegs of beer to Ft. Kearny for $6 each.

Four miles (7 miles.)
Junction with State Highway 10. South of here are many interesting historical sites. For information on these and other sites along this road, please see the entry for State Highway 10.

Seven miles (1 mile.)
Kearney.

Believe it or not in the late 1880s a convention was held in St. Louis in order to make Kearney the capitol of the United States. Folks must have decided that there was enough fertilizer around these parts without bringing in the politicians. In case you went to sleep during second grade geography and have been asleep ever since, the effort, thankfully, failed. A similar effort was undertaken to make Grand Island the capitol. (It also failed.)

Kearney and Kearny, for Nebraskans is the same thing. Both were meant to honor Gen. Stephen Watts Kearny, but someone, somewhere, began to misspell his name, so now, both spellings appear in various places. Kearney, the town, prefers Kearney.

Kearney is the home of several interesting museums and attractions. The Trails and Rails Museum is at 710 West 11th Street in Kearney. This fine museum is operated by the Buffalo County Historical Society and is located in the 1898 Union Pacific depot. It contains a fine collection of rare photos, diaries, letters and archives of the area's history. In addition, the first frame schoolhouse, built by the early Mormons, as well as the Freighters Hotel are on the museum's grounds. The museum, which is free to the public is opened during the summer months, and in winter by appointment.

The Old Baptist Church, corner of 22cd and 4th Ave. President Harry S. Truman attended services here during the 1948 Presidential campaign.

The Frank House is an example of midwestern elegance at its best. It was built in 1889 to impress out-of-towners, and it still does.

West on 25th Street (Highway 30) to College Drive. North on College Drive, one block. The Kearney Canal and Power Plant was built in 1886 and is still producing electricity.

Downtown Kearney has many buildings constructed during the boom years from 1885 to 1925. Many of these have the date imprinted somewhere above the first floor.

The Kenwood area, from the west side of 8th Ave. south to 13th, contains many fine examples of Kearney's Victorian houses.

Kearney State College is at 25th Street and 9th Ave.

Ft. Kearny Museum is one block north and one block east of the Interstate 80 exchange. This museum contains items from Ft. Kearny and the surrounding area.

Museum of Nebraska Art, 24th and Central Ave. This is an official collection of art about Nebraska or by Nebraskan artists, a fine and unique collection. It is located in the old Kearney Post Office, which is on the National Register of Historic Places. The museum includes work by over 250 Nebraskan artists. Some of the work of William Henry Jackson, George Catlin, Robert Henri, George Lundeen, Aaron Pyle and Grant Reynard is on display. The museum is open Tuesday through Sunday afternoons and is closed for major holidays.

There are many interesting historical and natural sites just outside of Kearney:

Two miles south of Kearney, on State Highway 44 and across the Platte River.

Location of 'Doby Town, which existed during Ft. Kearny's heyday. Named because it was built of adobe bricks. Here was located a well known house of ill repute.

Three and a half miles west of here was Platte Station, a Pony Express station. Near here also may have been another station known to early travelers as "17 Mile Station."

Two miles east on State Road L-50 East to Fort Kearny. This fort serviced the area from 1848 until 1871.

It served as headquarters for the military in western Nebraska for a good part of that time, and also as a reassuring sight to travelers along the Oregon Trail.

An "old" Fort Kearney had been built near Nebraska City, but it was soon clear that such a location had little value in protecting citizens on their way west along the Oregon Trail. So, in 1848 the new fort was being built.

In addition to those heading for Oregon, the California Gold Rush of 1849 brought at least 30,000 travelers through the Fort's parade grounds.

The Pony Express had a "home" station here, and later a telegraph office. The fort grew larger, and its significance and importance along with its size. Finally, however, the bloom of the westward expansion was off, the Indian wars settled, and the railroad built. There was less and less of a reason for the soldiers to be stationed at this once critical point in America's great land. By 1871 the usefulness of Ft. Kearny had largely been replaced by other forts, and this place was abandoned.

In 1928 most of the land was purchased from local farmers by the Fort Kearny Memorial Association, and eventually the area was made into a state park.

Along the banks of the Platte is the Kearny County Recreational Area and the Hike/Bike Nature Trail. Come on, get out of the car and see some of nature's beauty.

US Highway 30

*Continue **east on this road for seven miles,** When the road turns north to cross the Platte is Hook's Ranch, or Dogtown, a stage station and trading post at the junction of the Oregon Trail and the Ft. Kearney Trail from Nebraska City. An early pioneer wrote "Dogtown is the first settlement west of Marysville and an ugly one at that." This is also the location of Valley Station, a later-day stage stop, and Lowell Cemetery an early day cemetery.*

Along this stretch of county roads is the best place to view the early spring migration of the Sandhill Crane. This bird winters in South Texas and Mexico, and summers in northern Canada, but each year the entire flock of birds traverses a very narrow strip of land along the Platte River. You are now at the spot where the greatest concentrations of birds can be found. Bear in mind that the birds are very easily frightened, and contrary to what most people think, your car makes a much better blind than approaching them on foot. The birds are less likely to scatter when seeing a car than when seeing a person on foot.

The sandhill's deep honking, rattling call is distinctive, and is often how one first knows the birds are near. Some of the estimated 112 Whooping Cranes left in the world travel with the sandhills. The whoopers are easily distinguished from the sandhills, even at a great distance because of their bright, all white feathers. For more information about sites in this area, please see entry for State Highway 10.

One mile (1 mile.)

This structure is a cotton mill. A sight not particularly common in Nebraska. Cottonmill Park provides a little recreation for the weary traveler.

One mile (5 miles.)

Stop. Look east. Look west. This was known as the 1733 spot to early travelers because it was purported to be 1,733 miles to San Francisco and 1,733 miles to Boston.

Five miles (7 miles.)

Near here the first Mormons headed west sighted their first buffalo. This is the start of the area which held the massive herds of buffalo.

Seven miles (8 miles.)

Elm Creek.
Home of Chevyland USA. Yes folks. Just what you think. A

256

vast collection of Chevolet cars.

Eight miles (11 miles.)

Overton.

South five miles to a "T" intersection across the Platte River. A ***half of a mile*** to the east of this intersection was the campsite of the ill-fated Fletcher Cotton wagontrain.

On the night of August 4, 1864 the wagon train pioneers stopped to camp on the banks of a small stream. This was near the popular camping ground for pioneers known as Plum Creek.

The next morning the group moved out and started west over the Oregon Trail. They were never to make it to the next evening alive. You can follow their movements.

Drive ***west from this "T" intersection exactly two miles.*** It was at this spot where the party was attacked by Indians, probably Republican Sioux. All 11 men were killed and a woman was captured by the Indians. Nearly a year later she was found by a trapper up on the Powder River who traded for her. She was finally returned to her home in Iowa.

The remains of those killed were believed to have been buried near here. At a later date they were reburied at Plum Creek Cemetery, one and a half miles west, and a quarter mile north.

One half mile northeast of the cemetery, on the banks of Plum Creek, was the Plum Creek Station, which was the only station between Julesburg Colorado and Ft. Kearny which was not destroyed during the Sioux uprising of 1864. All 14 people at the station were scalped, however. They were buried at the Plum Creek Cemetery as well.

For other sites in this area, please see the entry for US Highway 183.

Eleven miles (4 miles.)

Lexington.

Lexington was founded after a Pony Express station and trading post known as Plum Creek (see above for Overton) started to grow.

The railroad came by on the other side of the river and the people moved north across the Platte and renamed their location after the battle of Lexington. (O.K., smarty pants, in what war was the battle of Lexington fought? Answer at the end of the paragraph.) Lexington had a reputation for being a pretty rough and tumble town as many gamblers and thieves held out here preying on pioneers headed west, and rich miners heading back east. After a long while the citizens took the law into their own hands and drove the banditos out.

The Battle of Lexington was in the American Revolutionary War.

Junction with US Highway 283. Please see entry for that road for sites along its route.

Four miles (1 mile.)

At this point in 1867 on the adjacent railroad tracks the Cheyenne Indians, led by Turkey Leg, derailed a train by destroying a small bridge. They were upset by the presence of the train in their territory. They attacked the train crew, scalped them and raided the contents of the train. After finding boxes of cloth, the Indians tied one end to their ponies and galloped for miles, stringing the colorful material behind them.

One mile (4 miles.)

Junction with State Road L 24-A.

South on L 24-A two miles. Just as the road turns west, and just before the second bridge across the Platte, on the southeast side of the road is the site of the Willow Island Station stage stop, a place to get a wet drink and a change of horses before moving on.

Four miles (6 miles.)

Near here in 1847 a group of Mormons led by Bringham Young came across a gigantic herd of buffalo. The herd stretched from the river to the distant bluffs and beyond.

The entire countryside in every direction was black with them and one member estimated that at least 10,000 were in the immediate vicinity.

Herds 50 miles long and 25 wide which took days to pass a given point, were not uncommon before 1860.

Six miles (10 miles.)

Cozad.

Cozad is located smack dab on the 100th meridian. This is the line many consider to mark the start of the true American West. (Or, for you Easterners, the start of the true American East!) It seems like a good candidate. From here to the west things seems to open up—crop lands are traded in for sage lands; crowded and bustling cities for open and endless skies. The land itself just appears to change around this point, and there seems to be a change too in the very air.

Cozad had at one time been the spot where the Union Pacific continental railroad tracks were to have joined. It didn't work out that way, so don't go looking for golden spikes anywhere.

Aside from naming a town after himself, the town's founder, John Cozad, bought 40,000 acres of land and started planting hay and selling lots for a new town in 1873. He believed the fine air around these parts would cure any ill. Cozad soon built a brickyard and a hotel. The hotel held new settlers while their houses were being built from Cozad's bricks.

Cozad was a good example of a frontier town's smooth man. He was a gambler and quite a cutup with the ladies. Cozad shot a man in town one gloomy day. Those who were there said he did it in self-defense, and a later investigation bore this out.

However, those were touchy days, and it never took much for a town to find an excuse to get a mob together for a lynching. Cozad, afraid for his life, gathered up his family and left his hotel and his brickyard and his town. Seems he headed east of the 100th meridian, changed his name and dropped into obscurity.

That seemed to be that until one of Nebraska's greatest writers, Mari Sandoz, started to investigate Cozad's history and wrote a book, *Son of the Gamblin' Man* which tells the story of this fascinating character's life. Other local historians, including Harry Allen, did much of the background work to discover the true story of what happened to the Cozads after they left town.

Cozad's son, Robert Henry, became quite well known as an artist, going by the name of Robert Henri, and there was an entire movement in American art "The Ashcan School" based on his non-traditional realism.

Just west on 8th Street off Highway 21, exit 222 from I 80.

The town's most beautiful and interesting attraction is the Robert Henri Museum and Historic Walkway. This was originally the hotel Robert Henry's father had built, and was Robert Henry's boyhood home. The museum is connected to several other of Cozad's famous landmarks by a walkway.

Many a child, traveling cross-country, has stood in front of the original Pony Express station and had their picture snapped by doting parents. A century old school house, as well as the old country church are a part of this tour.

A local author, Betty Menke has written a enjoyable and entertaining account of the Cozads and Cozad's history which is available at the museum and in local stores. The book's dollar and a half price is a steal.

Ten miles (5 miles.)
Gothenburg.

Gothenburg Pony Express Station is in Ehman Park along State Highway 47. Used as a Pony Express station from 1860-1861 and later as a stop for the Overland Stage. Small museum free, open most days.

The reconstructed station in Gothenberg is for tourists...to see where the Pony Express route was you must travel **south three miles** (see below) and then go **east one mile** to the Midway Pony Express staion. The station building there, now a ranch building, is the real thing.

Old Brown House Doll Museum, 1421 Avenue F, Gothenburg (1/2 block from Pony Express station). Museum of dolls and toys, small admission, open most days in all seasons but winter.

Lake Helen is on the north edge of Gothenburg on State Highway 47. It was originally built in the 1890s as a reservoir for factories the town hoped would be built nearby. The economic panic of 1893 put an end to those great plans, but the lake remained. It is now a park.

*Hiles Canyon is **5 miles south** of Gothenburg on State Highway 47. Named after early-day ranchers who had their Kokomo Horse ranch here. Kokomo was a famous racing horse. The owner of this ranch, and beautiful canyon was the first Gothenburgian (if that is what they are called) to own and fly an airplane.*

*Midway Station is **two miles south** of the Platte River on State 47. At this juncture there is a county road leading east. Take this road **one mile east** to the Midway Stage Station, which still stands.*

The cedar long house was used as a home station for the Pony Express as well as a Overland Trail Stage stop and a trading post. The building has two distinct types of log construction, the western half is a post and sill type construction, and the eastern part, a later addition, a saddle and rider design.

This little building has quite a literary history as it is mentioned in Mark Twain's Roughing It, *as well as Charles Dawson's classic* Tales of the Oregon Trail.

The Midway station was so named because it is midway between Kearney, Nebraska and Laramie ,Wyoming.

Ruts from the Oregon Trail are visible in the area.

Five miles (8 miles.)

To Interstate 80.

Three miles southwest of here was the Gilman's Ranch which served as a stage station for travelers on the Oregon Trail. The ranch had an iron pump which was a novelty. Ask at Gothenburg locally for directions.

Eight miles (9 miles.)

Brady.

This is beautiful country, with the cottonwood lined banks of the Platte and the wild hills to the north and south. This land seems unspoiled since the earliest times.

*One can follow the route of the Oregon Trail by going **south, one mile** past the Interstate, and then turning west. Follow the county roads as they zigzag westward and watch for historical markers, signs of the ruts from the trail and other sites all the way to North Platte.*

Nine miles (14 miles.)

Maxwell.

South of Maxwell, two miles to Interstate 80 and then south one and a half miles to Ft. McPherson National Cemetery. This is the most peaceful rest stop along the Interstate, no pun intended. Stop here and sit in the cool shade of the trees of this lovely, although isolated, final resting place for so many dearly loved fathers and sons.

Continue south 1/2 mile to the site of Cottonwood Springs stage stop and Oregon Trail station. This was one of the most widely used stops on the way west due largely to the springs just south of here. The state maintains a Special Use Area one mile south in the canyon.

This was also the site of Ft. McPherson.

*Go **west of here seven miles** to a tall hill known as Sioux Lookout. The view from the monument there is breathtaking. You can't get lost, the county roads to the northwest all head there.*

*Return to the south bank of the Platte River and take the county road **west eight miles** to the Fremont Slough State Special Use Area. One half mile west of here was a well-used ford across the river.*

Fourteen miles (13 miles.)

North Platte.

Junction with US Highway 83, and State Highways 70 and 97.

US Highway 30

For more information, and for information about sites along that highway, please see entry for US Highway 83.

This is the home of the Lincoln County Historical Museum (2403 N. Buffalo). The museum has several interesting buildings including the old Brady depot, a Lutheran church from Hershey, a one room school house and a log home. In addition a few of the markers which once marked both the Mormon and Oregon Trails have been brought to the museum for safekeeping. The ranch home which was once owned by Buffalo Bill is a half mile northwest of the museum grounds. It is owned by the State of Nebraska and is opened to the public.

The North and South Platte Rivers join just east of North Platte.

On November 7, 1958, during a world-wide rash of UFO sitings, a TWA pilot reported seeing a bright, lighted object flying at incredible speeds over North Platte.

South of town, on US 83, One and a half miles south of the Interstate exchange, and just to the west was the Cold Springs Pony Express station.

Continue south on 83 three miles to turn off for Mahoney Reservoir.

Turn *east and go five miles, then north three miles* to the 3,200 foot hill known as Sioux Lookout. This hill served as a look-out for the local Indians as they watched for buffalo, and for the whites moving along the Great Platte River Road. From this vantage point the Indians could signal hunters or warriors to attack. A statue of a proud Sioux in a double war bonnet was erected on the top of the hill in 1931, but vandals have destroyed much of the structure. Although the statue stands on public land, most of the routes up the hill are on private land. A move is underway to have the entire hill made into a state historical park.

For other sites near here see entry for Maxwell, above. The county roads which zig zag along the river to the southeast roughly follow the route of the Oregon Trail. For a refreshing break from the US Highway habit, takes these the *30 miles to the Brady turnoff.*

Thirteen miles (6 miles.)
Hershey.

Two miles south, just south of the Interstate is Hershey Special Use Area and the site of the Fremont Springs Pony Express station.

262

Six miles (12 miles.)
Sutherland.
Junction with State Highway 25 south. Please see entry for State Highway 25 for sites along this road.

Twelve miles (9 miles.)
Paxton.
North of here the large siphon tube which diverts water from the North Platte watershed to the South Platte is worth seeing. Paxton is also the location of a small museum in a reconstructed sod house. The bridge here across the South Platte is at the location of Ford Number 2, or Middle Ford, a popular crossing on the Oregon Trail.

Nine miles (3 miles.)
Along Highway 30 is a Pony Express Station marker. Alkali Lake Station was important to the Pony Express and to the military as a supply point. The station was located about one and a half miles southwest of the marker, on the south bank of the river.

Three miles (8 miles.)
Roscoe. This was a crossing of the South Platte during the Oregon Trail days. This crossing was used by very early travelers in the 1830s, and by later travelers along the trail. It was not a common crossing.

Eight miles (9 miles.)
Ogallala.
Sure, the Big Mac is here in Keith County. Supporters of Lake McConaughy spout facts and figures like waterfalls. For a number of those facts, please see the entry for the lake in the entry for US Highway 26. But many people miss the true beauty of Keith County because they simply come for the lake and nothing else. The real beauty of the county lies away from the marinas and beaches.
Start in Ogallala, a place for most people to stock up on gas, cold drinks, junk food and bait. Instead of the convenience store tour of the city, take some time here.
The city park, on the northern edge of the city, is the finest place to get away from the roar of the Interstate for miles. Let the kids play on the swings here while you put together a large lunch. Lean against the trunk of one of the old cottonwoods and elms and fall asleep in the shade, serenaded by locusts.

US Highway 30

On the way to the park (and yes, on the way to Big Mac, too) is the "Mansion on the Hill." This late Victorian house of brick was built in 1887 and is the oldest brick building in the area. It houses artifacts and displays of the town's exciting past. It is operated by the Keith County Historical Society.

The building cost $10,000 to build in 1887, although the brick was 16 inches thick and the stone trim had to be hauled from Lincoln. There are two fireplaces in the house and tile floors are from New Jersey. The stone near the front door was a carriage-step which allowed folks to step out of carriages with a bit more grace.

Three blocks west of the park on 10th Street is Boot Hill. This was the original cemetery for the town, and in addition to some fine, up standing citizens, many of the town's less desirable elements were buried here "with their boots still on." Usually the accommodations included a couple of canvas sheets between two plank boards. This is the place where the name "Boot Hill" for a cemetery originated.

The most curious story of this cemetery is that of Mrs. Lillie Miller whose perfectly preserved body was dug up 25 years after it was buried here. Miller died in childbirth in the 1860s. Years later her body, and that of her child's, were being exhumed for reburial at the new Ogallala Cemetery. Three of the workers passed out and a fourth ran from the site when their digging revealed Mrs. Miller's perfectly preserved body. Even the skin of her face appeared as soft and pure as the day she had given her life trying to give birth to her child. One of the great mysteries of this phenomenon was that the baby's body, which lay with Mrs. Miller, had not petrified. Mrs. Miller's remains were so heavy that a crane and a derrick had to be brought in to remove them from the site.

At the top of the hill is the gravesite of Rattlesnake Worley, a cowboy who was killed by an outlaw of the cowboy days over a nine dollar bet in a game of poker.

By the turn of the century most of Boot Hill had returned to sod and even the wooden markers which had located the graves had withered to dust. No marble or granite markers were placed in the original cemetery.

After the Civil War Texas cattlemen sought new markets for their cattle, and started heading them north on newly plotted trials. The Texas Cattle Road wound up through the Texas Panhandle, across western Kansas via Dodge City, and ended—as much as such a haphazard route ended anywhere—in Ogallala. Cattle ranchers from Wyoming, Colorado and Nebraska met the cowboys from Texas to buy their cattle. Later, cattle were shipped east via the railroad. During the cowboy heyday (roughly the 15 year span, 1870-1885, although the trail was used until 1895) Ogallala was as typical a Wild West town as could be found on any Hollywood set. Its few permanent residents waited peacefully through the winter and spring until the first of the cattle drives arrived in May or June. Then more and more drives arrived until the streets were full of hundreds of trail-weary cowboys looking for a way to spend their hard-earned wages and to let off a bit of steam. Saloons, brothels, gambling parlors and flop houses lined the streets. On the river bottoms south of town, 15 herds of 3,000-5,000 head each milled about.

The "old" downtown was a strip of businesses that lined Railroad Street and serviced the three to four month boom season of cowboys and cattlemen. Ogallala's celebration of its wild past surely pales in comparison to what it must have been like in those wild days.

In the current downtown, at the intersection of U.S. 26 and 2nd Street is one of those unusual places you can find ever so often in places like Ogallala.

The city's Fantasyland is a gigantic display of animated creatures. There is nothing quite like this place anywhere else in the state. The displays were originally built for a department store in Minneapolis, then later purchased by the Brandeis store in Omaha. Finally the city of Ogallala bought the entire collection and housed it to resemble the Walt Disney book *Fantasyland*. Many of the displays were created locally. Now it cost a couple of bucks to get in here, but kids under 6 are free, which goes to show you the philosophy the city fathers had behind this place. It'll be a place to remember.

Ogallala's Regional Arts Council is an active and strong arts organization which has brought fine cultural programs and events to the area. The council sponsors an artist in residence program and ballet. Symphony and drama are regularly featured in Ogallala.

One mile due south *of Ogallala, and just west of the road was Gill's Station a Pony Express and military supply station. Both the Oregon Trail and the Pony Express Trail crossed the road approximately one half mile south of the Interstate exchange.*

Nine miles (1 mile.)

Brule. Named after a branch of the Teton Sioux from the French word for the tribe.

One mile (3 miles.)

US Highway 30

South of here, on the south banks of the Platte River was a Pony Express station known as Diamond Springs Station. The building was made of cedar.

Three miles (6 miles.)

Oregon Trail marker. Just south of this marker on the South Platte was the Lower California Crossing, used by most of the pioneers headed west on the Oregon Trail. In those days the crossing was a dangerous one, the Platte sometimes could be a raging stream, and even in the best of times was 3/4 of a mile wide, swift and with quicksand which could bog down a wagon. Often several teams of oxen were used to pull a single wagon across the river at this spot. The Upper Crossing, used largely by freighters, was at Julesburg, Colorado.

On the south bank of the river was a small trading post known as Beauvais Station.

Just northwest of the highway is California Hill. This was one of the first large hills that the pioneers had to climb on their journey west, although it pales in comparison to hills they would later meet in Wyoming. The trail climbs 240 feet in a little over a mile and a half. Ruts are still visible on the hill.

Six miles (14 miles)

Big Springs.

The town of Big Springs may stick in the minds of some since it was the scene of a senseless and bloody bank robbery in the late 1960s. A lone gunman entered the bank and killed several people. A twisted and sad reminder of the violence that was once commonplace in the West.

The cowboy trails which passed through this area were active well into the 1910s when most of the land still had no fences. That era is still an active part of the living memories of many local ranchers and citizens.

Fourteen miles (7 miles.)

Junction with State Highway 27 north. Please see entry for that highway for information about sites along its route.

Seven miles (10 miles.)

Chappell.

This is the county seat of Deuel County, the town was named for an early founder, the county for an Omaha businessman.

Chappell is also the location of the Deuel County Historical Society museum. It is free and open to the public.

This is the most productive wheat raising area of the state and shortly after the turn of the century the area was swarming with homesteaders who were claiming land under the new Kinkaid Act.

Chappell is located on Lodgepole Creek, and from here west both the Interstate and US Highway 30 follow the creek. It was so named because the Indians gathered their lodge poles from its banks.

Chappell is also proud of the library's art collection which is one of the finest collections of art between Omaha and Denver.

Ten miles (17 miles.)

Lodgepole.

Here is the location of Lodgepole Museum one block north of the highway. One mile south of town, the access road to I-80 crosses over the Oregon Trail. A bit closer to the Interstate, it crosses the Pony Express route. (By the way, the state's highest point is near here, at least according to the folks who live here, but don't mention this to anyone in either Kimball or Banner County.)

The area between Lodgepole and Sidney was well known for the numbers of train wrecks that happened here. The reason seemed to be the tendency of the engineers to open the throttle and let her go, and the poor quality of the early bridges. This was also the site of several armed robberies of trains by bandits, possibly including some by "Doc" Middleton.

Seventeen miles (3 miles.)

Sidney.

Junction with US Highway 385. Please see entry for US Highway 385 for information about sites along this highway.

Sidney was as close as you could get to the Black Hills by rail, and when gold was discovered there in 1876, Sidney became a boom town, serving as a jumping off place for many of the strange characters the lure of gold brought out West. At one point Sidney had 23 saloons in a one block area. Nearly two thousand people passed through Sidney each day.

Train conductors usually announced the stop by saying "Sidney...don't get off here if you want to live." A well-documented story has it that at one saloon where a dance was in progress a man was shot and killed. Rather than stop the dance, the party people simply propped the corpse up in a corner. Before midnight another man had been killed. His body was placed in the same corner. Before dawn a third man was killed and the dancers decided enough was enough. The party ended.

In the 1880s a man was lynched from a telephone pole near the city's center in a grand case of misunderstanding. He was offered the choice of either jumping off the ladder, or having the ladder pulled out from under him. He chose to jump, saying, "I'll jump off gentlemen, and show you how a true man dies. Goodbye, one and all."

Doc Holliday, Luke Short, Bat Masterson, Wyatt Earp, and Dr. Walter Reed all spent time in Sidney. Calamity Jane gave birth to an illegitimate child here.

Don't let this history scare you off, though. Sidney is a clean and proud town and boasts several churches, good restaurants and friendly people.

Legion Park and Memorial Gardens, 10 blocks south of Highway 30 on 10th Avenue. Three railroad cars are here, as well as a pond stocked with fish for the young anglers. It has sunken gardens, tennis courts and a swimming pool. At the intersection of the highway and 13th Avenue is Cabela's Wildlife Exhibit. The display contains over 200 specimens of wildlife.

Ft. Sidney is located on Sixth Ave., just south of Highway 30. This is one of the most attractive and best run local museum sites. The staff has prepared brochures to explain the history of the fort, and are waiting to answer your questions. The museum is free and open all year round. Troops stationed here took part in the massacre at Wounded Knee when, as many claim, the Indian ceased to have an effect on the American West. The site includes the ammunition store-house, barracks, and officer's quarters. The fort was established in 1867 and abandoned in 1874.

This is the location of one of the best known and most frequently retold ghost stories in middle America. One day in 1868 a young woman, the wife of one of the officers at the fort, was carrying a load of clean clothes up the back stairs in one of the dwellings in the officers' quarters. She looked up at a strange sound, lost her balance, and fell down the steep stairs. When her husband found her, her neck was broken, and her face was frozen in a ghastly look of fear.

The husband, overcome by grief, ordered that the service stairs be sealed off. A pantry was built over the new wall, and at the top of the stairs, a closet was built in a bedroom to seal off the staircase.

Nothing more was heard about the incident until the 1930s when, suddenly, visitors and residents in the quarters claimed they could hear footsteps, and the sound of something falling, coming from inside the walls.

An old citizen of Sidney, Melchoir Herbert, who had been a soldier at the fort, began to tell people that the explanation was easy: the place was haunted. No one believed his story about the hidden staircase. He died in 1958 at the age of 91.

The sounds continued however, and in 1975, when the quarters were being renovated, a workman stuck his head inside some drawers in the pantry and discovered the staircase which had been sealed for over a hundred years. Suddenly, old Melchoir Herbert's story seem to make more and more sense.

The sounds have continued to this day, and they most frequently occur during the month of October, which some believe is the month in which the poor young woman died.

The Upper California Crossing branch of the Oregon Trail enters Nebraska from Colorado along the same route as the present-day US Highway 385. It follows 385 to its juncture with Highway 30 and then the trail is along the south side of 30 and parallels it all the way to Sidney.

A later branch of the Pony Express route also followed this path.

At the western edge of the city a marker designates the Deadwood/Sidney Trail. After gold was discovered in the Black Hills this trail became a very busy stage route, moving passengers and freight from the railroad in Sidney to the gold fields in Deadwood, South Dakota.

During one night in August of 1965, a rash of UFO sightings were made all over the Midwest. Reports came from Air Force bases and weather stations and individuals from Oklahoma to South Dakota and from several places in Nebraska. During that night Captain Lee Beekin, and four other men of the Sioux Army Depot in Sidney saw several objects in the sky.

Listen to Captain Beekin's report: "They looked like a naval ship going through the sky. There was a large one and four smaller ones flying in a triangle. They were all white."

Three miles (3 miles.)

Iris Gardens. If you like iris, you'll love it here. Over 800 varieties are displayed.

Three miles (3 miles.)

US Highway 30

Two miles north *on spur S17A: Sioux Army Depot and a fine museum on the campus of Western Nebraska Technical College.*

This place was established in the 1940s to produce ammunition for the war effort. Many of the buildings can be seen from the highway.

The tri-state area here (Nebraska, Wyoming and Colorado) contains the largest concentration of Intercontinental Ballistic Missiles of any place in the world, including Russia. Scattered across this area are missile silos containing 200 Minutemen III missiles.

The combined firepower of the missiles in this area is enough to wipe out the northern half of the world six times over. The combined firepower of the missiles in this area is equal to 45 times all the bombs dropped in the entire World War II.

One hundred years ago the Sioux fought the coming of the white man to their last breath. The Sioux believed in a vast power that would one day wipe out the earth. Let us all pray that they were wrong.

Three miles (6 miles.)

A rare glimspe of sod and rock houses which were once, not so long ago, the main type of dwelling in the greater part of the state.

Six miles (2 miles.)

Gunderson Mill. On the south side of the highway is the site of a mill established in 1878. It was a 36 foot square building and stood nearly 50 feet tall—quite a skyscraper in those days. It was the home of Snow Water Patent Flour...many would say a product far better than Powdermilk Biscuits.

Two miles (3 miles.)

Lodgepole Creek. They say that this creek is the longest creek in the world. That is if you define "creek" by saying it is smaller than a stream, larger than a slough and wetter than a wash.

The Point of Rocks to the north was a major landmark for travelers in the old days, and still is by those who travel this stretch of road regularly. The Sioux rolled rocks off of this mound to try and derail the trains that passed along here.

The point was used as a lookout for scouts keeping a watchful eye for those same Sioux as the railroad crews repaired track.

Just beyond here is a bend in the creek and the Hank Redington Ranch. The ranch is located on the Texas Trail—the trail up from the Lone Star State that was used for cattle drives to the railheads, the Blackhills and Montana. This ranch may have been the first ranch in the Panhandle.

Three miles (9 miles.)

Potter.

In downtown Potter (yes, there is a downtown) the Buffalo Bend Stageshow is an act you will not want to miss. This theater proves that artistic souls producing quality entertainment need not live in places like Lincoln or Hollywood. Shows are every weekend during the summer.

Potter is also the home of the Potter Museum.

The largest hailstone observed in the United States fell here on July 6, 1928. It was 17 inches in circumference and weighed nearly 2 pounds. Never mind it wiping out the corn crop, the watermelons were goners.

Nine miles (8 miles.)

Dix, in Kimball County. Kimball County is in wheat country, and chances are that's what you see growing all around the countryside. Alongside many fields are oil wells, more than 1,400 of them are in the county, drilled to depths of over one mile.

Nine miles (8 miles)

Kimball.

Junction of State Highway 71. Please see that entry for sites along its route.

Originally named Antelopeville, many people in Kimball are glad the name was changed to honor a vice-president and general manager of the Union Pacific Railroad.

The Plains Historical Society Museum is located at the corner of Second and Chesnut in the old Knights of Pythias Woodmen Degree of Honor Royal Neighbors Hall (don't ask how such a name came to be). It was built in 1905 and was used for lectures, meetings and the first movies ever shown in Kimball.

This is also the location of the oldest building on Main Street, the Old Stone Store, built in 1894 at the then high wages of $1.00 per day for the construction workers. It has served as a store, a rooming house, a ballroom and a saloon.

Kimball has two parks to rest at, as well as a public swimming pool three blocks south of the stop light and then east of Sixth Street nine blocks. One block north and five blocks east of the stop light is a marker commemorating the Lincoln Highway. This road, built in the 1920s, was the first paved, coast to coast road. It followed the general

271

route of the Oregon trail and was used by dare devil drivers who for years had driven across the continent for sport.

Eight miles (13 miles.)

Oliver Lake, a state park for visitors of all ages.

Southwest of here on a rise in the distance is a spot 5,426 feet above sea level, the highest in the state (never mind folks in Banner County to the north claim a spot in the outreaches of their county for the same honor, no one from the East Coast is going to imagine the state as anything but flat anyway, no matter what you tell them.)

Thirteen miles (0 miles.)

Wyoming border.

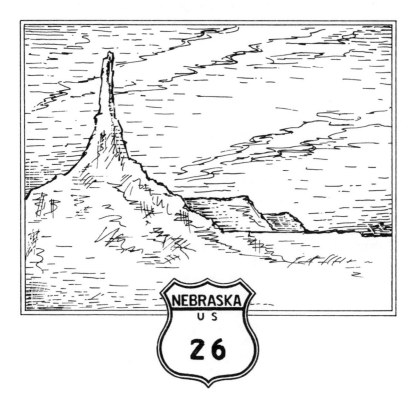

Zero miles (2 miles.)

Ogallala. Please see entry for US Highway 30 for information about Ogallala.

Two miles (25 miles.)

Junction with State Highway 61 north. Please see entry for State Highway 61 for information about sites along this road.

Ten miles to Lake C.W. McConaughy. Big Mac. The facts: It is 35,000 acres. It is Nebraska's largest reservoir, and therefore the state's largest body of water. Its dam is the longest dam of this type of construction in the world. The largest walleye caught in Nebraska, a 16 pounder, came from its cool deep waters. Many other record fish have been caught here. It has 105 miles of white sand beaches. It is the location of one of the largest open class inland sailing regattas in the U.S. Its shorelines offer crowded people-watching beaches, or remote campsites. Yes. It is all true. But one fact Big Mac fans often miss is that because of the lake more people pass through Keith County and see less than any other county in the state.

First of all, to really appreciate Keith County, to really fall in love with the place, go immediately to your local bookstore and buy a copy of one of the best book written in the state in the last 20 years, Keith County Journal by John Janovy Jr.

Next, drive away from the lake and see a number of the interesting sites around the place.

Twenty five miles (1 mile.)

Ash Hollow State Historical Park.

Through this deep canyon passed the Oregon Trail, and by the waters of the stream (now no longer in its original stream bed thanks to the construction of the highway) and springs, many thousands of pioneers camped.

Before the Oregon settlers passed this way, this area was home to many Indian peoples, including the Dismal River People, ancestors to the Plains Apache.

Before that this land was home to prehistoric rhinoceros and mastodons. The first whites to come this way were probably members of John Jacob Astor's overland party which came by here in March of 1813.

In 1835 a day long battle between the Pawnee and Sioux, traditional enemies on the plains of Nebraska, was won by the Sioux, and the Pawnee were forced to move down river to a place near present-day Grand Island.

A visitor's center in this fine state park will orient the traveler to the many interesting sites here. Be sure you ask for directions to the site of the trading post as well as the pioneer cemetery (perhaps hundreds of people were buried in the area, although only one grave site is marked); the old Fort Grattan where the Indians attacked an encampment of pioneers, and suffered terribly for this action some months later, and other places of interest.

According to Oregon Trail scholar and author Gregory Franzwa, who has written many fine books on the Oregon Trail, it is estimated that one out of every 17 people who started on the Trail died before reaching the coast. That would mean a grave site on the average of every 193 yards.

Just to the south is Windlass Hill, one of the first main hills the pioneers faced moving west. The arroyo, or wash that runs down the side of the hill started as wagon ruts over a hundred and thirty years ago. There are many pristine ruts still visible in this area, as well as an exhibit for tourists and an information booth.

Just at the north end of the park, and before crossing the river, a county road leads off to the west. Take this road **one and a half miles** to the grave of A. Kelly who died on July 14, 1852.

One mile (2 miles.)

Two miles east of Lewellen Highway 26 crosses Blue Water Creek. See below for description of the Battle of Blue Water.

Two miles (12 miles.)

Lewellen. Junction with State Highway 92 on the north side of Lake McConaughy.

Twelve miles (16 miles.)

Oshkosh, and b'gosh Wisconsin ain't got nothing on us! Location of the Garden County Historical Society and the county seat of Garden County.

*Take the county road **east out of Oshkosh 7 miles** to the Blue Water Battlefield Overlook. At this creek in 1855 Little Thunder's band of Sioux were eliminated in retaliation for the Grattan massacre.*

The Brule Sioux Indians had been accused of killing Lt. John Grattan and 28 men. A few weeks earlier Grattan and his men had been killed probably by members of Conquering Bear's band of Sioux, when they approached the band. Grattan had been sent to find and arrest an unknown Indian who had been accused of killing a single stray cow. The government ordered all Brule to move to the south side of the North Platte River. Little Thunder's band did not move and so a force of nearly 1,000 soldiers set out to force them to move. They met about a mile upstream from here and the underarmed band of Sioux were wiped out.

Sixteen miles (14 miles.)

Lisco. Named after a rancher who owned over 30,000 acres in this area. South, across the North Platte River was the Oregon Trail.

Fourteen miles (14 miles.)

Broadwater in Morrill County.

Morrill County was a critical one in the development of the American West as the Oregon Trail, the Mormon Trail, the Sidney to

US Highway 26

Deadwood Trail, the Black Hills Trail and one route for the Pony Express all passed through here, most of them along the banks of the North Platte.

In addition, several important landmarks of those trails are still visible today.

Just **three miles east** of here are Ancient Bluff Ruins, an eroded sandstone bluff which was a well-known landmark for travelers on the Mormon Trail since this was the first point one could see Chimney Rock (don't strain, Chimney Rock was much taller, and the air less carbon monoxided back then).

North on the road out of Broadwater, about **5 miles** to the Calvary Remount Station, used during the Indian Wars when Ft. Robinson was in its prime. This was the location of a battle between soldiers and Indians. Inquire locally for exact location.

North two more miles. Covalt Buffalo Herd. Ask for directions locally to view this fine herd ranging the grasslands much as they always have. Also on this road is the Nebraska Boys Ranch.

Cross the North Platte River at Broadwater and continue west on State Highway 92.

Three miles east is the location of a frontier post station on the Oregon Trail. This road east roughly follows the route of the Oregon Trail for about 45 miles to Ash Holow.

West on 92: You are now roughly following the route of the Oregon Trail. The trail runs to your south for the first 5 1/2 miles, when it crosses the road and is then on the north side of Highway 92.

At **eight miles** is the Junction of Highway 385 (see entry for US Highway 385 for more information on sites along this road.)

About **one quarter mile** past this junction, and an **eighth of a mile** to the **north** is the grave of Amanda Lamin, who died here of cholera crossing the continent in 1840. Her husband left his wagon train and returned alone to St. Louis where he purchased a granite marker for his wife, and came back with it with the next party headed west. You might say he was stupid, but his action did give his wife a kind of immortality since many history buffs, as well as local residents would not otherwise have known this poor woman's name who died so far from any home. The site is on private land, inquire locally for viewing.

A few ruts from the trail are still visible in this area, although recent farming has destroyed many of them. The Mormon Trail is on the northern bank of the river, and ruts from it are visible in places.

Inquire locally, at the Bridgeport Museum for directions to ruts.
Bridgeport via 92 is 16 miles from Broadwater.

Fourteen miles (2 1/2 miles.)

Bridgeport, the county seat of Morrill County.

Bridgeport is near the spot where the early Pacific Fur Trading Company employees, on their way to Astoria on the Oregon coast, camped during the winter of 1812/13.

In Nebraska, no accomplishment is too small, and Bridgeport boasts one of the largest, if not the largest International Harvester dealers in the world. If you have never been inside of a farm implement dealership, this is the one to see.

Bridgeport's State Recreation Area is a fine spot, and draws bird hunters from all over the Midwest because of its location on the flyway and the North Platte River.

The Bridgeport Museum is a must-see spot for travelers.

Five miles south of Bridgeport on State Highway 88: Jailhouse and Courthouse Rocks. These are two of the more significant natural markers on the Oregon Trail.

There are two stories of how Courthouse Rock got its name. One is that its shape suggested its name for the early travelers through the area. The other is that 12 outlaws were tried here, found guilty and shot to death on the butte's summit. Cowboys gave the name to nearby Jailhouse Rock, because, after all, what else is near a courthouse but a jail? The rocks actually looked different in pioneer days as the Brule clay and Gering sandstone which forms the buttes weathers easily in the harsh Nebraska storms.

Many, many seasons ago a Pawnee warrior challenged the wisdom of his entire tribe. His grandmother, whom he dearly loved, had been left behind on the prairie as the tribe moved to their winter quarters. The tribe left these old ones to die when they felt such people slowed the movement of the rest. Storms, raging Sioux and the displeasure of his own people would not stop this warrior.

He rescued his grandmother from her lonely death-spot, and brought her back to the tribe. Soon after the warrior was walking along the North Platte river when he found a great white horse, with fiery, pink eyes. It was said in the tribe that this great horse had been given to the warrior by the Great Spirits as a reward for saving his grandmother. From that time on the Pawnee began to change their custom.

With this great horse the warrior became famous in battles

277

with the Sioux. With this great horse the warrior managed to run down three antelopes and kill them all with a single arrow. For this, he won the love of a chief's daughter. Before long the warrior gained the status as a wise and powerful man in the tribe. It was here, atop of Courthouse rock, that this Pawnee wise man came to meditate and to receive the wisdom from the spirits of the other world. At this magic place then, the power of the Pawnee came to earth. Eagles and other dramatic birds roost on the rocks, perhaps carrying some of the Pawnee warrior's secrets.

The Pony Express route passed to the west of Courthouse Rock and joined the Oregon Trail just west of Bridgeport. Also to the west, along the creek bed, is a cliff which served as a post office for the travelers along the Oregon Trail. Here, under the words "Post Office" scratched into the sandstone, people left letters for those who were following behind them to find.

For a continuation of sites to the west along State Highway 88 see the entry for that road.

Return to Bridgeport.

Two and one half miles (5 1/2 miles.)

Pioneer Cemetery. The ruts of the Oregon Trail are visible on either side of this cemetery. Paul Henderson, who many consider to have been the greatest Oregon Trail scholar, is buried here within sight of the trail he loved. The first bridge across the North Platte River, the Camp Clarke Bridge, was built in 1876. This bridge was about three miles west of the present town, and Bridgeport was formed when the Burlington Railroad passed through the present site. The site is just north of here.

For the next several miles the Oregon Trail is to the north of the highway. Several trails important to the settlement of America's West come together here. The Oregon Trail, the Mormon Trail, the Pony Express Trail, the Sidney-Deadwood Stage Route and the continuation of the Texas Cattle Trail to Montana all pass near here.

Five and one half miles (1 1/2 miles.)

Five and a half miles past the cemetery stop the car. Here is a spot commonly known as the Jackson Panorama.

William Jackson stood here and sketched the scene before him in 1866. In front of him were hundreds of wagons, and several separate wagon trains, stretched out along the clearly visible trail passing Chimney Rock. In 1931 Jackson used the sketch to paint a large watercolor of the scene. The sketch and the oil painting are on display in the Oregon Trail Museum at Scotts Bluff National Monument.

One and one half miles (3 miles.)

Just to the south of the highway is Facus Springs, a watering spot along the trail, and the place where an early settler, Facus by name, was shot and killed.

Three miles (3 miles.)

Chimney Rock. This tall and unusual looking formation was the most often noted landmark on the Oregon Trail.

People who enjoy this kind of thing have located 97 individual references to the rock in pioneer diaries. Chimney Rock was probably first sighted by a white man in 1813 who was with a group of traders returning from Astoria on the Oregon Coast.

Pioneers scratched their names in the surface and camped near here as this was such a noted point of the trail and such a geological curiosity.

The tower is considerably shorter today than it was during the pioneer migrations. Wind, rain, and even target practice has shortened it since the pioneer days.

The State Historical Society, and the National Park Service, operate a small museum on Highway 26 at its closest approach. In addition, county roads lead to its base.

Just southeast of the base is an old cemetery with many unmarked graves believed to be from the migration time period.

Continue west on State Highway 92 at Chimney Rock for an interesting alternative route to Scottsbluff.

On State Highway 92 from junction of US Highway 26, south of Bayard:

Five miles.

McGrew. The Oregon Trail followed the route of present-day Highway 92. To the southwest of McGrew can be seen several landmarks of the Trail including Castle Rock, Table Rock, Steamboat Rock and Roundtop. These bluffs appear in William Jackson's famous panoramic painting of the Chimney Rock area which he originally sketched in 1866. The painting is on display at the Scott's Bluff National Historic Monument (see below.)

One and a half miles west of McGrew take the county road *on the south side of the road **west** for **one and a quarter miles.** On the south side of the road ruts from the Oregon trail are still visible. **Continue** on this conty road **west another three miles** when it rejoins Highway 92, or return to Highway 92 the way you came.*

Six miles west of McGrew *is the tiny town of Melbeta, just south of Minatare on US 26.* **One mile west** *of Melbeta is a marker commemorating the site of the Ficklin's Springs Pony Express Station. Both the Pony Express route and the Oregon Trail route crisscross Highway 92 several times between Chimney Rock and Scottsbluff.*

Eight miles west of Melbeta *is Scottsbluff and Gering. Please see entry for US Highway 26 below.*

Three miles (13 miles.)

Bayard. Bayard's Cemetery holds several unmarked graves which are believed to date to the days of the Oregon Trail. The Bayard area is known for its good trout fishing. Inquire locally.

Thirteen miles (8 miles.)

Minatare. Eleven miles north of here is the attractive Lake Minatare. See Scottsbluff, below, for further information.

Eight miles (2 miles.)

Just to the south of the highway is the site of Rebecca Winters grave. This is a very well-maintained grave dating to the Oregon pioneer days along the Oregon Trail.

The Chicago Burlington and Quincy Railroad changed the route of its tracks to avoid disturbing the remains of Rebecca. As the crews were building the line they came across a small mound, and across the top was a wagon wheel with a plank. The plank had an inscription which read, "Rebecca Winters, age, 50 years." The engineer of the survey crew moved the tracks to leave the grave alone.

Rebecca Winters was a Mormon who died of cholera in 1852. Her final resting place is 15 feet north of the railroad tracks, just as the highway swings to the north and away from them.

Two miles (8 miles.)

Scottsbluff.

This is the oasis of the Panhandle, many would agree. Friendly people, a cultured society, art, entertainment and history all await the traveler or resident at the Scottsbluff and Gering area.

As the highway enters Scottsbluff, Nebraska Western College is located on the eastern edge of the city. This is one of the largest colleges in the western part of the state. Its round buildings, resembling the pattern of green made by a pivot irrigation system, are unique.

The old Burlington depot is located at 14th and Broadway Streets. The Union Pacific depot is located on State Highway 71 in Gering. At Scottsbluff's Riverside Park is the largest zoo in western Nebraska. It is **one mile south** of 26 on State Highway 71. It also offers camping. Scottsbluff is the location of the West Nebraska Arts Center which offers exhibits of the art of the area.

The Scottsbluff/Gering area is hell-bent for promotion and has done a fine job in attracting businesses and conventions to the area. The towns boast several motels and quality restaurants and are proud of the area's interesting sites.

Ten miles NE of Scottsbluff is Lake Minatare State Recreation Area. Good fishing for walleye, perch and northerns. Public boat ramps and fishing. Near here are Nine Mile and Sheep Creek which offer good trout fishing.

Junction of State Highway 71. Please see that entry for sites north and south along this route.

Gering. Gering celebrates Oregon Trail Days during the third week in July to commemorate the first wagon train to reach the area. It is two days of fairs, food, and horseshoe pitching contests.

The North Platte Valley Museum is at 10th and J Streets in Gering and is open seven days a week.

The museum has many well-designed displays that provide a glimpse of the area's life before television. There is a recreated ranch house, cattleman's shack, pioneer home and blacksmith shop, as well as many other displays. The museum is known for its excellent chronology of the human habitation of the area.

Three miles to the west of Gering on State Highway 92, or west of Scottsbluff on Highway 29 and then south on 92 is Scott's Bluff, the must-see Scott's Bluff National Historic Monument.

(At the southeast corner of the intersection of Highways 92 and 29 was the approximate location of Camp Mitchell, an early military camp location for protecting the mail route.)

Scott's Bluff is an imposing bluff that pioneers moved under as they made their way through Mitchell Pass. It is estimated that a quarter of a million pioneers passed by this spot during a 20 year period beginning in 1843. They moved at an average of eight miles a day. The ruts left by their passing are clearly visible here as they move up through the pass at the base of the bluff.

The museum at the monument headquarters is a wonderful addition to the living history one can feel by walking through the pass itself. William Jackson's famous panoramic view of the area, painted from his sketch done in 1866, is on display here as well as many other exhibits.

In 1828 a man by the name of Hiram Scott, a lone fur trapper, died at the base of the bluff after he was abandoned by his companions. Since that time the bluff has been referred to as Scott's Bluff.

A trip to the monument is not complete without a side trip to the alternate route of the Oregon Trail through this area. **Go west on State 92** two miles to junction with State Highway 71. **Go south on 71 two miles.**

This county road which intersects the highway follows the exact route of one branch of the Oregon Trail.

Turn west here and go six miles. Stop the car.

Two miles in front of you is the route through Robidoux Pass and the site of the Robidoux Trading Post.

A later trading post was built two miles south of here and that site may be reached by turning **south** here and following the county road southwesterly for **three miles.** It is at the mouth of Carter Canyon. If you continue **west** here for another **two miles,** ruts from the Trail are visible on the southern side of the highway as the county road, and the old trail climb toward Robidoux Pass. Several marked and unmarked graves of pioneers are in this area.

Eight miles (6 miles.)
Mitchell.

To follow the approximate route of the Oregon Trail turn **south** at Mitchell and take the first west turn south of the North Platte River. Following these county roads as near to the river as possible will keep you along the same route so many hundreds of thousands of pioneers used.

A fine rock 'n' roller was born in Mitchell. Randy Meiser, originally a member of the band *Poco*, and later of the *Eagles*, was born in Mitchell.

Six miles (7 miles.)
Morrill.

Named for Charles Morrill who owned a large chunk of

Nebraska in the early days. After he contributed so much of his time and energy in helping the University, he was honored by having the state's finest museum, Morrill Hall on the University campus in Lincoln, named after him.

*Take county road L-79D **south out of Morrill and then take the first road west, south of the North Platte River Bridge.***

***Take the first right turn (north) in three miles. In one half mile** you will cross a small bridge. Stop the car.*

This is the valley of Horse Creek. In 1851 the United States Government invited Indian tribes from all over the west to meet at Ft. Laramie, 50 miles west of here in Wyoming, to try and settle centuries of Indian wars. To the surprise of everyone, thousands of Indians appeared at the fort for the talks. Since there was no good grazing land for horses, or enough water for those assembled, the Indians camped here, along Sand Creek and Horse Creek, so named for the good grass it provided their horses.

The treaty negotiations brought together tribes that had never met, from the Crow and Black Feet of Montana, to the Sioux and Iowa of the Great Plains. It is believed that here, along the banks of this sandy creek was the single largest gathering of American Indians ever.

Try to imagine these hills covered for miles with thousands of tepees and campfires. An astounding mixture of costumes, music and language now largely forgotten, was everywhere. There have been few people who have visited this site in the many years since that gathering.

The treaty was negotiated in part because the government realized that this route would soon become a popular one for the whites, and they did not want the Indians fighting while "citizens" were passing through. The treaty lasted three years until a white by the name of Gratten fired on some Indians accused of stealing a cow.

The Oregon Trail followed this same county road route. Just to the southwest here was the Horse Creek station, a station on the Pony Express and Oregon Trails.

Eight miles (0 miles.)

Henry, and the western end of US Highway 26 in Nebraska. Henry is located just on the better side of the Wyoming border. Just southwest of the town is the site of Red Cloud Indian Agency at the end of a dead end road as it reaches the river.

***South of Henry 3 miles** to where the Oregon Trail crosses State Road L-79C.*

Both CBS News and *National Geographic* magazine have called this highway one of the ten most beautiful in the country. It has been a route for travelers since there have been travelers in the state. Indians used part of the route and later the pioneers crossed the state along routes then known as the Old Freighters Trail, the Steam Wagon Road and the Nebraska City Cutoff.

Zero miles (9 miles.)
Nebraska City.
The state's most exciting and interesting state highway begins in this old river town. There is much to see in Nebraska City, for information please see entry for US Highways 73 and 75.
West of Nebraska City on State 2. This is the so-called Steam Wagon Road so named for the steam wagon that was supposed to make it to Denver and back twice a month. (See entry for US Highways 73 and 75 for details.)

Nine miles (4 miles.)
Dunbar. Dunbar was a stage station on Ben Holladay's Overland stage route and much later when the railroad replaced the stage route the town continued to hold on. The population of the town has not changed much in over 100 years.

Four miles (4 miles.)
At about this point the Nebraska City Cutoff of the Oregon Trail crosses the highway diagonally from the northeast to the southwest. For the next five miles it parallels State 2 on the south side of the road, about a half a mile from the highway.

Four miles (5 miles.)
Syracuse. Did the highway curve to miss Syracuse on purpose? A question more than a few Nebraskans have asked while driving from Nebraska City to Lincoln. Is this the highway? A question

more than a few Nebraskans have asked after missing the curve and heading up one of the town's residential streets.

Syracuse grew from a stage station on the Overland Stage route from the Missouri to Denver. This place had originally been known as Nursery Hill, after a spot just south of here on the stage route which had been the location of a trading post and stage station.

Junction of State Highway 50, please see that entry for more information about sites in this area.

Five miles (12 miles.)

Unidilla. The name means "meeting place" in Iroquois. There were no Iroquois Indians here, the town was named after a town in Illinois.

At the south end of the village is the Little Nemaha River and a state campground. Along the south banks of the Little Nemaha was the Overland Stage Route as well as the Nebraska City Cutoff of the Oregon Trail. Some traces of ruts are still visible in Otoe County. Inquire locally.

Twelve miles (4 miles.)

Turn off for Bennet.

On January 27, 1958 the mass murderer Charlie Starkweather killed two people who had stopped to help Starkweather and his girlfriend, Caril Ann Fugate, after their vehicle had gotten stuck in the snow. They forced the victims into a concrete cave two miles east of Bennet and killed them. In all, ten people were to be killed in the five day spree.

The Nebraska City Cutoff of the Oregon Trail crosses two miles south of Bennet

Four miles (8 miles.)

Cheney. An old community now nearly invisible compared to the spreading giant of Lincoln.

The Nebraska City Cutoff of the Oregon Trail crosses one half mile south of here. The road was also known as the Steam Wagon Road because it was supposed to carry steam powered wagons which everyone thought would be invented and would replace the horse.

There is a rare round barn south of Cheney. Ask locally for directions.

Eight miles (92 miles.)
Lincoln.
For information about the state's capital city, please see the entry for US Highway 34.

At Lincoln State Highway 2 is swept up by Interstate 80 and US Highway 34 does not resurface again until Grand Island. For sites between Lincoln and Grand Island along this route please see entries for US Highway 34 and Interstate 80.

Ninety-two miles (7 miles.)
Grand Island.
See entry for US Highways 34, 281, 30 and Interstate 80 for information about Grand Island and other sites in this area.

Seven miles (6 miles.)
Abbott, a scattering of houses on a bend in the road. Near here was the Robert Taylor sheep ranch which was one of the largest sheep ranches in a five state area. The ranch in Hall County alone took up nearly all of Prairie Creek Township, about 10,000 acres. At the turn of the century, before modernized haying equipment 1,400 acres alone were in alfalfa.
The railroad siding which was here was originally named Taylor's siding, but the railroad company didn't think it was enough of a neutral name to the place so it was renamed Ovina, from the Latin, ovis meaning sheep. *Taloris ovis.*

For the next few miles you pass through the prairie creek area. All of this land was once under the control of a Robert Taylor. During the great grasshopper plague of 1873 and 1875, this area was one of the hardest hit in the state. They destroyed virtually all of the green and living plants. Sulphur was used to try and smoke the grasshopper out of the corn.
A prairie fire swept through here in 1878, and later two men were found shot to death with cards attached to their shirts. The cards read: "Shot for setting the prairie fire."
In order to settle in this area one early pioneer drove his team of ten horses through 700 miles of winter snow in order to reach this area before others. Some of the snow was 12 inches deep.
In 1887 a 240 acre farm along Prairie Creek sold for $5,200 with house, grainery, running stream water and stock.

State Highway 2

Two miles north of Abbott and *three and a half miles west* (on county roads) to Runnelsburg. These are the ruins of the town of Runnelsburg which was more or less owned and operated by a man named R. S. Runnel. A stage route to connect Grand Island with the Black Hills was supposed to run through here, which gave Mr. Runnel much of his enthusiasm. The railroad replaced the trail, and the railroad passed south of here so Runnelsburg soon drifted into ghosthood. Mr. Runnel sold his farm for $14 an acre in 1884 and moved permanently to California.

Six miles (16 miles.)

Cairo. A railroad boom town, that boomed in 1887 as a result of the Grand Island and Wyoming railroad which passed through here. Cairo went from a corn field to a town of 250 in a few months. Folks here have no intention of letting it slip back the other way.

Since you are in Cairo, you might wonder where the Suez is. Well, it is a street here on the west edge of town.

For more information about sites in this area please see entry for US Highway 30.

Sixteen miles (11 miles.)

Ravenna, named after the town in Italy. Near here, in 1874 a pioneer brought the first shorthorn cattle into the area.

Location of Ravenna State Lakes, on the banks of the South Loup River.

Eleven miles (6 miles.)

Junction with State Highway 10 at Hazard.

One wonders why someone might select to live in a place named Hazard, however somewhere over 50 people have overcome their hesitation and call Hazard their home. The name is supposed to have been selected when the citizens could not find a name not already in use. "Well," one pioneer said, "we'll just hazard another name." The rest, as they say, was history.

The Beaver Creek Wayside Area, just west of the village is a nice out-of-the-way facility that allows non-motorized boats only. There is additional camping at Litchfield Recreation Area, six miles to the northwest on State 2.

For more information about sites along State Highway 10,

please see that entry.

Six miles (9 miles.)
Litchfield and Litchfield Recreation Area.

Nine miles (6 miles.)
Mason City. The stunning feature of Mason City is the work of its major artist Richard Martin, on the southern edge of the city. Martin creates sculptures of cats, dogs, roosters and other items from old tools and pieces of farm equipment. His entire yard and house is decorated with his work, the roof, the lawn, the porch and inside, so it won't be hard to locate the home of the master. In addition Martin creates wind sculptures that are balanced so that the slightest breeze sets them in motion. Martin doesn't sell his sculptures, by the way, although he has been known to give a few away.

Six miles (17 miles.)
Junction with US Highway 183, please see the entry for that highway for information about sites along that route.

Seventeen miles (8 miles.)
Broken Bow.

Yes, this county was named for THAT Custer. The hills of this county are good for raising alfalfa and cattle. Broken Bow, the county seat, was named when an early settler found a broken bow and some other Indian artifacts in a nearby burial ground about the same time the rest of the community was trying to think up a name for the town that was unique. For a long while pieces of this bow, like pieces of Christ's cross, showed up at various places around town.

There is a tour of the historic homes of Broken Bow. Ask at the library for information.

Custer County Historical Library and Museum is free and open to the public.

During one night in August of 1965, a rash of UFO sightings were made around Broken Bow and the entire Midwest. Reports came from Air Force bases and weather stations and individuals from Oklahoma to South Dakota and from several places in Nebraska.

A rancher near Broken Bow saw the objects as did several other people in the area.

Just west of town is a marker which celebrates the rebirth of the Grange movement in Nebraska when the Custer Grange met in 1911.

*Callaway is **20 miles southwest** of town and offers the Seven Valleys Museum with a large collection of Indian and pioneer artifacts.. It also has preserved the first Custer County courthouse— a long building. Near Callaway is the site of the Mitchell and Ketchum lynching, a part of a larger conflict between ranchers and pioneers during the 1870s. See entry for US Highway 183 north of Westerville for details.*

***Southwest of town, 15 miles on State Highway 21** to the South Loup River and the Pressey Wildlife Management Area which offers fishing, camping, bird watching and hunting.*

***Five miles north** take the right fork in the road and go one more mile to Dead Man's Canyon. This beautiful canyon was named after a battle which took place here in July of 1887 between two posses and other assorted lawmen and two men who were believed to have robbed several farm families in the area. One suspect was killed and the other fled on horseback.*

Eight miles (11 miles.)
Merna.

***Ten Miles north of Merna** on county road to Victoria Springs State Recreation Area.*
A series of springs once bubbled out of the sandstone here, creating different colored waters, depending on the chemical make up of the rocks through which they flowed. Early pioneers capitalized on the beauty of this area and set up trading posts to serve the tourist who sought out the springs. The waters were often used for their alleged curative powers. Today a pretty pond and a single clear springs are the center attraction for this out-of-the-way and quiet spot.

West of Merna 2 miles is Cedar Canyons, a waterless maze of canyon lands which are home to a wide variety of wild life. In addition to coyotes, deer, and other animals, this is a good birding spot, with occasional sightings of eagles, chickadees, cedar waxwings, owls and other fine feathered friends.

West of Merna on State 70 and 92 25 miles to Arnold.

In the late 1960s Arnold was renowned for its unfriendliness. Horror stories about people whose cars broke down in the town, and the universally rude and threatening treatment they received spred like wildfire. In 1968 a group of cross-country bicyclists paused at Arnold Lake Park and had two of their members beaten to a pulp by local cowboys. Two weeks later a lone bicyclist from Lincoln, unaware of the town's reputation, had the misfortune to break down on the outskirts of town. Without the intervention of a less blood-thirsty citizen he too would have suffered at the hands of the community.

Soon articles appeared in publications giving Arnold the title as the most red neck and unfriendly town in the state. Surely this isn't still true...

Eleven miles (21 miles.)

Anselmo. This small burg got its start thanks to the railroad. From here on the Sandhills dominate the geography. These sand hills are wet enough to support a rich texture of native grasses. The pioneers learned that plowing this land caused wind erosion. Now, a hundred years or better later, the same lesson is being learned again by those who insist on breaking through the grass in order to plant irrigated croplands.

The large church on the west side of town is the Catholic church and is known as the Cathedral of the Plains.

*To the **east six miles** to Silver Springs Recreation Area. The springs are there along with a log cabin built in the early days.*

Twenty one miles (10 miles.)

Dunning and junction with State Highway 91.

Fifteen miles north east on State Highway 91 to Brewster.
When you take out the road map of Nebraska and fold it in half the crease will split Blaine County in two. That might be the only reason why Blaine County might attract your attention. Take a look at that crease. Well, you might say, there seems to be a fairly good sized town there, Brewster, at the junction of State Highways 91 and 7.

The Dismal River flows through the area, and that river, despite its name, offers some good fishing and boating. So does the Loup. But outside of that, you might ask, what else could possibly be in Blaine County?

You are right about the river, it is a heck of a name for a pretty

State Highway 2

little river. Trouble is, Brewster, the county's seat and main town has all but dried up and blown away. All except for one place that not only has refused to give up the ghost but is actually bringing folks off the main highways to Colorado, the Black Hills and Yellowstone. Off those roads and out into the center of the Sandhills.

A trio of enterprising young men have taken over an old store in the town and turned it into "Doc Middleton's" an old fashioned saloon, restaurant, community center and news exchange. The place is named for a famous Nebraska outlaw who once owned a saloon in Brewster during one of his attempts to go straight. (For a more complete discussion of Doc Middleton, see entry for US Highway 20.)

The actual existence of the place owes a lot to the town spirit and sense of community. The population of Brewster has dwindled to somewhere between 20 and 40 from a peak of not many more.

When the men decided to open a place in Brewster no one in the town was telling them to go away. Instead, everyone pitched in and helped to build the saloon. In the first few months of operation, when the owners couldn't get to town because of other jobs, or work on their ranches, somebody nearby, oftentimes whoever was handy, would unlock the place and put on a fresh pot or two of coffee for the local folks who gather there in the morning. Fresh flowers appear on the tables due to the thoughtfulness of someone else.

Sounds a little unusual, even for the friendly Sandhills. Thing of it is, Brewster was just about dead and buried before Doc Middleton's opened. The town's population had dropped 50 percent in a few years, and the only thing in town besides a couple of houses were the courthouse and the post office. Now, with the restaurant, there's a place local folks can go and talk about the poor cattle ranching economy, the way the remaining empty buildings on the four block main street seem to be just blowing away, and county business, such as it is. But at least there's a place, and that helps explain the unusual community atmosphere you'll find at Doc Middleton's.

Expect to stand out like a sore thumb from all the locals who will most likely be gathered around a single spot in the center of the room. The place will grow quiet as you come in and everyone there gives you the once-over. After that, though, things return to the way they always are at Docs. Incidentilly, they don't serve breakfast, although they are open early in the morning for coffee and conversation.

Hows the food? How else do you think the food would be at a place like this?

Brewster is probably the smallest county seat in the country.

The area's most notable claim to fame was having the number one high school football champions a few years back.

After filling up at Doc Middleton's a drive southeast toward Taylor on Highway 91 is a must. The beauty of the Loup River Valley is unequaled.

Ten miles (14 miles.)

Halsey. This is the gateway to the Nebraska National Forest, a man-made forest of beauty.

It is something of a matter of pride that the Nebraska National Forest— the Halsey Forest is entirely artificially planted. Outsiders raise their noses when told this information.

Established in 1902 by Teddy Roosevelt, the area contains 93,000 acres. The forest was the idea of Charles E. Bessey, a famous University of Nebraska botanist who knew that the Sandhills could support a large forest.

Between 1903 and 1921 13,500,000 seedlings were set out. In the last year alone 2,200,000 jack and yellow pines were planted. They first tried planting the seedlings directly into the soil, but the plants did not survive.

Eventually it was discovered that if a trench was built the trees had a much higher rate of survivial. The planting crews would follow a horse drawn plow and trench which made furrows in the grasses of the hills. Trees are now transplanterd to Niobrara division in Cherry Co.

Don't come here expecting the close-in forests of other areas. The sparse hills and coolies hold enough trees to qualify as a forest in Nebraska.

Fourteen miles (15 miles.)

Thedford, the county seat of Thomas County. Please see the entry for US Highway 83 for more information on this town rich with history and life.

Fifteen miles (11 miles.)

Seneca. An interesting and previously unknown method of keeping track of time was developed by Senecans who kept shades up and doors open so that the sun would shine onto their floorboards. People called around to check and compare when their shadow claimed it was high noon. In this matter, little by little a Seneca Standard Time was agreed upon, and you could be reasonably certain that when your shadow said it was noon, everyone else saw their shadows as noon too.

Horse races were often held on Railroad Street to determine the fastest local horse.

Seneca, in the extreme western edge of Thomas County was founded in 1888 and was named for the Seneca Indians. In the old days at its peak, during the 1920s, Seneca had three grocery stores, a telephone office, dress shops, a theater, post office, two auto dealers, a livery stable, two large hotels, two banks, and was a division point for the railroad.

When the courthouse in Thedford was destroyed by fire in 1920 Seneca residents pounced on the opportunity and demanded an election to move the county seat to their town. They lost by a vote of 362 to 514.

In 1948 during the presidential campaign President Truman stopped by for a barbecue in Seneca. The town had gas lights, a movie theater, electric lights, an ice making factory before any town for miles around had these services.

Slowly the railroad began to lose interest and money in Seneca. In 1968 the last railroad train came through town. Despite the slowly shrinking size, Seneca has survived. Today the town has a population of, well, somewhere under a hundred.

The Seneca Church was built in 1909, and since with the town's declining population it has been difficult to keep a vital church membership. Still, there are those who believe wherever there are two or more...

The Seneca Cemetery dates from 1899.

Seneca was home of a farmers' union which was half social organization, half cooperative farm effort. The union movement, which was big in the 1920s, has largely died out in the Sandhills.

During the blizzard of January, 1949 a southbound passenger train stalled in Seneca and the passengers spent several days in the depot and Ruby's Cafe until the tracks could be cleared. The cafe had people sleeping on tables and chairs and did more business in those couple of days then it had ever done.

Four miles north on county roads to the site of Buffalo Flats. The post office in this area was a cracker box in the home of one of the residents. People came by to pick up mail there.

The church at Purdum was built in 1908. The cemetery predates the church by about 25 years.

Near here is the Lone Star Cemetery, a small cemetery dating from the turn of the century.

Eleven miles (25 miles.)
Mullen.

Mullen is the county seat of Hooker County. Mullen was named after a local agent of the railroad when the town was founded. It is the county seat of the sparsely populated Hooker county. So sparesly populated, in fact, that Hooker County is the least populated county in the state. Note that the license plates here begin with the rare number 93, indicating that out of the 93 counties in the state, Hooker is last in population. This is not a shameful thing, on the contrary, Hooker residents feel a kind of pride and honor at having what no other county has as much of: empty space.

No, the county was not named for the businesswomen who worked in Mullen a century ago, but rather after a noted Civil War general.

Mullen is at the very heart of the Nebraska Sandhills, a unique geological and ecological formation unlike any other place in the world. The Sandhills were laid down thousands of years ago after the great ice sheets rolled back to the north. At first settlers believed the sandy and rolling hills would be good for nothing better than scattered cattle grazing. However, in time they learned that areas of the land supported some crops. When the gigantic Ogallala aquifer, an enormous underground sea of water, stretching over the entire state of Nebraska, and going as far south as Texas, was utilized, farmers began to reap the harvest of crops grown on the hills.

Today a developing controversy centers on land use in the Sandhills. Some claim that the pivot irrigation systems which have turned the land into large circular gardens of green crops, is depleting the nutrients from the soil, as well as adding to the erosion of the hills and the depletion of the aquifer. Others claim that everyone should leave the care and husbandry of the land to those who know the land the best, namely the ranchers and farmers who have spent their lives here. In any event the Sandhill region of Nebraska is a special and remote gift for all people to visit and to marvel over.

South of Mullen, five miles to a narrow paved road leading off to the west. Down this road 15 miles to the banks of the North Fork of the Dismal River, cross the river and continue another eight miles to the

295

State Highway 2

banks of the South Fork and the site of the North and Cody Ranch. This grassy expanse of hills was once the range of thousands of buffalo, antelope and deer. In 1877 William F. Cody, who would later become world renown as Buffalo Bill, along with Major Frank North, purchased a herd of cattle at Ogallala and spent a good part of their summer driving them to this range land. Here the men started a ranch that would become known as the North and Cody Ranch. Not much is known about the success of this ranch, or Buffalo Bill's part in it, but for years the ranch was made welcome to any traveler who happened this way. In later years many dignaiaries were entertained here. Today the quiet and peaceful river flows through beautiful country of grasslands and thickets along the banks.

Twenty five miles (1 mile.)

Whitman, in the heart of the Sandhills.

"It's a great country for cattle and men," said pioneer Ellen Moran, "but hell on horses and women."

The earliest settlers around these parts were people with names that hinted at pioneer spirit. People like Old Gus Buchfinck, Fetus Carrothers and Bryant Greathouse, who homesteaded in the late 1880s near Whitman. These men came to the area in covered wagons looking for good, cheap land for cattle and families. Some, like George Moran, husband of Ellen, were lucky. They had 13 children, and nearly single-handedly populated early Whitman.

Others, like Effie Brown, weren't so lucky, she was shot to death in the Whitman Hotel by her husband in 1900 after he had gotten drunk in the local saloon.

Here was the Whitman Barn which served as a supply point for wagon trains heading for places as far away as the Snake River country of Idaho, and the Arkansas River to the south.

The Whitman post office which is the oldest in Grant County, was established in 1887.

Whitman once served as a major cattle shipping point for railroads. Special Saturday evening runs made shipping easy for the local cattleman. Sixty or more cars of beef was not an unusual train length in Whitman's shipping heyday. Also, of lesser importance, were the 4 passenger trains a day that once stopped here.

As the highway passes near the railroad tracks: this was once all cattle yards and stock pens for cattle awaiting shipping.

Whitman's hotel cost 35 cents in its heyday during the early years of this century.

Whitman at its peak during homesteading years and when the Kinkaid Act opened the Sandhills in 1900, had two hotels, two livery stables, two doctors, two general stores, pool hall, lumberyard, photo shop, drugstore, icehouse, cattle yard, coal chutes for trains, a barbershop, and a blacksmith (who had a shop across the south side of the railroad tracks). Fred Troop's saloon was the busiest of the 7 saloons.

The brick bank, which still stands, dates back to the town's big days around the turn of the century.

The Whitman firehouse was the post office in 1928.

In its 100 years of history, there have been only five robberies in Whitman. All of them have taken place at the post office. The total stolen during these five break-ins has been $72.38.

Just north of the school is the old parsonage of the Methodist Church, built in 1898.

The IOOF Hall was once a pool hall. In 1976 the pay phone on the main street of Whitman was purcahsed by the Whitman Women's Club extension group "Out Our Way." The phone is a useful item for stranded tourists.

On a nice hill overlooking the village one quarter mile south of town is the cemetery. The oldest grave is from 1888. Included here are the graves of the Weaver family's five children, who all died within a 7 month time span in 1889. The Weavers were the owners of Whitman's first big store.

While the homesteaders, who were called Kinkaiders because of the act of Congress which allowed them to settle this land, helped the economy of the area, they were usually the butt of jokes.

"You know what an S.O.B. is, don't you?" a rancher, even recently said, "Well, a kinkaider is 10 times worse than that."

North of Whitman: This road was once the main wagon road north to the Black Hills. In 12 miles the road crosses the Middle Loup

River. Here was a common resting place for wagon trains heading north. Teams were watered in the sluggish waters of the river, and teamsters could decide if they really wanted to continue on this madness, or return to Whitman.

North of Whitman 18 miles. *This area was once the common first night camping ground for wagon teams leaving Whitman.*

Southwest of Whitman: *Here the last free land in the state of Nebraska was opened for homesteading and settled. Most of the land had once been deemed a "forest preserve" by the state, but when the attempt to grow trees failed, it became homesteading land. Many homesteaders, hearing that the land was a "forest preserve" came expecting to see lots of green. They were disappointed.*

Tracks were 640 acres for the Kincaiders of 1913. Tracks were given out during a week long drawing, done in Hyannis. One hundred numbers were drawn each day, and the winners could then file claims on their choice of a section of land. This became Whitman's largest "boom" time with tents on the streets of those hoping to win at the drawing.

One mile (4 miles.)

The airport is to the north of the highway. Here in 1938 a mail bag containing 374 letters and 2 packages gained a page in history by being the first, and last, airmail delivered to the town.

Four miles (7 miles.)

North of here at the old Monahan Ranch during the gigantic prairie fire of 1892 Sidney Manning had just started back for Whitman when he noticed the fire sweep over a ridge and race toward him. Manning survived the fire by jumping down an open water well. "I didn't know if I would drown or burn," Manning said. The wind of the fire swept a large pile of cattle chips into the well and on top of Mr. Manning. Nothing Manning said about the chips has survived.

This fire covered hundreds of square miles and is possibly the worse natural disaster in Nebraska's history.

Seven miles (8 miles.)

Hyannis.

The Hyannis County Courthouse is the home of the Grant Co. Historical Society Museum. Many fine displays of the local area's history can be seen here. It has limited hours, but can be opened by appointment. The courthouse was the central location of many famous Grant County Sheriffs.

This town, as well as Whitman and Ashby, were named after towns in Massachusetts by early settlers from that area.

Oldest building in town is the house lived in by Ada Coons. This was the first building in town and still stands. It was built in 1887.

The Bank of Hyannis was built in 1915. When first built as a bank, the south half of the main floor was used as a saloon.

Bud Moran, who still is talked about in these parts, was the first sheriff of the territory which now includes Grant Co. While in Whitman, Bud Moran held a madman in the jail for safekeeping. Three men had brought him in and left him in Bud's office.

Listen to Bud tell it: "He was so violent the cowboys which brought him in had roped him. When they left, he informed me that he was the devil and made a leap at me. He tried to bite me. I was sure scared then. I didn't have time to run, so I just throws him over my shoulder out of sheer terror of him. When he hit the floor that took some devil out of him, and I was on him before he could get up and put the handcuffs on him. He looped his arms around a dog I had in the office and bit its ear off. When I tried to pry his mouth open he swallowed the dang thing, eyeing me resentful-like all the time."

Main Street on east side: Dredla's building built in 1914, was the site of the Ashley Store which also served as post office from 1906 until 1918.

Near this building was the first drugstore in town and although the owner was not a pharmacist, he did quite well by selling medicines which contained a fair amount of alcohol, and also, we might assume, headache remedies.

The barber shop has been in existence since 1938.

West side: The hotel was built in 1898 by Sherman Sears and has always looked pretty much the same as it does today. The door on the north was for men, and the one on the south for women only. This was so that the women would not have to pass by the men who gathered in the lobby and talked about the things that interested them, namely women. The third floor was not as nice as the other floors and the manager would rent these rooms to cowboys, ranch hands and other individuals he might consider less than refined. The rooms here were cheaper, however.

The building next to the hotel was built in the late 1880s as well, and has served as a tack shop for a great part of that time.

Next to the Masonic Temple and Post Office stands a building that was once completely remodeled after a cowboy came into the building on his horse. Seems that he had just gotten off a long week of branding and was wanting a bit of excitement. His horse ended up having the most excitement, it fell through the floor which was the intial reason for the extensive remodeling.

The last building on Main Street was the site of the first Bank of Hyannis which was built in 1893.

Beems Gas Station was built in 1930. We thought you would like to know.

The Baptist Church uses a part of the original Hyannis Opera House which was built in 1896 at a cost of $745.

Near the lumberyard is an old house that was built in the late 1890s and later moved into town. In its basement a local inventor built and rebuilt a perpetual motion machine. The machine was often being repaired and there are not many who saw the thing run, however it was a contraption of spokes and a wheel, filled with water. For a while the machine was displayed in the store.

At Hyannis Park was the site of the first school house: 1888.

Train depot on the tracks was built in 1901. Here Teddy Roosevelt spoke in 1904. He came to town on a special train, made his address from a specially built bandstand near the tracks. There was a very large crowd for the only President to visit in the history of the town.

In 1896 a party of people broke into Whitman County Courthouse and took all of the county's records. The records were then hidden in a blowout south of town. As a result Hyannis became the county seat in 1897.

The town library was the recipient of an unusual gift in 1942. The Omaha World Herald sponsored a scrap metal drive for the war effort, called the "Scrap Harvest." Grant County was the winner of the competition raising nearly 650 pounds of scrap per capita. The old wagon wheels, guns and tools today might have brought a much higher price than the $1,000 the county won, but for Vernon Moran, who collected 96,953 pounds of scrap by himself, the honor far outweighed the prize. The money was used for the library.

The rodeo grounds, near the football field, hosts the most popular event in these parts. "The Old Timers Rodeo" includes a parade and the celebration draws thousands to Hyannis. The tradition of a rodeo here dates back to the late 1880s.

Frye Lake, north of town is a good fishing spot.

The Hyannis Cemetery is on the hillside to the north and affords a view of the beautiful Sandhills of the surrounding country side. The oldest gravesite is from 1890. A local eccentric, Major Guelliner, demanded he not be buried "like everyone else." He is buried with his head to the east.

West of Hyannis. Here was once St. Mary's Cemetery. Here was the grave of Mart Managan. Managan dug his own grave, built a fence around the site, purchased a coffin and placed it in the open grave covered with a piece of tin. He lived for 12 years after this, but was confident of his burial arrangements. Little did he know that the small cemetery, including his remains, would be moved to the cemetery in Hyannis to make way for the Grant County airport.

Eight miles (5 miles.)
Ashby
This rustic western town has had it all: shoot 'em ups, a blacksmith shop, a church that was once a store, and even a cowboy's ghost.

At a dance hall in Ashby a man who had been a Lieutenant in the Army always made everyone stand and salute him when he walked in. Once, when someone new to town didn't, the Lieutenant shot him. The man had a wad of bills rolled up and placed in his pocket which stopped the bullet. Nothing is known about the eventual outcome of this story.

301

State Highway 2

Charlie's Store is the location of the town's store since 1914. Once there were two stores in Ashby, within yards of each other. The store's former owner, Edward Montgomery, was not happy that another store had started in town. In 1921 the new store burned to the ground. The cause of the fire was never determined.

In 1920 a common sight was John Halloren and the owner, Edward Montgomery, riding up and down Main Street on their horses, whooping and hollering and carrying on. The two men would be stark naked. Most town folk knew they had probably been snipping a bit of alcohol. Charlie's is a good place to stop off for a cool bottle of pop and friendly conversation.

The present school was built in 1915 after a series of one roomers. All 12 grades were not taught in Ashby until 1930.

Ashby started as a railroad town in late 1800s. The oldest thing in town is the lumberyard, which has been in existence since Ashby's earliest days. The flush bathrooms were added in 1976. The cement structure on the north side of the railroad tracks was the base for the water tower which once was Ashby's source of water for train, town and business.

The Ashby church, on Main Street, was once a building for one of the town's three lumber yards. In 1920 it was purchased and a steeple was later added to the storefront structure. The addition was built in 1977.

An old shack on Main Street was once known as King's Place and was where old bones were brought duing WWII to be made into calcium.

The Ashby Town Hall, now the location of the Veterans Club, was famous across the Sandhills for having the best dance floor in the area.

The cemetery is east of town and the oldest grave is that of an infant who died in 1915.

There was an old cowboy named Dubs who lived in Ashby. He built himself a shack on some land just west of town and kept pretty much to himself, remembering the old days of cattle drives and camping under the stars.

Dubs would walk into town every once in a while to check his mail and get groceries. It was a pretty uncommon thing to see a cowboy walking, but he seemed to like the exercise.

Then he stopped showing up. After a few weeks some folks decided to go out and check on the old timer.

What they found was Dub, sitting in a chair in his shack, stone-cold dead, his face frozen in a silent scream of fright.

Since that time residents of the area report seeing an old cowboy walking alongside of Highway 2, just on the western edge of town. There are those who swear that when they see this man he looks as if he is from another age.

The road southwest of Ashby was formed when a man drove his car to Denver, and marked his route by painting the fence gates blue.

This road, in 30 miles, leads to the southeastern edge of the vast and beautiful Crescent Lake National Wildlife Refuge, and eventually to State Highway 27. Please see the entry for State Highway 27 for more information.

North, 14 miles to Old Mason, or Stansbie/Perrett Cemetery. About 20 graves including Roberta Wilson's who was found by settlers and buried after a blizzard on Feb. 9, 1891.

Five miles (14 miles.)
Five miles to the south are located Big and Little Buckboard Valley where various skeletons of horses and the ruins of old buckboards have been found. No one knows more details about the lonely pioneers who may have perished here.

The highway east and west of here is a particularly straight east/west line. This is indirectly thanks to the United States Army. The Army had this idea that its soldiers could meet the 20th Century on bicycles. In an attempt to prove so they had three companies of men bicycle from Montana to St. Louis in 1897. At this point they were having so much trouble that they followed the rail road tracks in order to make their way. Their path later served as a road, and now it is this stretch of Highway 2.

State Highway 2

For more information about these bicyclists, please see entry for State Highway 27.

Part of the original pioneer wagon road is visible on either side of the highway east and west of here.

Fourteen miles (8 miles.)

Ellsworth. Once the headquarters for the gigantic Spade Ranch. Junction of State Highway 27 north. Please see entry for that road for information about sites along its route.

Three miles north, Morgan's Cowpoke Haven Museum and Tack Shop. You are not a true traveler of the wilds if you pass up a place with a name like this.

Eight miles (24 miles.)

Lakeside: WWI potash was mined here, making this a temporary boom town.

Junction for State Highway 27. You are near the heart of Mari Sandoz country. Please see entry for State Highway 27 for more information about sites in this area.

Twenty four miles (18 miles.)

Alliance. Junction with US Highway 385. Please see that entry for more information about sites along its route, and for information about Alliance.

Eighteen miles (12 miles.)

Hemingford.

An old song of the Sandhills is sometimes still sung around these parts. It is commonly called "The Kincaider's Tune" after Sen. Moses Kinkaid who helped to open this area to the last batch of homesteaders in 1904:

> The corn we raise is our delight
> The melons too, are out of sight.
> Potatoes grown are extra fine
> And can't be beat in any clime.
>
> The peaceful cows in pastures dream

And furnish us with golden cream.
So I shall keep my Kinkaid home
And never far away shall roam.

If the homesteader had a different view of the country, there
are other appropriate verses:

I've reached the land of drouth and heat,
Where nothing grows for man to eat.
For wind that blows with burning heat,
Nebraska land is hard to beat.

Al Reneau was a ranchman's name,
Skinning Kinkaiders was his game,
First mortgages only, at a high percent,
Work you down on your cattle to the last red cent.

The Nebraska Sandhills are a unique geological area unlike
any other in the world. The name is misleading for the Sandhills
contain thousands of lakes and marshes as well as meadows and
even some forests. They were created by the wind and by erosion
after a great inland sea dried up, some 100 million years ago. The
great ice sheets further transformed the area so that today these hills
constitute one of the most productive cattle range lands in the world.
Just like the thousands of buffalo that once roamed this area, the cattle
now feast on the rich grasses of the delicate hills.

The area is ideal for birdwatches and nature lovers. Secluded
lakes and meadows provide homes for shore birds, cormorants and
phalaropes as well as hawks, larks, and golden eagles. Deer and
pronghorn antelope populate the area as well. Elk have been reintro-
duced to the Sandhills and range in Box Butte County.

Twelve miles (9 miles.)

Junction of State Highways 2 and 71. They follow the same
route from here north to the South Dakota border.

Nine miles (8 miles.)

On the Dawes/Box Butte County line: Marsland.
Marsland is located on the Niobrara River. This was a major
stage and Deadwood Trail stop. Horses were changed here, and
travelers could get a bite to eat, a sip of whiskey and other pleasures.

305

In the back of one saloon the owner stacked all of the empty whiskey bottles. It was said the stack was as high as a haystack. The unusual name came from a man who was from Lincoln, and there are more than a few locals who will tell you Mars is exactly where many Lincolnites seem to come from.

Marsland reached its peak when the railroad came its way. It became a major shipping point for the ranches in the area. This town once had a hotel, livery stable, creamery and a water mill. Now a few buildings remain, but most of the glory of this town is left to the ghosts who inhabit it.

Seven miles east of here via the county road is Box Butte Reservoir, good fishing and boating.

West of Marsland for the 20 miles to Agate. The road follows the Niobrara River on the south, and, on the north, the road follows the Fur Trader's Trail which was used by the earliest white travelers in this area.

Agate: Agate National Mounument. See Sioux County, State Highway 29. It is 22 miles north of here on State Highway 29 to Harrison.

Nine miles (8 miles.)

One mile east of State Highways 71 and 2:

Belmont. A ghost town founded in 1886 by a dairy farmer. The dairy used a treadmill with dogs to power it in order to separate the cream. Two dogs worked while the third rested. Each dog worked for 10 minutes, and rested for five. Not bad hours for a dog. The town once had nearly 50 buildings. Most of these are gone although the brick school building and a few others still stand.

A short walk north of Belmont will take you to an unusual sight in Nebraska. Here is the only railroad tunnel in the entire state. It was built in 1888. Nebraskans are so sensitive about being considered the flatlands that a special marker has been placed here to let the tourists from Oklahoma know there are tunnels in this state. Don't tell any Oklahoman that the tunnel has not been used since 1983 when a by-pass was built.

From here to Crawford State Highways 71 and 2 roughly follow the old Sidney to Deadwood Trail. The Trail was used by huge wagon trains to supply the Red Cloud Agency, where as many as 13,000 Indians were camped, as well as to service Deadwood once gold was discovered in the Black Hills. Many clear ruts can be seen still on this route. Keep your eyes open for the easiest route up and through the hills, and you'll spot them.

Eight miles (17 miles.)
Crawford. See US Highway 20 entry.

Seventeen miles (0 miles.)
Follow the signs 17 miles to Toadstool Geological Park. Camping and picnicking and water is available here. This extensive park is a geologist's dream. Cottonwood Creek flows through the park. It was somewhere along this creek where Crazy Horse took his 1,500 people to camp after he surrendered at Ft. Robinson in May of 1877.

You are in the vast Ogllala National Grasslands. For more information on this area see the entry for US Highway 20.

Highways 2 and 71 end at the South Dakota border.

Zero miles (24 miles.)

Highway 275 enters Nebraska in southeast Omaha as it crosses over the Missouri River from Iowa. For information about Omaha please see entry for US Highway 75.

Twenty four miles (2 miles.)

Junction with US Highway 6, Dodge Street, Omaha. Please see entry for US Highway 6 for information about sites west on this highway, and US Highway 75 for information about Omaha.

Two miles (4 miles.)

Turn off to Elkhorn which was a Union Pacific station in 1865. It was first named Chicago, then Douglas, then Elk City and finally Elkhorn. Elkhorn is the home of the German Farmers Mutual Fire Insurance Company which was the first non-native company of its kind.

Four miles (10 miles.)
Valley.

The Valley Community Historical Museum is preserving items of local heritage including prehistoric bones of the giant mammoths to items from the pioneer life of the Valley area. The museum is in the 1873 school house, which also served as a Baptist and Catholic church before becoming the museum. The museum is free and open on Sunday afternoons or by appointment. This pretty little town was founded in 1864 and is still home for over 2,000.

Ten miles (11 miles.)
Fremont. For information about Fremont, please see entry for US Highway 77.

Junction with US 77 and US 30. Please see entry for those highways for information about sites along their routes.

For eleven miles north of Fremont US Highway 275 and US Highway 77 follow the same route. For information about sites along this stretch, please see entry for US Highway 77.

Eleven miles (3 miles.)
Junction US 275 and US 77. US 275 leaves 77 and branches off to the west.

Three miles (7 miles.)
Hooper. The main street of Hooper is considered by many to be one of the best preserved nineteenth century main streets in the state. The construction is of native brick and cast iron and all but two of the contiguous buildings were constructed in the 1890s.

Main Street is listed as a National Preservation Site because of its unique architecture.

The Wickwire Hotel was built in 1885 when a local farmer decided to branch out from growing hogs and corn. The building is made from locally produced brick and at one time the main floor had a lobby and a "sample room" for traveling salesmen.

Hooper was once known for its hog cholera serum plant. We just thought you might like to know.

Seven miles (1/2 mile.)
Scribner. Yes folks, this town was named after Charles

Scribner of the famous New York publishing house which did not publish this book. Scribner was the son-in-law of one of the founders.

The museum is located in the old Milligan Building, built in 1884. The town hall was built in 1906 of local brick. The Soll Opera House was built in 1898. Patrons hoisted themselves to the second floor theater with a hand-pulled elevator.

The Harder Hotel. Built in 1901.

The Musbach Museum. This was a dry goods store, and was donated to the city to use as a museum.

East of Scribner on Bridge Street, then turn north on the first county road east of the Elkhorn River Bridge. The Scribner Brickyards were built in the 1890s. One of the "bee hive" kilns can still be seen as well as the brick horse barn. This is one of the few remaining nineteenth century brickyards in the state. Near here was the Black Hills Wagon Trail.

Just west of Scribner on 275 is the Mr. Cottonwood Historical Marker. To quote: "It grew from a trackwalker's probing staff thrust into the ground in 1871 by the late Herman Wegner. Protected through the years by the C & NW Railroad and after by a city ordinance. A living symbol planted unwittingly, made by God, protected by Man."

One half mile west, and one half mile south of Scribner is the location of the old Peeble Mills built in 1868.

Eight and one half miles west of Scribner on county roads is the site of Glencoe, post office established in 1871.

Three miles (1 mile.)
Junction for Snyder.

Four miles west of junction: Snyder.
Snyder town hall was built in 1903 and has recently been renovated.

The Snyder Opera House was built in 1900 and had a main floor restuarant and saloon, and a second floor entertainment hall.

Five miles west of Snyder: Dodge. You are in Dodge City, Dodge County and oddly enough the names are not related. The county was named after an Iowa Senator, and the city after an early pioneer. The town hall was built in 1895 and the bell tower once held a large fire bell.

One mile (1 mile.)
One mile east to Dead Timber State Recreation Area.

310

One mile (7 miles.)
Crowell. Crowell was founded in 1883.

Seven miles (7 miles.)
West Point. This town, located on the lovely Elkhorn River, is one of the state's oldest settlements. It was founded in 1857 by a man who set up a brickyard and a sawmill. A small war broke out between the founder of these businesses and two other competing ones. We are talking real bullets and real hangings here. The opposition set fire to the mills, shot at the owner and hanged one of his workers.

West Point was so named because the settlers thought of this place as the furthest West the white settlement of America would get for a while. Try explaining this to the folks in Newport, Oregon.

West Point is the location of the Cuming County Museum, located in the old train depot. The museum itself is quite old and its exhibits are in fine condition.

On the east edge of West Point is Wilderness Park, 120 acres set aside for the enjoyment of human and animal alike.

Northwest of West Point Highway 275 parallels the lovely Elkhorn River. Just off the highway between West Point and Beemer, is the De Witt Cemetery, designated as an official Nebraska Historical site. It is at the oldest settlement in Cuming County.

North east of West Point 10 miles on State Highway 9 and then east for eight miles State Highway 51 is the John G. Neihardt Center to honor one of Nebraska's greatest writers. See the entry on US Highway 77 for more information.

Seven miles (7 miles.)
Beemer. Beemer also has a wilderness park, this one is 230 acres and provides access to the Elkhorn.

South of Beemer, two miles on county roads: Immanuel Lutheran Church. This is the oldest Missouri Synod Lutheran Church in the state. It was established at this location in 1868.

Seven miles (1 mile.)
Wisner. For as long as there has been a Wisner (since 1871) this town has served as a feeding and shipping point for livestock. Thousands of cattle are fed along the lots which cover the sloping bluffs along the highway. Anyone from Nebraska knows what the

smell really is. The smell is the smell of money.

By the way, Cuming County is known as the livestock capitol of Nebraska.

Twenty miles east of Wisner on State Highway 51 to the John G., Neihardt Center to honor one of the state's finest writers. See the entry for US Highway 77 for details.

Five miles (1 mile.)

Junction with State Highway 15, north. For information about sites along this route, please see entry for State Highway 15.

One mile (8 miles.)

Just south of the highway: Pilger.

One of Nebraska's least recognized yet most famous Hollywood actors came from a farm just south of this small rural community. Blue Boy, a prize-winning Hampshire Hog had a nearly starring role in the movie "State Fair." And you thought it was just Marlon Brando who was from Nebraska!

Junction of State Highway 15, south. For information about sites along this route, please see the entry for State Highway 15.

Two miles north of Pilger is a recreation area with an inviting 40 acre lake.

Eight miles (8 miles.)

Junction with State Highway 57, five miles south to Stanton. Please see the entry for State Highway 15 for information about Stanton.

Eight miles (10 miles.)

Norfolk.

Junction with US Highway 81. Please see the entry for US Highway 81 for information about Norfolk (yes, the hometown of Johnny Carson) and for sites along the route of Highway 81.

Ten miles (7 miles.)

The Elkhorn River. This river is one of the more popular rivers in the state for recreational purposes.

Two tenths of a mile past the river, on the right is the site of the Pawnee Battleground. In 1859 the Pawnee "agreed" to give up their land on the Platte River and move further north. However, soon after, just as they were about to start their migration, a group of settlers near present-day Fremont had an altercation with the Pawnee. The whites say the Indians robbed a man. The Indians, although no one listened, say a white man raped an Indian. In any event the Pawnee fled up the Elkhorn River. General John Thayer was dispatched to follow them. He encountered the Pawnee at this spot on the morning of July 12, 1859. The Pawnee surrendered six men and paid for damages the whites at Fremont demanded. Although this is still called a battleground, there was no battle here to speak of.

Seven miles (5 miles.)
Millstone State Camping Area.

Five miles (7 miles.)
Tilden. This town lies in the counties of Antelope and Madison. It was named after Samuel Tilden who lost the Presidential race in 1876 to Rutherford Hayes.

An unknown hack writer by the name of Ron Hubbard was born in Tilden. He later fooled around with an electrical machine much like a lie detector and decided to create a religion based on this and his idea of perfect science fiction. From his efforts a group known as the Scientologists were formed, and L. Ron Hubbard became famous.

Since then, no one in Tilden believed Hubbard's thinking was ever quite clear.

Seven miles (6 miles.)
Oakdale.

Tintern Monastery. This is a special and an unsual place. This monastery was founded by the Monks of Tintern, an order based on the teachings and visions of Father Clifford Frank. This is the first order to be established since the 13th Century, and the first order ever to originate in the United States. For visits to the monastery, ask directions in Oakdale.

Six miles (17 miles.)
Neligh, county seat of Antelope County, and home of the Neligh Mills. The Antelope County Historical Society is located on the highway and is open Friday and Sunday afternoons.

Neligh Mills is a branch museum run by the Nebraska State Historical Society. It was built in 1873 and was the most important flour mill in northeast Nebraska. It continued to produce flour until the 1950s. The mill was powered by water from the Elkhorn River.

In this area are the Antelope Historical Museum and various historical markers. This is a must see point of interest if you are traveling in this section of the state.

Just west of Neligh is the junction with State Highway 14. For information about sites along its route, please see the entry for State Highway 14.

Seventeen miles (11 miles.)

Six miles north, just on the county line, is the highest point in Antelope County at around 2,100 feet.

Eleven miles (0 miles.)

Junction with US Highway 20. It is 13 miles to O'Neill. Entry for US Highway 275 ends. For more information about sites along this route, please see the entry for US Highway 20.

Zero miles (5 miles.)

    Missouri River and the Iowa border.

    US Highway 20 enters Nebraska at South Sioux City in Dakota County. Dakota County was named for the tribe of Indians known as the Kacotah, or Sioux who lived in this area for a long while. South Sioux City is a part of a community that spans three states.

    Sioux City proper is in Iowa, and North Sioux City is in South Dakota. It is pretty plain, however, that South Sioux City, Nebraska is the finest looking of all three.

    South Sioux City itself had one time been the location of four different towns which eventually merged to form a single entity.

    Down along the shore of the Big Muddy Missouri River you will see the largest marina anywhere along its banks.

    While watching the boats, reach down and take a handful of the soil here. You can only find this particular soil—a wind blown remnant from the Ice Age known as loess—one other place in the

315

US Highway 20

world, and that is in China.

When Prohibition was adopted in Iowa, South Sioux City got quite a reputation as a center of vice. Saloons which featured women of the night, fist and gun fights, and gambling and dancing were the highlights of those days.

Five miles (4 miles.)

Jackson—a sleepy community in the shadow of the three big sisters to the east.

Just north of here was the original site of the quiet town of St. John's, founded just before the Civil War by a Catholic priest who wanted to set up a missionary for the Omaha Indians. The priest went away to serve in the war, and the town moved to this location in order to avoid the threat of flooding by the Missouri. Later the town's name was changed to Jackson.

Four miles (23 miles.)

Junction with State Highway 12. For information about sites along this route, please see entry for State Highway 12.

Twenty three miles (2 miles.)

Intersection of US 20 and State Highway 15.

Two miles north of this intersection is the location of the old town of Norris, abandoned after it was bypassed by the railroad. One mile further east and a quarter mile north is the location of the old Norris Cemetery. For information about other sites north and south on 15, please see the entry for State Highway 15.

Two miles (1 mile.)

One mile east of the intersection of US 20 and this county road is the location of the former town of Claremont Junction. The town eventually died, which is what happens when you are known as a former town.

One mile (14 miles.)

Laurel.

In the town cemetery, on the southwest corner of the village, is the grave of a Mrs. Gleason who was born in the 18th century and died in the 20th.

The junction with State Highway 15, south is here. For a continuation of sites along that route, please see entry for State Highway 15.

Fourteen miles (4 miles.)
Randolph.

Randolph is known as the honey capitol of the world. When you buy that Sioux Bee Honey, keep in mind that the honey may be packaged elsewhere, but Randolph's 16,000 colonies of bees (or roughly 160,000,000 bees), which produce more than a million pounds of honey each year, is where it really comes from.

Four miles (6 miles.)
Junction with US Highway 81. For sites north and south along this highway, please see the entry for US Highway 81.

Six miles (13 miles.)
Junction with State Highway 121. To the north are such sites as the Wild Horse Holding Facility and the best pastry this side of heaven. For information about these and other sites, please see the entry for State Highway 14.

Thirteen miles (12 miles.)
Plainview. Well, yes, but there are people in the Bronx who would trade this view for theirs any day.

Junction with State Highway 13. For information about sites along State Highway 13, please see entry for US Highway 81.

Twelve miles (11 miles.)
Junction with State Highway 14. This highway runs from the Kansas border to the border with South Dakota. For information about sites in this area and along its route, please see entry for State Highway 14.

Eleven miles (11 miles.)
Orchard. This town was named for the miles of apple orchards planted here in pioneer times.

According to Lilian Fitzpatrick's fine book *Nebraska Place-Names,* Antelope County was named to remember an antelope one of the first settlers shot for dinner while guiding an early group of tourists through the area in 1867.

From Orchard to O'Neill US 20 passes through or very near to a half dozen or better small communities both dead and alive. The highway parallels the Elkhorn River and winds its way uphill. As the road slips past hills speckled with yucca the entire sense of western

US Highway 20

America begins to unfold. Or, for those of you traveling east...the entire sensation of the peopled and cultivated eastern America begins to reveal itself.

Eleven miles (13 miles.)

Junction with US Highway 275, south. For information about this highway, please see entry for US Highway 275. US 275 joins US 20 at this point, northward.

Thirteen miles (8 miles.)

O'Neill.

At 4,000 proud and friendly folks, O'Neill is the largest town in any direction for close to 100 miles. Its location in the heart of the Elkhorn Valley makes it an ideal place for both the small garden farmer as well as the rancher. I wouldn't get the oxygen masks out just yet, but O'Neill is at nearly 2,000 feet in altitude and from here westward the gradual climb to the continental divide is apparent.

O'Neill is the county seat of Holt County and the courthouse is the center of the town's activities. The peaceful and quiet streets around the Courthouse simply shadow a much wilder and reckless past.

During the early years of this century O'Neill was known as one of the roughest towns around. To give you an idea just how rough things were around here, a man by the name of Barrett Scott, who was the Holt County Treasurer, took off for Mexico with his pockets apparently full of the county's money. He was found and brought back to O'Neill to face trial.

He was released on bail, but while free he was kidnapped. His body was found 30 miles north of here on the banks of the Niobrara River. Scott's body was wrapped in a horse blanket, and the hanging rope was still around his neck. A boot heel mark was in the middle of his forehead, and his body was mutilated.

Forty men were arrested and a dozen were brought to trial. None of those 12 ever served time for Scott's murder. By the way, no one has so much as stolen a dime from the coffee fund much less embezzled county funds since that day.

O'Neill was founded by, and named after, John J. O'Neill who was quite a flamboyant character in his own right. He was an Irish-American and spearheaded a group to encourage Irish settlement of the American West. The first colony to settle under O'Neill's director-ship was right here in 1874. O'Neill had earlier fought for the Union in the Civil War and had commanded a Black infantry. Later he was a major figure in the so-called and short-lived Fenian invasion of Canada.

The town of O'Neill was one of the oldest towns in the state to traditionally have Sunday shopping hours for most stores. This was originally (and is still true) to help service those out-of-towners who could only make it to town on the weekends.

Eight miles (10 miles.)

Emmet, named after an Irish patriot.

North of here, all the way to the Niobrara River, some 30 miles distant, are numerous Indian burials, often located on small hilltops. These burials were encased in limestone rock slabs and were regarded by the ancient peoples who once lived here as sacred places. Don't disturb them, think how your would feel if someone dug up great grandfather Herkimer.

Ten miles (30 miles.)

Junction with State Highway 11. For information about sites along this route, please see the entry for State Highway 11.

Atkinson. The second settlement founded by John O'Neill and his Irish. In case you wondered, no, the town did not look like this in the late 1870s when first settled. A small lake just outside of town provides camping and recreation facilities.

Thirty miles (9 miles.)

Bassett and the junction with US 183. For information about Bassett and points south, please see the entry for US Highway 183.

Nine miles (3 miles.)

Long Pine is a half mile south of the highway.

This tiny town with the attractive name would be called Mazi-sneede Wachishka if the white settlers had not translated the name of the local creek from its original Omaha. Just outside of the town is Long Pine Recreation Area, another fine and beautiful area for the camper, hiker, fisherperson and nature lover.

One half mile past the turnoff for Long Pine the highway crosses the canyon which is formed by Long Pine Creek. Who says Nebraska isn't beautiful? Good fishing here.

Three miles (6 miles.)

Junction of US 183, north. Please see entry for US Highway

183 for information about this area.

As you come in sight of Ainsworth you enter an area known as Bone Creek. This area was named because of the thousands of buffalo skeletons which once littered the floor of the valley.

Six miles (10 miles.)
Ainsworth.

Ainsworth was named for a railroad construction engineer and was founded in 1883.

The Civil War Memorial at the County Courthouse park was built in 1948 because of the donation of a Civil War veteran, L.K. Alder. Alder volunteered at the age of 17, and served nearly two years under General Sherman, and accompanied Sherman on his famous "march to the sea." The Nannie Osborne homestead is the oldest structure in Ainsworth. The home was built in 1879. Nannie was divorced from her husband when she moved to Ainsworth from Ft. Hartsuff, 70 miles to the southeast. It must not have been easy for a divorced, single woman in 1879, especially one who wanted to build such a fine home.

Sellors Memorial Museum. This small but interesting museum was not built by pioneers, but by as a memorial to all Brown County pioneers. The logs were cut from trees along the banks of the Niobrara and hauled here in 1936. It was expanded in 1967.

North out of Ainsworth for 13 miles on county roads until you reach Plum Creek. Here are many fossil beds in the limestone of the deep canyon along the creek. Camels, rhinoceroses and prehistoric horses have been found in these fossil beds.

Ten miles (11 miles.)
Turn off to Long Lake on Highway 20.

Some miles south of here, at the junction of Long Lake turn-off and Elsmere Rd. was the site of the only sod high school ever built in the United States. This is no pioneer story. Lakeland High School that once stood here, and was built entirely of sod, was constructed in 1934. That's right, 1934.

Because of the Depression and the drouth, many students in the isolated western part of Brown County were going to have to drop out of Ainsworth High School. For eight years a total of 33 students attended the small campus-like high school which consisted of the school, a barn and a his and a hers two seater.

All of the buildings, including the privies, were made from native sod. The school marm and her family lived in the sod school.

The instructor, Mary Holm, cooked her family's meals on a Coleman stove.

All parents are required to stop here a moment for this place is the original prototype of all those "when I was your age, we had to ride 20 miles on horseback to get to school" stories. Most students arrived by horseback, and many lived over five miles away. They arrived by traveling across country, stopping to dismount and open, then close numerous gates.

Mrs. Holm was not the only teacher. Two others worked at the school in the seven years it existed.

South on Long Lake Rd to Long Lake Recreation Area. Local folks will tell you that the best fishing to be found is in Long Lake. Don't believe them. There's good fishing there, all right, but to find the truly great spots you need to act like you are a local person and just listen. (Fishing hint: It rhymes with June and spoon.) A fine camping area is located here.

One half mile to Johnstown. Small community of windmills, horses, and houses. Johnstown was once the home of John Berry who drove the mail stage to Ft. Niobrara.

Eleven miles (19 miles.)
Wood Lake in Cherry County.

Cherry County was named for a soldier who was killed near Ft. Niobrara. It is said that Cherry County is the largest county in the United States. If that turns out to be only local boosterism, bear in mind that this county is larger than Connecticut, Delaware and Rhode Island combined, and a lot more livable, many Cherry County citizens might add.

Wood Lake was a name given to this town by early settlers. They knew it meant that here, finally, were some trees around a small lake, but others not from around here might think it implied a lake in the woods.

Nineteen miles (2 miles.)
Junction with US Highway 83. For information about sites along this highway, please see the entry for US Highway 83.

Two miles (3 miles.)
The highways cross the Niobrara River, Nebraska's wildest river, at the Bryan Bridge, named for William Jennings Bryan,

US Highway 20

Nebraska's only presidential candidate (unless you consider Gerald Ford, who was born in Omaha). The man lost three times. Don't worry, the bridge is probably safe. The river here is extremely beautiful as it winds through a shallow canyon.

Three miles (11 miles.)

Valentine.

The canoe and white-water capitol of Nebraska.

This is the county seat of the vast Cherry County. This is as close as you'll get to the way life was in the Old West. The town is proud of its ranching and farming history and the flavor of the west is everywhere here. Lake Minnechaduza on the northern edge of the town was formed in 1892 when a local flour mill dammed the Minnechaduza Creek for a mill run. The name is from the Indian name for the stream.

Valentine is the home of the Cherry County Historical Museum at South Main and Highway 20. It is open six days a week during the summer months, and three days a week during fall and spring. In winter it is opened by appointment only. The museum contains pictures, articles and other materials that show the history of Cherry County, Ft. Niobrara, Valentine and other local communities. Some of the unusual items include a baptismal font, the weapons and disguise used in a train holdup in 1890, one of the first typewriters, a vast collection of arrowheads and Indian artifacts, a button collection, a research facility containing many printed county documents and a log cabin built by Valentine's first postmaster and moved to the museum grounds in 1982.

Valentine is also the canoe outfitter headquarters for trips on the Niobrara. Several outfitters and rental places abound in the community for the spectacular trip down Nebraska's beautiful Niobrara. There has long been talk of designating the 20 mile stretch of the river near here as a wild and scenic river which would allow for protection and tourist regulation of the river.

Four miles east of Valentine on State Highway 12 is the Ft. Niobrara National Wildlife Refuge. This area is home to many of the large animals which once roamed this area including buffalo, elk, antelope and deer. A small herd of longhorn cattle were introduced here not long ago. It is over 20,000 acres and was originally set aside by President Theodore Roosevelt. The Niobrara formed a 100 deep canyon through part of the refuge, and streams enter the canyon in waterfalls.

Many fossils have been collected in this area. Near the refuge headquarters is the site of the original Ft. Niobrara which includes a museum. The fort was built in 1880 to protect settlers from the Sioux.

The refuge is one of the finer areas in Cherry County. For more information about other locations along Route 12, please see entry for State Highway 12.

Follow State **Highway 97 southwest** *out of Valentine* **25 miles** *to the Samuel McKelvie National Forest. After about 15 miles the road crosses the Niobrara River. It was near here that Doc Middleton had a hideout.*

At **32 miles** *from Valentine on State 97, is the turnoff for Snake River Falls. Snake Falls is the most dramatic waterfall in the state and is the highlight of the beautiful Snake River. The Snake River plunges over a 22 foot cliff in a deep canyon. Behind the falls is a natural cave which was used for years by horse thieves and other banditos. Today it serves as a cool place for local children to cool off in late July.*

At **34 miles** *the Merritt Reservoir provides fishing and boating and flood control, but destroyed some of the most beautiful river scenery in the state.*

There is camping in the national forest, with developed sites at Merritt Reservoir and at the National Forest Headquarters 19 miles south of Nenzel west of Valentine (see below).

Ask at the museum for directions to the Bowering Bar 99 Ranch which was a ranch willed to the Nebraska Game and Parks Department and is the state's first living-history ranch.

At Valentine are the junctions of State Highway 12 and US Highway 83. Please see those entries for more information about sites in this area.

Eleven miles (8 miles.)

Crookston, where a mill on the Minnechaduza Creek was an important early-day business.

Eight miles (12 miles.)

You have passed into (or from if you are headed east) Mountain Standard Time while traveling through the rolling Sandhills.

Twelve miles (7 miles.)

Nenzel at the junction of State Road 16F.

US Highway 20

South on 16F for 20 miles to the campgrounds of the Samuel McKelvie National Forest. Along the way you will pass a few scattered and old homestead ranches, including that of the historian and early politician A.E. Sheldon whose History of Nebraska *is still a viable history of the state.*

Seven miles (15 miles.)

Cody. If you missed the western flavor of the area so far, Cody, named after a local pioneer and not Buffalo Bill, should give you an idea.

Ten miles south of here, on private land, are the Boiling Springs, one of the great natural wonders of the county. Ask locally for directions and permission to visit the place.

Fifteen miles (9 miles.)

Eli, notable for its name which was after Daniel Webster Hitchcock, whose nickname was "Get-There-Eli." For a long while this town was known by the full Get-There-Eli.

Nine miles (30 miles.)

Cottonwood Lake Recreation Area. An 80 acre lake stocked with fine fishing fish.

Merriman,. Just to the west of the recreation area is at the junction of State Highway 61 at Merriman. This highway travels through some of the most isolated territory in the state. It is 70 miles to Hyannis down this road. This road is only meant for the traveler seeking complete isolation and beauty. For those of you interested in Highway 61 revisited, please see entry for State Highway 61.

Thirty miles (15 miles.)

Gordon.

Gordon was the part-time home of Nebraska's most famous outlaw, "Doc" Middleton. He was born in Texas under a different name and arrived in the Sandhills region in the late 1870s, having already killed a number of men in Texas and Kansas, as well as being on the Texas Rangers "Most Wanted" list for stealing horses. (A crime considered by many to be worse than murder.)

After being held in log chains in a log jail in Sidney for stealing 34 horses, Middleton escaped during the night by shoveling a tunnel to the outside.

On another occasion Middleton was chased by a posse from Ogallala to Sidney, during which he crossed the Camp Clarke Bridge near Bridgeport in Morrill County with his reins in his teeth and his .45s blazing the night sky, traded his horse for another and escaped the pursuit of the posse.

He later spent much time around Bassett, Neligh, O'Neill and Atkinson as many of those area ranchers were on friendly terms with the outlaw.

In 1885 Doc Middleton wrote a short article about his life in the Gordon paper. "It is utterly false that I stole horses from either stockmen or citizens. On these occasions I resorted to a game of bluff to protect myself and made it work. I do not deny that I drove off horses from the Indians. I did do that, but it was not from choice that I did so. I have sowed my wild oats and reaped the harvest and now, having settled down in the determination to be a man among men, I can afford to tell the truth, I claim that among those who know me best, my word is as good as that of any man and will not be doubted."

It was generally agreed, however, by those who knew him best, that the Badlands Badman was "an outlaw and a killer who was also gracious and refined, a gentleman of the road who would steal your horse but pay for his dinner."

Doc Middleton had a wife and children. One of his sons, Ponca Bill, once said that his father always buried the men he shot, which was more than some could say...and he always came home at least twice a year. An excellent book on the life of Doc Middleton was written by Harold Hutton of Bassett. Some copies of the book are still available at bookstores throughout the state.

Visit the Mari Sandoz room in Chamberlin-Hobbs Furniture store, a private collection of Sandoz memorabilia. It is free and open working hours during the week.

Ask at the Mari Sandoz room for a copy of a short walking tour of Gordon.

Junction with State Highway 27. South of here are many sites that the author Mari Sandoz wrote about in her famous book, *Old Jules*. For information on these and other locations, please see the entry for State Highway 27.

Fifteen miles (9 miles.)

Rushville.

Don't laugh at this small Nebraska town. More famous people have visited it than will ever visit you or I. These have included Buffalo Bill, Presidents Teddy Roosevelt and Calvin Coolidge, John J. Pershing, Fredrick Remington and many others.

US Highway 20

Home of Sheridan County Museum, a small but interesting county museum worth the hour spent inside. Near here is Smith Lake, noted for a long while for its good fishing.

Junction with State Highway 87. This road has many interesting sites along its route, including many places the author Mari Sandoz wrote about. For more information please see entry for State Highway 87.

An interesting circle tour which will allow you to view many sites of interest in the history of the relations with the Sioux Indians can begin at Rushville. For a description of this tour, please see entry for Hay Springs, below.

Nine miles (2 miles.)

Turn off to Walgren Lake. *The lake is **five miles south.***

Walgren Lake is an alkali lake, and home of Nebraska's only known sea monster. This monster was well known in pioneer days, and many a modern sighting has reinforced its existence.

In 1921 a rancher was passing near when his horses reared up. He looked out across the lake and saw an animal spouting water about 150 yards from shore. He estimated that the animal was 10 feet long, a yard wide and was dark in color.

Later that same year it was seen again, with the same description, Once again, late in 1921 two state workers heard a very loud splash near the shore, although they did not see anything.

Then in August 1922 several witnesses saw a 20 foot long creature in the shape of a fish.

In 1923 an association was formed to drag the lake and catch the monster. Everything was set until the landowners of the lake learned that the association was going to charge admission and asked for a cut. The plan fell through.

As it is said in these parts, any devil who can scatter fossilized bones over the Sandhills to confuse those of little faith, can put a sea monster in an alkali lake.

Two miles (10 miles.)

Hay Springs.

***North** of Hay Springs on county graveled roads are many interesting historical sites. About **15 miles** north is the location of the Spotted Tail Indian Agency, 1874, as well as the "chosen land" of Crazy Horse.*

***Another five miles** brings the brave traveler to the site of Camp Sheridan, established to keep the Sioux in toe and to protect the* *early settlers.*

***Five miles to the east** is Beaver Wall, an escarpment with breath-taking views which increase in grandeur with every mile. From the top one can see from the Black Hills to the buttes at Crawford, a distance of nearly 150 miles.*

Swing back south on the marked gravel road toward Rushville and pass through Metcalf Game Reserve. A great place to hike, since the county road is the only road through the preserve. Wild turkey, deer and antelope are common here.

***Twenty miles south** to return to Rushville, or go back the way you came to Hay Springs.*

Ten miles (2 miles.)

Dawes and Sioux Counties were once a part of a single large county known as Sioux County which encompassed an area from the North Platte River to the state line. In the late 1800s they were divided into approximately their present sizes.

Here, where the Little Bordeaux Creek crosses the highway, was the location of a village named for the trader, James Bordeaux. A farmstead and a railroad siding are all that remain of the community.

The long ridge you see in front of you is Pine Ridge, a series of bluffs, hills and escarpments which cut across this corner of the state.

It was near here that one of the most incredible stories of the Old West took place. In 1823 a man named Hugh Glass set out for the Yellowstone with a party of prospectors and explorers. Near what would one day be either Nebraska or South Dakota, he was attacked by a grizzly bear.

The bear tore at Glass' flesh, leaving gaping holes in his sides, arms and legs. The rest of his party, certain that he would die, left two men to watch over him and bury him when he died. After five days the men grew restless and stole all of his belongings: his gun, knife, and supplies and left him to die alone with the coyotes and wolves.

Instead, Glass survived and slowly crawled 100 miles to a fort on the Missouri in what is now western South Dakota. He rested a few days until he found a party heading for the Yellowstone. He set out with them, still very weak, but in search of the men who had left him.

A few days later this party was attacked by a party of Arikara Indians who killed everyone in the party except for Glass. Glass continued on alone and nearly two months later he reached the Yellowstone.

However, the men who had abandoned him, he soon learned, had returned down river to Ft. Atkinson near the present-day town of Ft. Calhoun, north of Omaha. Glass immediately turned around and, rigging a canoe out of buffalo hides, began to float the river.

He hooked up with a party of couriers delivering supplies to various Army outposts. Along the way these men were attacked by more Arikara, and—you guessed it—Glass escaped.

He strayed across this part of Nebraska and walking and floating various rivers he eventually made it to Ft. Atkinson about a year to the day after he had been attacked by the bear.

The men he sought were at the fort, but by then Glass had cooled some, and in time the men ironed out their dispute and became friends. Glass' story is told in verse by Nebraska's poet laureate, John Neihardt (see entry for Bancroft).

Two miles (5 miles.)

Near here was the site of the Sweat Colony, a religious utopia movement of the late 1880s founded by Levi G. Sweat from Missouri. The colony made up a good portion of the area's earliest white inhabitants, a few of their descendants still populate the area.

Five miles (1 mile.)

Museum of the Fur Trade has exhibits on the fur trade in North America. The trading house of James Bordeaux (1837-1876) is located on the grounds. The exhibits include weapons, furs, trade goods and an Indian garden with many of the plants used by local Indians. It is open every day during the summer, and during the winter by appointment. Don't be put off, the superintendent will open the museum for you. It is a good idea to call ahead of time, however.

Within a **quarter mile** *of here are a handful of historic locations. About a quarter mile to the* **east** *turn north on the road which curves north across the railroad tracks.*

Just to the west, and visible from the road, is the site of the Joseph Bissonette's log trading post which was in operation from 1872-1877. The Nelson saloon, post office and stage station are also located here.

In about **a half a mile** *this road crosses Bordeaux Creek,* **three miles** *downstream and on the west bank was the location of a commonly frequented Sioux campsite.*

Six miles to the northeast *you might catch a glimpse of Sheridan's Gates, two buttes through which the military road led to Camp Sheridan.*

One half mile east of the museum the scenic Bordeaux Road runs south through table lands and canyons until it connects with *US 385, 15 miles away.*

About *four miles south* on this road, along the west bank of the creek was Spotted Tail's camp from 1870-1872. The road intersects with King's Canyon Road about six miles south at a place known to locals at "the Cliffs."

One mile (2 miles.)

One mile west of the Museum of the Fur Trade: Take Slim Buttes Rd. north. That farmstead on your right also served as an old dance hall many moon ago.

Two miles (3 miles.)

Chadron.

If there ever was a town that once had saloons with swinging doors, cowboys who used their 45s to finish any and all heated discussions, and other wild types, Chadron was it. Some might say that there is still a bit of this Old West flavor to the place.

Some of Chadron's early citizens such as ranchers Charles Coffee (not from Columbian mountains) and Bartlett Richards are members of the Hall of Great Westerners at the National Cowboy Hall of Fame in Oklahoma City. During the Massacre at Wounded Knee in 1890 many of the surrounding area families gathered in Chadron for protection. They needed none, the Indians were wiped out fairly thoroughly.

Chadron's most famous citizen might well be Milford (Dub) Miller who was a tackle for the Chicago Bears from 1934 until 1937. Miller wasn't quite a refrigerator, but the Bears were considered the best team in the nation. At the time of Miller's seasons with the Bears a good professional football player made about $125 per game. That figures out to something like $2,500 per year, including bonuses. Miller, who is remembered locally as a good, kind-hearted man, died in 1981.

Another unusual Chadron resident was Clyde Beedle, an eccentric strongman who entertained people from everywhere with his amazing feats of strength. Beedle was well-known for being able to drive a spike through a one inch thick board with his bare hands. He often could be seen pulling the 4 ton fire engine across Chadron's First Street by his teeth. He also amused himself by bending a 3/8ths inch bolt into a circle, by tearing a deck of cards into quarters, and diving over straight back chairs while carrying 35 pound weights in each

US Highway 20

hand. Perhaps one of his most inspiring activities was to tie a rope around his neck and then get four strong men to pull with all their strength. Beedle did not choke. He died in 1975 at age 81, but before his death he was still able to squat press 250 pounds, and bench press 325.

First off, put this book on the seat of the car and drive directly to the Chadron Chamber of Commerce and pick up a copy of their excellent *People and Places From the Sidewalks of Yesteryear—A Walking Tour of Chadron.* This little book, also available at some bookstores, will provide an enjoyable afternoon in the town on an easy and rewarding one mile tour.

You could drive, but better yet, get out of that gas-hog for a moment, and walk south on Main Street from downtown. Chadron has many Victorian houses, as well as other classic styles such as bungalow (usually a low-slung, comfortable looking sort of house with a wide porch on several sides), and Georgian Revivial. Many of these styles, as well as some other eccentric ones can be seen in the blocks immediately adjacent to downtown on Main Street.

Also stroll around the streets that run parallel to Main. Among the other things you will see are the old houses that once belonged to one of Chadron's founding families, the Coffees. (No, they didn't go to pot, nor were they half-perked.)

Chadron's downtown contains some unusual and historic buildings. Perhaps one of the most unusual is the Blaine Hotel at 2nd and Bordeaux streets.

The hotel opened in 1892, and a year later this building served as the starting place for an event known as "The Great Cowboy Race" where hundreds of cowboys raced from Chadron, Nebraska to Chicago, Illinois. Some dignitary stood on the balcony just above the main entrance and fired a gun into the air and all that was seen then was a cloud of dust fading off in the direction of Chicago.

The World's Fair was going on in Chicago, and hell, that seemed as good a reason as any to have a race. Among the competitors was the outlaw "Doc" Middleton (see entry for Gordon Nebraska, above). The Humane Society was dead set against the race and they kept a careful eye on the entire affair, following the horses' conditions through the 1,000 mile race. Although lots of cowboys started the race, only 9 or so were serious about it. The prize was $1,000. The first man to reach the finish line (which was the entrance to Buffalo Bill's Wild West Show) took 13 days and 16 hours.

Across Bordeaux Street is the Niles Hotel, once used by the railroad to house work crews.

Don't sell Chadron short. Near here were the law offices of Fannie O'Linn, the first woman postmistress in the state as well as the first woman in Nebraska to be admitted to the bar. The story goes that she owned land west of here, hoping to sell it to the land company which would then form a town named after her. The price was too high and instead the land company bought some land further east.

For a long while people believed that the town was named after Pierre Chadron, an old-time French fur trapper and squaw man who trapped in these parts. That's a pretty nice bit of romantic stuff fit for a Mitchener novel, but in the late 1970s researchers determined the town was more likely named after Louis Chartran a trader and trapper.

Either way the ghosts of these old pioneers haunt the coolies and hills of the area to this day. At 2nd and Main the white brick building was the home of a bank when it was built in 1885, and catty-corner is the First National Bank building which was built in 1917 by C. F. Coffee (no drip, this guy).

It was at this location on July 4, 1900, that Teddy Roosevelt stood in the noonday heat and spoke to the thousand or better gathered there. His speech was more than likely the same one he had given across the Panhandle, but the crowd cheered all the same.

Roosevelt liked this neck of the great American woods, and it is easy to see why.

At the corner of 2nd and Chadron Streets you can see two curbs, as the older one, when the streets were wider, is still visible. On the east side of Chadron Street hitching rings are still visible. There are those from the eastern part of the state who might want to believe these are still used by wild cowboys. I'm not going to tell you any differently.

City Hall (234 Main) was built in 1917, and the Pace Theater, next door was built in 1925. The first movie to be shown in the Pace was "Sea Hawk," not a talkie, so a local band provided the music. Across the street is the old Opera House , built in 1888. Many of the buildings on that side of the street are brick, and date from the late 1880s. This is because most of the rest of the town was destroyed by a fire in 1887.

331

US Highway 20

The Federal Building, now the Post Office, at 278 Main was a pork barrel project of Moses P. Kinkaid. Yes, the same Moses P. who revised the homesteading act and invited thousands of farmers to try their hand at making the Sandhills bloom. These homesteaders were known by the then derogatory name "Kinkiaders."

Unlike many other counties in Nebraska, Dawes County had a reasonable way of determining which city should be the county seat. Instead of fisticuffs, or gunplay, or outright skullduggery, the citizens of Dawes voted for their county seat. The county court house at 4th and Main reminds some of the Nebraska statehouse in Lincoln.

Some blocks from here $26,000 was found stashed in the basement of a house at the corner of Fifth and Maple. The money was mostly in silver dollars and was found shortly after the owner, John Sweeney, died in 1959. The money was hidden in the cellar, behind two locked doors. There were 105 glass jars filled with silver dollars wrapped in $20 rolls. Fifty-two more jars were found in an old trunk and a cream can. Fifty-three other jars were later found stashed in the basement, some bills were in jars, or paper bags with the amount written neatly on the lid. Sweeney was a bachelor and worked for the railroad all of his life. The house was appraised at $1,430.

Chadron State College is at the southern edge of the town. The Military Road which ran from Ft. Robinson to Camp Sheridan, cuts across the campus.

South of town five miles is the wonderful Dawes County Museum. It is open every day during the summer months and on many weekdays during winter. For a description of this museum and the many historic sites within a few miles of it, please see entry for US Highway 385.

Go north one mile on the eastern edge of Chadron to the site of Chadron Cemetery, which is now abandoned. Several gravesites are still marked. Just west of town is the junction with US Highway 385, south. For information about sites along this route, please see entry for US Highway 385.

Three miles (1 mile.)

Junction for US Highway 385 north. Please see the entry for this highway for information about sites along its route.

Just to the north of the Chadron Airport, along the White River was the location of the great Sundance which was held in 1877 by all the Sioux tribes in the area. This great dance was one of the last great gatherings of the Sioux. The Sundance involved testing a man's courage and spirituality by having him stand and stare at the sun.

332

Some participants were also hung by large bone hooks which had been pierced through their breasts. The ones who endured this dance gained great respect and honor in the tribe as shamans and because they were to have atoned for the wrong deeds to the entire tribe.

The butte to the south is named Trunk Butte for somewhat obvious reasons.

One mile (7 miles.)

A road known as Deadhorse Run goes south off of US 20. It follows Chadron Creek to US 385.

About **1 1/2 miles west** of Deadhorse Run is an alternative route to Whitney along the banks of the White River.

A small but still kicking town founded in 1885, Whitney was once considered as a possible county seat. The population is less than 100 and many empty buildings attest to the fact that Whitney has seen better days. Near here a large Sioux lodge once stood on the banks of the White River. Whitney Lake, two miles to the northwest is a good fishing and skiing spot. Whitney may also be reached by following US 20 for another 7 miles and then taking the paved road two miles north (see below).

Seven miles (3 miles.)

Turn off to Whitney. Straight **west** of here, **two miles,** along the banks of the White River Crazy Horse set up his camp after moving away from Ft. Robinson. See also entry directly above.

Near here the highway crosses the White River. To the east, on the east bank of the river was the site of the Whetstone Indian Agency which existed from 1872 until 1874.

Just south of this site is the location of an old military campsite used often during the Indian "troubles." The careful explorer can still find the rifle pits dug by the soldiers. Please observe no trespassing signs, and respect private property. Also please observe the rather large western diamondback rattlesnake crawling around your Reeboks.

Just to the west, on the north side of the river was the location of a long time Sioux camp.

Ask locally for directions.

Three miles (6 miles.)

Historical marker. **Two miles north** of here is the location of Crazy Horse's camp of 1877. To the south can be seen Crow Butte. See below, entry for Crawford for a description.

Six miles (4 miles.)

Crawford.

The cultural center in downtown Crawford displays the finest in regional arts and crafts. The White River Park has been stocked with trout for children under 16 years of age. Crawford also boasts a fine city park, and a swimming pool on First Street near Highway 20. Calamity Jane lived here for a while.

For tours along State Highway 71 and 2 north and south out of Crawford, see entry for State Highway 2.

For a dramatic look at a piece or two of the Old West, follow this side trip out of Crawford:

*Go **east** out of Crawford on the County road. You will pass Crow Butte to the south of this road.*

Crow Butte was the location of a major battle between warring Indians. It seems the entire thing started when Crow Indians raided James Bordeaux's Trading Post, some 25 miles to the east in 1849. They were alleged to have taken 47 horses and 35 mules. The leader of the raiding party was a Crow named White Bear. Bordeaux gathered together a band of Brule Sioux fighters like Red Leaf, Cloud Man and Two Strikes and followed the Crow.

A major skirmish happened a few miles to the north of here on the banks of the White River. Some of the Crow escaped, but the remainder fled south, the Sioux in hot pursuit. The Crow were backed up against the north face of this butte. They abandoned their horses and then climbed up the single trail to the top of the butte. The Sioux camped below and waited for the Crow to come down for want of water.

For the next three days and nights the Sioux could hear the Crow singing and caught glimpses of them dancing at the top of the butte. Fires lit up the sky from the top of the butte at night. Finally a Sioux scout found a long rope made of rawhide, hair and horse ropes. The Crow, some time before, had slipped down the butte using the hastily made rope. The body of a Crow was found at the bottom of the cliff, a victim of a long fall off the rope. Other Crow had stayed behind to keep the fires burning at night to distract the Sioux. Their fate can only be imagined.

For years this Butte was called "Place Where the Crows Danced" or "Dancers' Butte."

*In another **2 miles** turn **south** and follow White Ash Creek for* *a Nebraska wilderness experience. This rugged and yet beautiful area is open to camping and picnicking.*

*About **5 miles** along White Ash Creek the road rises to the top of Pine Ridge. Swing west here for **another mile** or so to Squaw Mound, the highest point on the Pine Ridge escarpment. Continue past the Ponderosa Special Use Area to State Highway 2.*

***West** of here **four miles** is Deadman Creek, reached by county roads. The creek was named by the Indians who feared its powers of evil. They would not go near the place. Deadman Road, which follows the creek, is roughly the same road used by fur traders in the very earliest years of white occupation of this area. **Three miles west of** Deadman Creek is the ghost town of Glen. Although local folks may resent being called ghosts, this town has seen its heyday as a cattle shipping point.*

*If you made it to Glen, you are now following the White River upstream toward its source. To the north is the Peterson Deer Refuge, and **ten miles west,** just south of the T intersection is the ghost town of Andrews. Andrews was a major railroad shipping center. **Three miles to the north on 2 return to Crawford.***

Four miles (1 mile.)

Fort Robinson.

This is one of the finest in the Nebraska State Park system. Not only is this spot critical to the history of the state, but also to the history of the Native American in the Midwest. It is a park with complete tourist facilities, and yet has enough wide open spaces and wilderness for the individual who wants a bit of alone time.

Through the cooperation of the State Games and Parks Department, the State Historical Society and the University of Nebraska this park offers a paradise for naturalists, photographers, historians, kids, adults and just about anyone. The staff can tell you much more about the significance of this spot than ten books like this so pull in and look around.

One mile (5 miles.)

Smiley Canyon Road. This is the old Highway 20 route which ceased to be used because of all the winter accidents here. This is a beautiful canyon in any season. The road reunites with Highway 20 in about five miles and is the more beautiful route.

Five miles (8 miles.)

Historical Marker concerning the Cheyenne Outbreak. The

335

US Highway 20

road toward Harrison passes the Ft. Robinson timber reserve to the north, and the White River Valley and the Peterson Deer Refuge to the south. At the top of the ridge you are just shy of being 5,280 feet above the sea. That's one mile to you metric folks.

Eight miles (7 miles.)

The winter of 1949 is considered by many in these parts to be the worst winter ever in the Pine Ridge country. During the month of January alone 61 inches—that's five plus feet—fell near Chadron. For a good part of that month the temperature never got above zero. The worst single day of a two month long bad spell was on January 2. For three days the winds blew at hurricane force and the snow continued to fall. Drifts up to 40 feet tall were what the survivors saw when they finally climbed out of their houses. Some places reported that nearly 3 feet of snow fell in two and a half days.

Freight and passenger trains were nonexistent, the first one finally reached the Sandhills on January 28th, after being dug out by the 5th Army. The Army brought in small tanks to provide relief, but they too were slowed by the storms. There were reports of people stranded in their ranch homes for 4 to 6 weeks before finally hearing the low roar of the Army's tanks.

Thousands of bales of hay were air lifted to the livestock in the area. The losses weren't as great as some blizzards, but still many cattle died as a result of the storms. Some estimates put the number at nearly 200,000 cattle and 150,000 sheep.

Still, other animals somehow survived. Pigs, buried in a snow drift for 32 days were found alive. So were geese, horses and cattle.

Many people died in trying to walk a few hundred yards from stalled cars to ranch houses. Others survived, but remembered the winter of '49 as the all-time worst, even more of a disaster than the great blizzard of 1880- 81.

Seven miles (3 1/2 miles.)

*Turn **north** on Pants Butte Road for **five miles** to Sowbelly Canyon and Coffee Park. A lovely small park for day use only. It is run by the city of Harrison and often over looked by the traveler. Swings, picnic facilities and the beautiful outdoors are its greatest features. You may wish to continue to Sowbelly Canyon Road and follow it for **five miles** into the town of Harrison rather than return to Highway 20.*

Three and a half miles (9 miles.)

Harrison.

Please see entry for State Highway 29 for information on Harrison and for information about the remote and beautiful sites north and south of here.

Nine miles (1/2 mile.)

Just before the Wyoming border: Here from the late 1880s until the 1940s was a major railroad siding for shipping cattle out of the grasslands. Such sidings were an extremely important part of ranch life. Often thousands of cattle and a good many cowboys would be here on a Saturday afternoon waiting for the freight to pull up to the siding so that the cattle could be loaded on for shipment.

One half mile (0 miles.)

Wyoming border.

This tour begins at the junction with US Highway 20, eight miles west of South Sioux City. For more information about this area, see entry for US Highway 20.

Zero miles (8 miles.)
Junction with US Highway 20, eight miles west of South Sioux City, Nebraska.

Eight miles (5 miles.)
Ponca. Ponca is one of the oldest towns in the state, it was surveyed in 1856. The town's name is from the tribe of Indians that once lived here and who were banished to Oklahoma during the Civil War. (See entry for Santee Indian Reservation, below, for a more complete description of these people.) A walking tour of Ponca's historic buildings is available. Ask locally for a copy.

Be sure to try and catch the Ponca Rodeo, held each summer.

One of the finest for miles around.

Two miles north of Ponca: Ponca State Park. This park is *1,000 acres of some of the finest woodlands in the state. These hills and valleys attract cross-country skiers in winter and backpackers and horse packers in summer. A fine example of the quality of Nebraska State Parks.*

Five miles (6 miles.)

Take county road to north eight miles to Ionia Volcano. When Lewis and Clark passed this way in 1804, they recorded this bluff overlooking the Missouri in their journals.

The chemical make up of this clay and shale cliff causes it to smoke when fresh rock is exposed to water, hence the name. The Ponca held this cliff to be a sacred place. Its purpose in their world was to serve as a place to purify and clarify the soul. No one was allowed near here unless they had prepared with many days of fasting and prayer. If properly prepared, and with a pure heart of simple faith, the Great Spirit might still speak to those who listened.

Downstream of here, along the west bank of the river, Lewis and Clark reported large mounds which indicated an Indian village of great size had stood there not long before.

Six miles (6 miles.)

Newcastle. A town that was nearly dead when, in 1893, it persuaded the railroad to bring a spur this way. It then thrived until the mid 1930s when the railroad stopped sending trains this way to collect local crops. It is still alive, although once again a shadow of its former self.

Six miles (2 miles.)

Maskell. The surrounding hills and valleys were inhabited by a greater population of prehistoric mammals and historic Indians than by the peaceful and gentle farm dwellers who dot the countryside today. Indian burials in this part of the world were on top of the hills, and because of this, the hills were believed to have a life of their own.

Two miles (3 miles.)

You have just entered Cedar County. This scenic county is rich in natural beauty, but you will have to leave the main highways to see the best part of it.

Three miles (1 mile.)
Turn off to Wiseman Monument. See below.

One mile (5 miles.)
Junction with State Highway 57. *Turn south on 57.*

In about seven miles on the west side of the road an iron fence marks an ancient private cemetery for the Morten family.
In another mile and a half the road swings to the east, then after a mile, to the south again. Just after this curve is the site of the Old Territorial Military Road which ran from Plattsmouth to Niobrara. The trail began in 1857. On the south side of the lane which leads to the family home, the ruts of this road are still visible. This is private property, please ask to see the ruts.

Return a quarter mile north to the intersection with county road. Go *east one mile.* In the field to the south are buffalo wallows and a trail used by buffalos. Both the wallows, and the game trail may still be visible in places. This land belongs to the Anderson family. Please ask their permission to view the ruts.

Return to State Highway 57. Continue south. At the third intersection with county roads, turn east and go three miles. Turn south and go one half mile.

Just to the northwest of the bridge which crosses the creek is a long stretch of ruts from the Old Territorial Military Road of 1857. Also at this location, just to the east of the road was the site of St. Peter's Trading Post and Stage House which serviced travelers on the road.

Retrace route one mile north to intersection with State Highway 84. Take 84 west nine miles to Hartington. See the entry for State Highway 15 for information about Hartington.

Return north, six miles to intersection of State Highway 57 and 12.

Five miles (11 miles.)
The town of Wynot, Nebraska, a question some people have answered with satisfaction. In the old days an elderly German woman

answered every question posed to her with (you guessed it) "Why not?" Soon it became kind of a local joke to answer everything with "W'ynot." When it came time to name the town there really wasn't much of a choice.

You are entering one of the more interesting areas of Cedar County. Among many other tales, several ghost stories have circulated for years about this once very populated and important location in Nebraska.

*North from Wynot past the Catholic cemetery, go **one mile.** Take the right fork and go for another quarter mile. This old mill served an important function of providing flour and feed for local farmers. The mill building was built in 1868 and served as a flour and saw mill until the 1930s.*

***West from this T intersection one eighth of a mile** to a monument commemorating the first school district in the county.*

***One half mile further west** to the "Y" in the road. In the crook of this "Y" on top of the hill was Ft. Jackson, built in 1864 to protect local citizens from attacks by Indians.*

***West two miles to State Road S-14H, then north three miles** on State Road S-14H. One mile west of here is the brick house of the Lammers. They are the only remaining early-day pioneer family in the county. The house is located on the original homesteading site and is 120 years old. The bricks were made on the property. One mile southeast of this intersection is the St. Helena Catholic Cemetery. It is the 4th oldest cemetery in the state and there are graves which date from the early 1860s.*

***One mile further north** on State Road S-14H to St. Helena and the site of the Felber Tavern. For over a century, this was the center for information, comfort, supplies, gossip, card games, booze, neighborly conversation and news.*

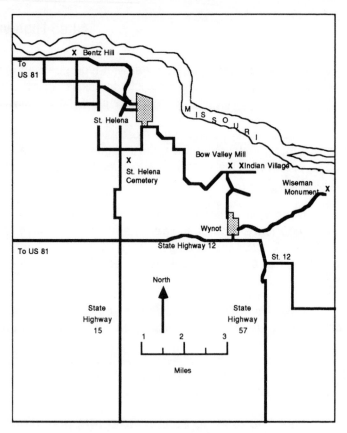

Northwestern Cedar County

West one quarter mile of St. Helena, then north on graveled road for one and a half miles, then west for two and a half miles. On the northwest corner of this intersection is the site of the Bentz Hill Massacre. Dr. Lorenzo Bentz was killed here by Indians in 1864 as a warning to other settlers who might be so silly as to try and settle in this area.

West five miles to US 81. See entry for US Highway 81, or, to continue with State Highway 12 tour return to the mill site.

At the mill site, go one quarter mile east. Hill on the north side of the road was the site of a large Indian village which stood here nearly 900 years ago. Tradition has it that the Indians who lived here were unfriendly, and when the first settlers came this way the other local Indians called the long since abandoned site, "Bad Village." However, many others believe that this name indicates not the *character of the inhabitants of the village, but rather the evil spirits that existed and still exist there. In any event, the village was unusual since the Indians who lived there, or the ones who came after, built a wall around the entire place to keep others out, or to keep something in.*

*   **One half mile further east,** just as the road turns south is the location of the first courthouse in the county. The building was never completed and the structure was used instead for church services. This is also the location of "Old St. James." The town later moved to its present site, 1 1/2 miles south of here.*

*   **One and a half miles south:** Unincorporated village of St. James. Location of the first church in the county, a Methodist-Episcopal Church.*

*   **East out of St. James 3 miles** to the site of the Wiseman Massacre. On a Tuesday afternoon July 23, 1863 Indians killed Mrs. Hansen Wiseman and her five children. Her husband was in Yankton buying supplies for the family. This incident set off a series of killings on both sides that only ended after the government set up Ft. Jackson near St. Helena.*
*   You are near the banks of the Missouri here, just a half mile north for a nice view.*

Eleven miles (5 miles.)
Intersection with US Highway 81. Please see entry for US Highway 81 for information about sites along this route.

Five miles (7 miles.)
Crofton. A small village named after Crofton Court in England. North on 121 from here to Devil's Nest a lookout over the vast Lewis and Clark Reservoir.

Devils Nest, now, in part, a private recreation development, has been known for centuries in this neck of the world. It is a meadowy, tear-drop hilled, chalk cliffed, wooded wonderland of wilderness. It also can be reached by traveling west from US Highway 81 just south of the border.

Seven miles (5 miles.)
Turn off for Bloomfield. This is the location of the Wild Horse Holding Pens. For further information about this site and others in this area, please see entry for State Highway 14.

Five miles (11 miles.)

You have just entered the Santee Indian Reservation, location of the Santee Sioux since 1868.

The Santee were moved here from their homelands in Minnesota and the Dakotas after they had fought against the whites in an "uprising." This was one of the most concentrated attacks the Indians ever made on the white intruders. Because of the Civil War, the Indians believed that the whites would be weakened and that the Army would have their attention on the War Between the States. In 1863 several attacks took place simultaneously all across the West. The Santee in Minnesota made the most serious of these attacks, destroying all the stage stations for hundreds of miles along trails, and attacking settlers and towns.

The government captured 500 Indians in Minnesota and sentenced most of them to die. That saintly President, Abraham Lincoln, commuted the sentences of all but 38 of them. As a result the government decided to ban the Indians from Minnesota, and brought them here, and formed this reservation as a kind of prison camp, really.

Trouble was, this was Ponca land. In order to solve this slight problem, the goverment forced the Ponca to leave their land and they were forcibly removed to what we now call Oklahoma. Along the way to Oklahoma, a great Ponca chief—Standing Bear—lost his son to illness. The chief turned around and, carrying the body, attempted to return to his ancestral home along the Missouri to bury his son. He was stopped by troops in Nebraska. However, citizens and friends in Omaha fought for the chief's rights and eventually the courts made a famous decision, some 100 years after the Constitution was adopted. They decided that "an Indian is a person within the meaning of the law."

Eleven miles (1 1/2 miles.)

Junction with State Road S-54 D. *Nine miles down this road to Santee. This is the metropolitan center of the Reservation.*

The Santee Reservation is one of six reservations in Nebraska. The others are: the Omaha and Winnebago in Thurston County. The Fox and Iowa in the extreme southeastern corner of the state, and a small piece of the Pine Ridge Reservation in the Panhandle county of Sheridan.

One and a half miles (4 miles.)

At the western boundary of the Santee Indian Reservation is the Bazile Creek Wildlife Area. Bring your binoculars for fine views of wildlife and their habitat.

Near here is a chalk cliff known as Maiden's Leap, with a profile resembling a woman's face. Legend has it that Jesse James jumped from the cliff to his horse to escape a posse which was closing in. A ferry crosses the Missouri just north of here, and although there is a toll, it is a wonderful ride for the kids and the adults with young hearts. There isn't much reason to leave Nebraska, so turn right around and ride the ferry back.

Four miles (1 mile.)
Niobrara.

Junction with State Highway 14. For further information about sites in this area, please see entry for State Highway 14.

Niobrara has one of the oddest histories of any town in the state. The town was once located on the site of a Ponca Indian village. After hearing of the beauty and productivity of this land, a small group of pioneers set off to settle the area in May, 1856. They reached this spot, and while hundreds of Ponca Indians watched, the settlers marked off the land which is now considered "Old Town." They built cabins and a small fort. The Poncas, as might be expected, did not appreciate this occupation. In the winter of 1856 they tried to run the settlers off. The Indians burned all of the buildings except for the small fort, where the settlers held them off. The men spent the winter living in the tiny cabin, and soon the town became the first county seat of Knox County.

In 1881 the rising waters of the Missouri caused Niobrara to move for the first time. They moved buildings and homes a mile and a half to the southwest. That should have been enough movement for one town, but with the creation of Lewis and Clark Lake in the 1960s and 70s, the ground water began to rise and Niobrara was forced to move again. It is hoped that between God and Man, Niobrara has seen its last of moves.

Niobrara was the home of a well-known 24 piece Indian band, that is, a musical band, which toured the midwest in the early years of this centruy.

One mile (16 miles.)
Niobrara State Park. Camping and Picnicking.

Sixteen miles (4 miles.)

State Highway 12

Monowi. A small Boyd County town with a name that means "snow-on-the-mountain-flower."

Boyd County is one of the more remote, and less frequented counties in the state, and as such can boast of some of the most beautiful, and least viewed beauty around.

Boyd County, like Keya Paha County to the west, is bordered on the south by the lovely Niobrara River, Nebraska's great treasure.

Four miles (3 miles.)

A sign on Highway 12 directs the traveler to Sunshine Bottom. It is said that the robins stay here all winter long, for the valley is warmer than any of the surrounding area. The valley is being discovered, however, and homes are creeping up its sides. Glimpse it quick.

Three miles (10 miles.)

Lynch.

Turn north here at school house and go 1.5 miles to the site of an old Indian village. This rather large village covered nearly 2 square miles. Remember that taking items from a ruin is not only an assault on the rights of everyone, it is now a criminal offense.

Wolf Island is in the Missouri River near Lynch. The island was named by local folks for...well, you figure it out.

A trip north of Lynch to the Missouri would be well worth it, since much of the traffic touring the river bank on the more frequented highways will be avoided.

Ten miles (3 miles.)

Intersection with US Highway 281, south. Please see entry for US Highway 281 for information about this area.

Three miles (5 miles.)

Spencer.

Junction with US Highway 281.

For information on Spencer please see the entry for US Highway 281.

On the hillside between Spencer and Butte the word "Angel" can be seen carved out of the trees. It is easier to see in winter. No, the Almighty hasn't spoken here, just a local farmer and an idle tractor. The farmer's name is...well, you get three guesses.

Five miles (4 miles.)

South on this county road for two miles.

One of the more unusual items in this area is the round barn located on private land southeast of Butte. The round barn was a popular style of barn building in the late 1800s. Some claimed that such a design was the ideal way to build for convenience, economy and ease of operation. The idea was that feed for the stock could be placed in the center, and the stalls would radiate around the location, so that the least bit of work had to be done to distribute the feed.

In addition, many cowboys used the round barn for horse stock, using the round yard outside for breaking and training the horses. Go through the southeast gate and follow the road to the bottom of the hill to inspect the barn. If you aren't from around here ask at the Reiman's Ranch for permission to inspect the round barn. And always remember to close gates behind you.

Four miles (12 miles.)
Butte.
Junction with State Highway 11. For more information about sites along this route, please see entry for State Highway 11.
For information on Butte, please see entry for State Highway 11.

Twelve miles (5 miles.)
Twin Buttes. If you are not here at either Christmas or Easter you might appreciate knowing that the large cross at the top of these buttes is lit during those holidays. If you are here then, you have to wait until dark to appreciate it.

Five miles (12 miles.)
Location of White Horse Ranch. For years Ruth Thompson raised her albino horses at the ranch. From this stock several generations of horses have populated ranches and horse barns all over the world. Thompson only comes to the ranch part of the year now, and she no longer breeds the horses, but every year around Father's Day, albino horse breeders congregate here to show off their pure white, albino stock.

Twelve miles (15 miles.)
Cross the Keya Paha River, which flows out of the Rosebud Indian Reservation in South Dakota to join with the Niobrara River 20 miles southeast of here.
The name is from the Dakota Sioux and means "river with the turtle hill."

Fifteen miles (8 miles.)
      Burton. A tiny town made up of a collection of small churches.

Eight miles (5 miles.)
      Junction with US Highway 183. Please see that entry for more information about sites in this area.

Five miles (3 miles.)
      Springview.
      For information on Springview please see entry for US Highway 183.

Three miles (30 miles.)
      South on county road five miles to the site of Meadville, on the banks of the Niobrara. This ghost town provides a fine view of the Niobrara. This town was founded by a gentleman named Mead, the post master, road builder, ferry boat operator and roadhouse owner. The story is that Mead studied for the ministry, but then lost the faith. He came to Keya Paha County and started his various businesses along this spot on the river. He was a wild and reckless man until a traveling minister by the name of Captain Charles Frady came to Meadville and preached. Mead was so inspired that he regained his faith to such an extent that one Sunday he shot at swimmers bathing in the river who were not keeping the Sabbath holy.

Thirty miles (11 miles)
      The turn off for Smith Falls. If you are this close, you must turn off to see the tallest waterfall in the state.
      Four miles south on Smith Falls Road to the falls which cascades from a creek 52 unbroken feet down to the Niobrara River.
      For the lion-hearted:
      At the "T" intersection in four miles turn left, and then an immediate right. One hundred yards down this road park the car and follow the path over the covered barbed wire to a hand-powered cable car. You may stand in this car and turn the crank to wheel yourself over the middle of the swift, deep, Niobrara River. Look upstream and on the far bank for the best view of the falls.
      Those less fool-hearty:
      At the "T" intersection in four miles turn right, and go 200 yards. Cross the Niobrara over wooden bridge and park the car. Walk

back across the bridge and look downstream for a partial view of the falls.

Eleven miles (4 miles.)

The Fort Niobrara National Wildlife Refuge. This area is home to many of the large animals which once roamed this area including buffalo, elk, antelope and deer. A small herd of longhorn cattle were introduced here not long ago. It is over 20,000 acres and was originally set aside by President Theodore Roosevelt. The Niobrara formed a 100 foot deep canyon through part of the refuge, and streams enter the canyon in waterfalls. Many fossils have been collected in this area.

Near the refuge headquarters is the site of the original Ft. Niobrara which includes a museum. The fort was built in 1880 to protect settlers from the Sioux.

The refuge is one of the finer areas in Cherry County.

Four miles (0 miles.)

Valentine.

Junction with US Highways 20 and 83. For information about Valentine, please see entry for US Highway 20.

For further information about other sites in this area, and along these highways, please see entry for US Highway 20 and US Highway 81.

Bibliography

An Architectural Album, Compiled by the Junior League of Lincoln, Nebraska, North Printing, Lincoln, 1979.

Andreas, A.T. *History of the State of Nebraska*, Unigraphic, Evansville, IN, 1975.

An Informal History of Nemaha County, 1854-1967, (np), (nd).

Arthur County Historical Society, *History of Arthur County*, (np), (nd).

Bailey, Edd H. *A Life With the Union Pacific,* Saltillo, St. Johnsbury, VT, 1989.

Bailey, Barbara. *Picture Book of Nebraska*, Whitman, NY, 1956.

Baltensperger, Bradley H. *Nebraska, A Geography*, Westview Press, Boulder,1985.

Banner County History, Bayard N E (nd)

Boyd County Nebraska, 75th Anniversary, 1966.

Boye, Alan. *A Guide to the Ghosts of Lincoln, 2nd edition,* Saltillo, St. Johnsbury, VT 1987.

Brown, Elinor. *History of Lancaster County, Then and Now,* self-published,Lincoln, 1971.

___, *Nebraska Travel-Rama,* Midwest Publishers, Ceresco, NE, 1973.

Brubaker, Ethal. *Our Nebraska*, Johnson Publishing Co., Lincoln, 1963.

Bryson, Conrey. *Winter Quarters* Deseret Books, Salt Lake City, 1986.

Carpenter, Allan. *Nebraska*, Childrens Press, 1978.

Cather, Willa. *O, Pioneers!* , Riverside, Boston, 1913.

___. *My Antonia*, Knopf, NY, 1918.

___. *A Lost Lady,* Knopf, NY 1923.

Cedar County Historical Society, *Pioneer Families of Cedar County,* (np) 1967.

Centennial History of Hamilton County, Hamilton County Centennial Association Aurora, NE, 1967.

Centennial Year, Grand Island, Nebraska, Centennial Souvernir Book Committee, Grand Island, NE 1970.

Bibliography

Copple, Neale. *Tower on the Plains Lincoln's Centennial History, 1859-1959*, Lincoln Centennial Commission, Lincoln, 1959.

Cornerstone-Historical Preservation in Nebraska V. 1-, Nebraska State Historical Society, Lincoln, 1979-.

Crabb, Alexander R. *Empire on the Platte,* World Publishing, 1967.

Creigh, Dorothy W. *Nebraska, A History,* W.W. Norton, New York, 1977.

___. *Nebraska, Where Dreams Grow,* Miller and Paine, Lincoln, 1980.

Dick, Everett. *Conquering the Great American Desert,* Nebraska State Historical Society, Lincoln, 1975.

___. *The Sod-House Frontier,* Johnson Publishing, Lincoln, 1954.

Duell County Historical Society, *Duell County, Nebraska,* (np) (nd).

Dustin, Dorothy D. *Omaha and Douglas County, A Panoramic History,* Windsor Publishing Co. Woodland Hills, CA, 1980.

Dundy County Heritage, Dundy County Extension Council, Pruett Press, Boulder, (nd)

Eiseley, Loren. *All the Strange Hours: The Excavation of a Life,* Scribner, NY, 1975.

___, *The Emense Journey,* Random House, NY 1957.

___, *The Firnanebt of Time,* Atheneum, NY, 1960.

___, *The Night Country,* Scribner, NY, 1971.

Fitzpatrick, Lilian L. *Nebraska Place-Names, including selections from Link,J.T., Origin of the Place-Names of Nebraska,* Bison, Lincoln, 1960.

Federal Writers Project. *Nebraska, A Guide to the Cornhusker State,* Viking, New York, 1934.

Flodman, Mildred. *Early Days in Polk County,* Union College Press, Lincoln, (nd).

Fradin, Dennis, B. *Nebraska in Words and Pictures,* Childrens Press, 1980.

Franzwa, Gregory M. *Maps of the Oregon Trail,* Patrice Press, Gerald, MO, 1982.

From 'Hoppers to 'Copeters: Stories of Nuckolls County for 100 Years, Nuckolls County Committee, 1967.

Gaffney, Wilbur, ed. *The Fillmore County Story,* Geneva Community Grange, Geneva, NE 1968

Garfield County Historical Society. *Garfield County Roundup; A History of the People,* Quiz Graphic Arts, Ord, NE, 1967.

Graff, Jane. *On a Bend inthe River: The Story of Seward and Seward County, Nebraska,* Henderson, NE 1967.

Grant County, *Its Friends and Neighbors,* Grant County Historical
        Society, 1980

Greeley County Historical Society. *Greeley County History,* (np), (nd).

Haines, Aubrey L. *Historical Sites Along the Oregon Trail,* Patrice
        Press, Gerald, MO, 1981.

Hayes County Historical Society. *History of Hayes County,* (np), (nd).

Henry, Stuart. *Conquering Our Great American Plains*, E.P. Dutton,
        New York, (nd).

*Historical Markers in Nebraska, compiled by National Society of DAR
        in Nebraska,* Franklin Press, Beatrice, NE, 1951.

Historical Sites Around Fairbury (brochure), Jefferson County Histori-
        cal Soceity, (np) (nd).

Historical Booklet Committee. *Honor Our Heritage:Portrait of Prog-
        ress in Phelps County,* (np), 1973.

History of Colfax County, (np) 1967.

Homestead Centennial, Beatrice, NE 1962.

Horan James D. and Sann, Paul. *Pictorial History of the Wild West,*
        Crown, New York, 1954.

Horgan, Paul. *Graet River: The Rio Grande in North American History*
        (2 Volumes) Rinehart, NY 1954..

Hutchinson, Duane. *Doc Graham, Sandhills Doctor*, Foundation
        Books, Lincoln, 1971.

Hytrek, Anthony J. *The History of Fort Robinson, Nebraska From
        1900 to the Present*, Chadron State College, Chadron,
        NE 1971.

Important and Interesting Sites in Nebraska, Nebraska State Histori-
        cal Society, Lincoln, 1961.

Janovy, John Jr. *Keith County Journal,* St. Martins, New York, 1978.

Johnsgard, Paul A. *Those of the Gray Wind: The Sandhill Cranes,* St.
        Martins, NY 1981.

Johnson, Niel M. *Portal to the Plains: A History of Washington
        County, Nebraska,* Lincoln, (nd).

Jordon, Robert P., *Nebraska, The Good Life,* National Geographic
        Society, Washington, D.C., 1974.

Kleofkorn, Wiiliam. *A Life Like Mine,* Platte Valley Press, Lincoln,
        1984.

Kooser, Ted. *Not Coming to Be Barked At: Poems,* Pentagram Press,
        Millwaukee, 1976.

Kuzma, Greg. *Adirondacks,* Bear Claw Press, Ann Arbor, 1978.

LaMere, Oliver, and Shinn, Harold, B. *Winnebago Stories*, Rand
        McNally, New York, 1928.

Lass, William E. *From the Missouri to the Great Salt Lake: An Account*

Bibliography

of Overland Freighters, Nebraska State Historical Soci
ety, Lincoln, 1972.

Manson, Mae. Prairie Pioneers of Box Butte County, Iron Man
Industries, Alliance, NE 1970.

Mattes, Merrill J. The Great Platte River Road, Nebraska State
Historical Society, Lincoln, 1979.

McDermott, Edith S. The Pioneer History of Greeley County Nebraska, Citizens, Greeley, NE, 1977.

McKee, James L., and Duerschner Lincoln, A Photographic History,
Salt Valley Press, Lincoln, 1976.

___. Lincoln, The Prairie Capital, An Illustrated History, Windsor
Publishing, Woodland Hills, CA, 1984.

Morton, J. Sterling and Watkins, Albert. Illustrated History of Nebraska (3 Volumes), Jacob North and Company, Lincoln,
1913.

Morris, Wright. God's Country and My People, Harper & Row, New
York, 1968.

___. Ceremony at Lone Tree, Atheneum, NY, 1960.

___. Field of Vision, Harcourt, Brace, NY, 1956.

___. Fork River Space Project, University of Nebr., Lincoln, 1981.

Mufon Symposium Proceedings, Dayton Ohio, 1978.

Nebraska History Magazine, Nebraska State Historical Society, Lincoln, various dates.

Nebraskaland Magazine, Lincoln, NE., various dates.

Nebraska Travel, Nebraska Department of Economic Development,
Lincoln, 1972.

Neihardt, John. Black Elk Speaks, University of Nebr., Lincoln, 1961.

___, The River and I, University of Nebr., Lincoln, 1974.

___, The Cycle of the West, University of Nebr., Lincoln, 1972.

Newman, Peter C. Caesars of the Wilderness, Vol II, Penguin,
Toronto, 1987.

Nicoll, Bruce N. Nebraska: A Pictorial History, Bicentennial Edition,
Universitry of Nebraska Press, Lincoln, 1975.

___, and Keller, Ken R. Know Nebraska, Johnson Publishing Co.,
Lincoln, 1951.

O'Gara, W. H. In All Its Fury—The Great Blizzard of 1888, J & L Lee,
Lincoln, 1988.

Olson, James C. History of Nebraska, University of Nebraska Press,
Lincoln, 1966.

Perkey, Elton A. Perkey's Nebraska Place Name, Nebraska State
Historical Society, Lincoln, 1982.

Perry, Alice P. History of Cass County, (np) 1967.

354

Powers, Lester C. *Hitchcock County, 1873-1973,* Hitchcock County News, Trenton NE 1973.

Rogo, Scott D. ed. *UFO Abductions True Cases of Alien Kidnappings,* Signet, New York, 1978.

Rosicky, Rose. *A History of Czechs in Nebraska*, Eastern Nebraska Genealogical Society, Fremont, 1976.

Russell Ed. *The Lives and Legends of Buffalo Bill,* University of Oklahoma Prtess, Norman, 1960.

Sandoz, Mari. *Old Jules,* University of Nebr., Lincoln, 1969.

___. *Son of a Gambling Man,* Potter, NY, 1960.

Scheele, Roy. *Pointing Out the Sky: Poems*, Sandhills Press, Ord, NE, 1985.

Sheldon, Addison, E. *History and Stories of Nebraska*, University Publishing, Lincoln, 1913.

___. *Nebraska, The Land and the People,* Lewis Publishing, Chicago, 1931.

Scott, Lynn. *The Covered Wagon and Other Adventures,* University of Nebr., Lincoln, 1987.

Sidney: *The Magestic High Plains,* Spelts-Bailey, Grand Island, 1987.

Sioux County*: Memoirs of its Pioneers,* Harrison Sun-News, Harrison, NE 1976.

Stevens, Morgan. *Memories of Perkins County*, Stevens Co, Astoria IL, (nd).

Story, Ronald D. ed. *The Encyclopedia of UFOs*, Dolphin, New York, 1980.

Strait, Treva. *The Price of Free Land,* Lippencott, NY, 1979.

Thedford, Nebraska, (np), (nd).

Tobias, Nebraska (np), (nd).

The UFO Evidence, National Investigations Committee on Aerial Phenomena, Washington D.D., 1964.

Valley County Historical Society, *A View of the Valley: Valley County, Nebraska,* (np) 1973.

Wayne County Historical Society, *Wayne County Anecdotes and Historical Notes*, (np), (nd).

Where the Buffalo Roamed Stories of Early Days In Buffalo County, World Publishing Co, Shenamdoah Iowa, (nd).

White, John B. *Published Sources on Territorial Nebraska*, Nebraska State Historical Society, Lincoln, 1965.

Wilson, James C. *Itzatenango and Friends*, Moo Cow Press, Santa Fe, 1974.

___, ed. *Saltillo Review*, Lincoln & Santa Fe, Vols. 1-5, 1971-1976.

Index

Index

Index

F

Fairbury, (County seat), 167
Fairmont, 138
Falls City (County seat), 1-2
Falter, John, 1
Farwell, 105
Father Flanagan, 19
Ficklin's Springs Station, 280
Field, Richard, 227
Filley, 165
First Plymouth Congregational Church, 197
Fletcher, Alice, C., 47
Florence, 15
Florence Museum, 16
Floyd, Sergeant Charles, 49
Folk School, 105
Fonda, Henry, 251
Fonenelle, Logan, 24, 80
Fontanelle (Ghost town), 24
Fontanelle Orchard, 24
Fontanelle Forest, 15
Ford, Pres. Gerald, 19
Fort Atkinson, 22-23
Fort Calhoun, 22-23
Fort Garber, 109
Fort Hartsuff, 89
Fort Hartsuff State Historical Park, 99
Fort Independence, 251
Fort John, 149
Fort Kearny, 7
Fort McPherson National Cemetery, 236
Fort Niobrara National Wildlife Refuge, 322, 349
Fort Robinson, 335
Fort Sidney, 240, 268

Fort Valentine, 99
Fossil beds, 144, 320
Franklin (County seat), 174
Franzwa, Gregory, 274
Freeman, Daniel, 166
Fremont (County seat), 42
Fremont, John C., 85
Fremont and Elkhorn Valley Rail road, 42-43
Fremont State Park, 244
Fremont Springs, 53
Fremont Springs Station, 262
French, Daniel Chester, 196
Frenchman River, 191
Fugate, Caril Ann, 205

G

Gage County Historical Museum, 166
Gandy, 120
Garland, 209
Garret, Jeremiah, 180
Gavins Point Dam, 72
Gehling Opera House, 1-2
General Crook House Museum, 17
Geneva (County seat), 66
Genoa, 78-79
Gering (County seat), 281
Germans, 59, 70, 117, 183, 250
Ghost towns. See names of individual towns: Arbor, Athens, Camden, Catherton Dunlap, De Soto, Glen, Marsland, Montrose, Norris, Omadi, Omega, Riverview, Rock Bluff, Runnelsburg, Shea, Swan City
Gibbon, 253

Index

Index

Index

Index

Index

952 952015